The Development of Imagery
and its Functional Significance
in Henry James's Novels

by

ALEXANDER HOLDER-BARELL

HASKELL HOUSE
Publishers of Scholarly Books
NEW YORK
1966

PREFACE

> One's work should have composition,
> because composition alone is positive
> beauty.   *Henry James*

The English novel before James is by no means without imagery. From its beginnings we find all novelists making use of it to a greater or lesser extent. But with none of them before James—Hardy, Meredith and George Eliot excepted—does imagery form an organic and significant part of their art. It is used almost solely for decorative purposes, in order to colour and enrich the prose. In comparison with his predecessors the imagery in James's works strikes us at once as being something quite different from decoration. We are aware that without it his novels and stories would lose their deeper meaning, their life would vanish. The images in his work indeed form such an organic part that the whole would be destroyed were one to attempt to tear them from it.

Images—particularly metaphors—in James's novels are an essential part in his expression of eternal values. They help considerably in raising and widening his themes to a statement of universal and lasting truths. So Proust's dictum that metaphor alone can give a sort of eternity to style finds its undeniable confirmation in James's work.

It is the purpose of the present study to show the development in James's application of imagery and to demonstrate how the functional significance of his metaphors underwent a similar development. The functions fulfilled by images—other than decorative—are multifold in James's work. Several groups have been established and analysed in successive chapters, with a rising line in functional significance up to the transition from mere metaphor into general symbols.

The analysis of some of the more elaborate metaphors has made it inevitable to extract some essential pictorial passages only from their context in order to avoid extended and disadvantageous interruptions in the flow of the argument. An appendix has therefore been added which gives some of the major long passages, containing functionally significant images, in their entirety.

ACKNOWLEDGEMENTS

I wish to acknowledge my deep gratitude to Professor Henry Lüdeke who has supervised the growth of this dissertation and who has, with his paternal understanding and patience, and with his critical and constructive advice, helped me considerably in writing the present thesis. I am also deeply grateful to Miss Claire Benedict and the Cooper Fond, with the help of which I was able to carry out the necessary initial research work at the Bodleian Library, Oxford. I should also like to thank those who have helped me with the manuscript: Mr. Jan Stevens and Dr. James Day for their advice concerning the language, and Mr. Werner Diehr for his reading of the proofs. And last but not least I owe my deepest gratitude to my wife whose patient assistance in many respects has been my constant and encouraging companion.

CONTENTS

Preface 5

Acknowledgements 6

Chapter 1: The Significance of Imagery in the Work of Henry James 9

Chapter 2: The Rhetorical Image 17
   A. Comparison and Simile 17
   B. Metaphor 21

Chapter 3: The Expanding Image 24
   A. Revised Images 24
   B. Added Images 25
   C. Obscuring Images 28
   D. Comic Effects through Images 30
   E. Illustrative Images 32
      1. General 32
      2. Path Images 35
      3. Light Images 36
      4. Theatre Images 38
   F. Emphasizing Images 41
      1. General 41
      2. Key Images 47
      3. Images Based on Games 50

Chapter 4: The Characterizing Image 55
   A. Spoken Images 55
   B. External Characterization 62
   C. General Characterization 66
      1. General 66
      2. War Images 71
      3. Animal Images 76

Chapter 5: Images Expressing the Abstract in Terms of the Concrete ... 81
   A. The Poetic Metaphor 81
   B. Thoughts and Ideas 88
   C. Feelings 101
   D. States of Dependence 106

Chapter 6: The Constructive Image 117
   A. Iterative Imagery 117
      1. Water Images 117
      2. Architectural Images 124

3. Flying Images 129
4. Princess and Dove Images in *The Wings of the Dove* 132
5. Minor Forms of Iterative Imagery 137
  B. Preparatory Images 139

Chapter 7: The Transition from Metaphor to Symbol 148

Notes 159

Appendix 186

Bibliography 212

CHAPTER 1

The Significance of Imagery in the Work of Henry James

It was Aristotle who recognized the pre-eminence of the metaphor over other means of diction. Metaphor was, according to him, the one thing that could not be learned from others; it was the sign of an original genius. Though he used the term in a wider sense, Aristotle conceived of metaphor as a much simpler form than we do in the twentieth century. Many of his examples have lost their originality and have become an integral part of our spoken language as "dead" imagery.

Poets tend to make the most extensive use of imagery. The dramatist at once encounters more difficulties in its use. A drama is comprehensible only "through a series of impressions, successively". But time is very much in favour of the dramatist. He can count upon making his effect on the listener or reader in one "sitting". There is a continuous succession of impressions from the beginning to the end. A novelist's laws are in many respects completely different from those of the dramatist. Successful use of functional imagery in prose needs a great deal of virtuosity and mastery.

The comparatively young literary form of the novel has only recently discovered how successfully imagery can be used for certain functions in prose, in spite of the many limitations in comparison with poetry and dramatic art. Imagery, as far as it was introduced in the early novels, was not very significant, because the novelists of the eighteenth and nineteenth centuries were not yet mainly interested in the psychology of their characters' actions. Their art is still largely descriptive. Many of the Victorian novelists introduced a great deal of imagery for decorative and ornamental purposes only, which is stressed by the fact that the majority of it consists of comparisons and similes, and not of the more powerful metaphor.

There are mainly two distinct groups of imagery: "dead" and "created" images. Those of the first group have become part of our everyday language and have almost completely lost their metaphorical character. The functional significance of such images is almost nil.

The nineteenth and twentieth centuries have produced a great number of theoretical works on the nature of the various forms of imagery[1]. Whereas the results in the case of simile and comparison are essentially the same, they are rather diverse for metaphor; a fact which should give us a first hint that metaphor is a much more complicated form of imagery than simile. Its roots are not so easily recognized, because it is the result of a deep process in the mind of its creator. Whilst many comparisons are not more than an afterthought, metaphor in its highest form is the only way to express certain things. Deutschbein pointed out that metaphors sometimes have a strongly psychological character and meaning: "As far as they are not merely of an ornamental and purely decorative character, they take away the veil from the soul of a human being; they disclose his innermost feelings and show us not only on what his attention concentrates (sphere of facts) but above all what his thoughts are preoccupied with and where his fancy likes most to dwell[2]." It is this taking away of a certain veil from the soul of a character which shows us one of the necessities for the use of metaphors. Neither simile nor comparison could be used to the same effect. They can at the utmost express a strong impression of conception. An analytical writer who is largely concerned with the psychological development of his characters must suffer from the insufficiencies of ordinary language. Hence he most frequently uses imagery as a resource to overcome such difficulties successfully.

Elster, in his *Prinzipien der Literaturwissenschaft,* says that it should always be possible to replace a metaphor by a term taken from the ordinary world of mental experience. In the case of the original metaphor just the contrary holds true. We use "terms" taken from the world of experience, in order to render explicable what is part of another, the inward world. And yet, Elster's statement is not completely wrong, as there are at least two different kinds of metaphors. His assertion refers to a type which we may call "conscious". It is not introduced in order to remedy an incapacity of the language, but to heighten the significance of a passage. One of the main characteristics is its intensity. It is true that such metaphors could be replaced by a term, or rather a number of terms, taken from our world of mental experience. But as soon as they are introduced in order to fulfil definite functions they are indispensable. We can, however, only understand this function entirely, if we are able to answer the question why a writer has introduced a certain image. What does it take the place of? What does it indicate? Thus we have to find out first what caused the image, then its meaning, and thirdly its purpose or function. In the case of "spontaneous" imagery, cause, meaning and function fall together and form a unit. The cause is the insufficiency of the language. The function is to make good this lack of adequate expressibility; and this function contains at the same time the meaning. Often, therefore, the functional intensity of such originally conceived metaphors is not so high as in the case of consciously introduced metaphors. Imagery of the latter kind is mostly caused by the need of a writer to produce certain effects on his readers.

A common way of approaching imagery is to classify and catalogue it. This method necessarily tears the images out of the respective situations. Such a method can, at the utmost, help us to become aware of iterative imagery.

Another method is to interpret imagery out of its context because its full significance can only be recognized if it is seen as part of an organic growth. By using this method more satisfactory results will be achieved, not only in the case of poetry and drama, but also in that of prose. Here, images are rooted fast in the plot itself, and form a highly organic part of it, with the exception of those which are merely introduced for decorative purposes.

In prose, imagery tends to be precise, to render inwardness as exactly as possible; or in other words: it tries to make inwardness part of the outward, comprehensible world. Its aim is to explain, to emphasize.

If we take a writer like Henry James, we begin to realize that one has to be extremely careful in attributing any such generalizations to his art. In a novel like *The Awkward Age* we cannot miss its strongly dramatic conception; if we read *The Wings of the Dove*, do we not sometimes have the impression that we are reading not prose but poetry? These two examples have been chosen at random; yet any of James's novels and tales leave similar impressions with a careful reader.

The dramatic influences on his art are easy to trace, because he himself frequently discussed this problem in his critical essays, especially in the prefaces to the first collected edition of his novels and tales[3]. We can choose almost any one of them, to find at least one, if not several, such recollections of his lifelong preoccupation with dramatic art, his continuous wish to write plays. Discussing "Julia Bride" he writes that "the number of a young lady's accepted lovers" would certainly have much to "say" to her "general case". "*What* it might have to say (of most interest to poet and moralist) was certainly meanwhile no matter for *a priori* judgement—it might have to say but the most charming, the most thrilling things in the world; this, however, was exactly the field for dramatic analysis, no such fine qualities being ever determinable till they have with due intelligence been 'gone into'. 'Dramatise, dramatise!' one had, in fine, before the so signal appearance, said to one's self[4]." Only by dramatizing would one "see"; in other words, through a dramatization he hoped to achieve an analysis as close and complete as possible. Dramatic presentation and imagery were the two devices which allowed him to objectify his indirect approach to the matters with which he was dealing.

Many critics have tried to find the most ingenious explanations for the change in style between the work of the young and the mature novelist: "Les critiques sont tous d'accord pour constater que la différence est très grande entre les premiers romans de James et ses derniers, et nombreuses sont les explications qu'on en a fournies; mais personne ne me semble avoir vu que cette différence est due en grande partie à l'évolution de Henry James pendant les années où il écrivit pour le théâtre" writes M. Leon Edel in his thesis[5]. The evolution he speaks of was very considerable during James's dramatical years in the early 'nineties, and its influence is always strongly felt in all the subsequent productions, especially in the "architecture" of the later novels with their constant alternation between analytic and purely dramatic scenes. Such architectural principles can easily be understood if one is ready to acknowledge James's preoccupation with drama as the result of a deep artistic interest, which had already begun to take root in the very young artist, and occupied his mind constantly until his very last years.

Although imagery is as important as drama in James's fiction, there are no remarks on it in his critical prefaces. When he there speaks of images and poetic pictures he has something quite different in mind. He never touches upon the function of imagery, and we have to ask ourselves whether there is an explanation for this fact. His notebooks give us a unique picture of his method of creation. He never sat down to work out an idea for a story immediately. His first step, always, was to make a note of the possible "germ" of an idea. He then let the "seed grow", and waited to see whether the idea would be "fertilising" "in the long run"—whether there would be any "upspringings" in the seed. When the idea had really taken root in his mind, he repeatedly made further notes, which show a development of the original idea. Thus the germ grew and grew over the course of many years, sometimes amounting to over a decade. Only then, after long years, when "the persons and their actions were vividly present to [his] inward eye" did he start to work out his plot more carefully by writing a scenario which he usually seems to have followed closely in actually writing the story[6]. By that time his inner vision of each character was extremely vivid. He appears to have seen every detail. His experience in life and his exceptional gift as an observer allowed him to attribute so many observed phenomena to each of his characters that they turned out to be not mere creations of an artistic mind, but really living persons. Thus James's "inner eye" saw some of his characters as flying high up in the air, as wild beasts, as precious pieces of a collection, as floating in an endless sea, as being in the same boat with someone else and so on.

Another source from which to study James's way of working is Miss Theodora Bosanquet's excellent little book[7], from which we get a lively picture of how he created when he had taken to the habit of dictation. "He 'broke ground'", writes Miss Bosanquet, "as he said, by talking to himself day by day about the characters and construction until the persons and their actions were vividly present to his naked eye. This soliloquy was, of course, recorded on the typewriter[8]." And he was not easily satisfied with putting into words what his "inward eye" saw. It saw such a tremendous number of things that he sometimes must have felt rather despairing about the limited possibilities of the language. Imagery must then have appeared to him the only possible, adequate way of conveying his visions.

12

We may conclude from the above that James's imagery is by no means far-fetched and artificial, as some critics have maintained, and as it might sometimes appear to a superficial reader. On the contrary, it is the direct outcome of an inner vision of his characters. If Dr. Johnson said of Dryden that sometimes "he seems to look round him for images which he cannot find", one could say the exact contrary about James whose imagination was singularly fertile and whose mind must have been crowded with images of all kinds. He stored them there until they were needed for one of his characters. Not only his novels and stories are full of them, however, but also his critical works, especially the prefaces. But is not the use of imagery for explaining highly theoretical matters the best proof of its profound, indeed almost unique, suitability for such difficult subjects?

He did not feel it necessary to deal critically with them, although he was most careful always to find the best and most exact formulation of a thought. Words were, for him, "not enough for the things of the mind", and we know from his friends that in conversation he always struggled hard in order to "convey his precise meaning". As ordinary expressions very often proved inadequate imagery became for James like a second mother-tongue in order "to express in terms of experience thoughts lying beyond experience, to express the abstract in terms of the concrete, to picture forth the unfamiliar by means of the familiar, to express insensuous thoughts by sensuous terms[9]".

The remarks on James's working methods, his long years in creating a work, raise the question how far we may and must consider "conscious" metaphors, and sometimes even comparisons and similes, as original. Was not most of his imagery original by the time he wrote the stories, when it had become, through the long melting process within his mind, an integral and organic part of his inner vision? His revisions of his early novels show us how unsatisfied James often was, however, with the way he could express his inward pictures and how organically connected with his inner vision his images were.

When he prepared the first collected edition of his novels and stories, he altered large parts, in some novels and tales almost every sentence. Again, critics did not pay enough attention to these revisions, although they are in many ways informative. We can follow them here only as far as imagery is concerned. If we examine them in the three early novels *Roderick Hudson, The American* and *The Portrait of a Lady,* we come to the conclusion that alterations are the most frequent where imagery is involved. James either revised already existing images, or sometimes enlarged them, or even introduced completely new ones. On re-perusal he became aware of the subtlety lacking in the presentation of his characters. He felt that some of his creations were not plausible enough because he had not yet been able, in his early creative years, to translate his inner vision adequately. In his revisions he tried to correct this defect as much as possible. By altering the imagery, he hoped to give his readers a more comprehensible picture of some of his characters. Images alone could help him in this endeavour because only through them could he render his subjective vision sufficiently objective. Many critics have reproached James for obscuring his early novels through his revisions. This impression is certainly a great deal the result of James's altered or newly introduced images. It is true that the text comes to lack straightforwardness and simplicity, but on the other hand James is very often able to convey a much more intense meaning. One has to examine the later images all the more carefully, as their weightiness is much greater when compared with earlier examples. These are, in general, much simpler; their meaning is, on the whole, distinct and clear. And the performing of more than one function by a single image is not as frequent as in the later fiction. Owing to this multitude of purposes fulfilled by one and the same image, the late novels often show a strong tendency towards ambiguity.

One of James's chief devices was his "central consciousness" which he used as a mirror or reflector in order to eliminate the presence of the author in the novel itself. He tried to maintain this centre in as few persons as possible. But only in *The Ambassadors* did he succeed in keeping up one single consciousness throughout an entire book. It is very likely that that is why he considered this novel his best work. In the preface to *The American,* James writes of Christopher Newman, the American hero of the novel: "the interest of everything is all that it is *his* vision, *his* conception, *his* interpretation: at the window of his wide, quite sufficiently wide, consciousness we are seated, from that admirable position we 'assist'. He therefore supremely matters; all the rest matters only as he feels it, treats it, makes it[10]." Although this quotation concerns but one character in a particular novel, it can be applied to the central consciousness in any of James's novels and stories. He developed to great perfection this device of a central mirror. There is a much weaker treatment of it in the early works; and this is certainly a reason why they are, on the whole, much easier to read, because they do not require the same concentration as his late works of fiction. James more and more demanded the unrestricted attention of his reader, and there can be no complete understanding of the meaning and significance of his fiction, if one follows, as he wrote himself, the "usual stupid routine of skipping and halting and letting slide".

Although most of James's fiction, even his last novels, shows a shifting of the central consciousness between at least two persons (as for instance in *The Golden Bowl*), there is always only one *central* reflector at a time. Thus all the reflective parts in a novel by James give the impression of being large monologues in a drama. Here they are spoken, there we read them; but the result is the same. On the one hand, then, we have the comparatively few images used by persons when actually speaking. On the other hand, there is an overwhelming number of "thought" images; and they can fulfil two simultaneous functions: in the first place they provide us with a rich impression of the central, thinking, reflecting character himself. We are able to draw certain conclusions from the kind of images he uses, and we then understand why this central consciousness had to be laid in a highly intelligent, observant and responsive character who was able to register every detail his life came in contact with. In the second place, these same images may provide us with useful characterizations of many other persons who come into contact with the central reflector. As James himself said, it is "as mirrored in that consciousness that the gross fools, the headlong fools, the fatal fools play their part for us—they have much less to show us in themselves[11]". It depends on the central consciousness how far we see the other participants in the "drama" as fools or as other more or less intelligent persons. Through these "reflected" images, and with the aid of a few spoken ones, we have to examine on what plane James intended to place certain persons socially, intellectually and emotionally.

It is mainly a result of James's dramatic conception of his novels and tales that the plot works up to a first important climax which is laid in the middle of the story; not necessarily in the middle as far as the organic development is concerned, but certainly with regard to the external lapse of time. The first half of a Jamesian novel takes the form of an exposition, "insists ever on figuring to me as the stage or theatre for the second half[12]". The second half, then, contains the development of the premises. The first part is largely static, whilst the second tends to be dynamic and dramatic. Revising his novels, James felt that he had "in general given so much space to making the theatre propitious" that the two parts "often proved strangely unequal[13]". In many cases this is true for the "organic centre"; as far as the temporal centre is concerned, however, it has in most cases "succeeded in getting into proper position[14]". Such effective conclusions of the exposition we find, for instance: in *Roderick Hudson* when Roderick and Christina Light disappear alone together for an hour; in *The Portrait of a Lady* when Isabel Archer has been given unlimited freedom by the large amount of inherited money; in *The Old Things* when Mrs. Gereth stipulates the condition under which alone she would be ready to send the spoils back to Poynton; in *The Ambassadors* when Lambert Strether writes the letter of great consequence about Chad's life in Paris to Mrs. Newsome; in *The Wings of the Dove* when Kate Croy reveals to Merton Densher her dreadful plan in connection with Milly Theale's illness; in *The Golden Bowl* with Charlotte's and Amerigo's being alone at Matcham, their secret vow and journey to Gloucester. Apart from such high central climaxes there are, of course, many others in the course of the stories. For any of them we can ask the same question: how do images contribute to the building up of such climaxes?

As James's style changed considerably, we can witness a continuous development in his use of imagery and its significance. Within each of the following chapters the selected novels will therefore be analysed in their chronological order. As it is beyond the scope of the present thesis to include all James's novels for a close analysis of the imagery, the stress has been laid on six novels, chosen from the early, middle, and late periods. They are: *Roderick Hudson, The Portrait of a Lady, The Old Things*[15]*, The Ambassadors, The Wings of the Dove,* and *The Golden Bowl.*

The aspect and the importance of imagery in James's work is usually overlooked in critical treatises. But the late F. O. Matthiessen realized not only the eminent importance of James's revisions, but also that of his imagery[16], although he analyses the novels generally, and not from a special angle. Every now and then we find a few remarks, a chapter or an article on James's imagery among the large body of literature about him. But in many of these cases we only find incidental intimations; or then only one special kind of his imagery is taken into consideration[17].

CHAPTER 2

The Rhetorical Image

Just as most people use many rhetorical images every day without being aware of them, so many writers introduce them quite unintentionally. It would indeed be very hard to find any prose which is without them. They are there, and yet many readers take no notice of them at all, read over passages which are full of such images without attributing any special meaning to any of them. This is the best proof that their significance must be extremely small and—if the writer has introduced such images with a specific intention—cannot lie in the single image itself but in the effect they produce as a whole. It can best be described by a comparison with the *bassus continuus* in a musical composition. The thorough-bass can very seldom be heard by our ears very distinctly, although it contributes an essential quality to the colour of a tone-sequence. It does not constitute the melody, and yet is very important for the character of the tonal quality; and a musical piece would sound somewhat different were the thorough-bass left out, although we would have no difficulty in recognizing the particular composition. The rhetorical images which a writer employs provide a similar kind of background or accompaniment. It is through them that a text receives a particular colour, which is, however, never the same colour with different writers, though they all take their examples from the same stock. It is a particularly Jamesian habit to alter such common images slightly and thus make them his own characteristic creations.

A. COMPARISON AND SIMILE

Dialogue and soliloquy take up the greater part of a Jamesian novel. Mere description occurs but occasionally. Hence James has to make a frequent use of simple imagery. It would strike the reader as unnatural if his characters did use elaborate images when talking to one another. They use expressions like "you alone look as if you had a little of the milk of human kindness left", "Why did I find her standing there like a goddess who had just stepped out of her cloud?", "He's as big a donkey as his mother", "I'm behaving like an angel", "I've been like a lamb": they are all images which we may hear from people in our daily lives. But already in the dialogue James shows a tendency to replace such common images by some that he has newly created[1]. This becomes fully apparent when we come to the rhetorical images introduced apart from the dialogue. Images like "with bare shoulders as white as snow", "She could not only sing like a lark", "as fresh as a rose" are extremely common in Thackeray's novels and those of other Victorian novelists. They are a characteristic of their styles, but not of James's. Thackeray uses them as mere decoration; for the reader they have no significance at all. We tend to pass over such "dead" images without receiving a clear and lasting picture in our minds. Common images of the nature which Thackeray frequently used are very rare in James's work[2]. If ever he introduces them it is almost always within the dialogue. Otherwise he often alters them in order to avoid old and well-worn pictorial expressions[3]. Such images mark the transition from the merely 'common' to the typically Jamesian rhetorical comparisons and similes, as for instance: "the lightning flashed and vanished, like the treble shrilling upon the bass[4]." In this connection it is noteworthy that George Eliot, whose considerable influence on James is undeniable, shows the same tendency to avoid common images. The lack of their existence in her novels is even more complete than in James's. With both novelists the main aim in avoiding the conventional and in trying to find original formulations seems to be the same, namely to convey as clear and intense a picture as possible. James, in the example quoted above, does not shrink from comparing a visible phenomenon with an audible one. George Eliot had not yet gone that far when she said of Dorothea Brooke's voice that it was "like the voice of a soul that had once lived in an Aeolian harp". But the tendency towards originality is apparent. When Dickens, on the other hand, introduces the somewhat unusual similes "as good as gold and as true as steel", he hastens to add, almost as an excuse, that "those were her [Peggotty's] similes". An even more striking comparison from *Roderick Hudson* reads: "the moods of an artist, his exaltations and depressions, ... were like the pen-flourishes a writing-master makes in the air when he begins to set his copy. He may bespatter you with ink, he may hit you in the eye, but he writes a magnificent hand[5]." Whilst we read this image a vivid picture begins to take shape in our minds. But what is more important is the circumstance that we are able to translate this picture very easily into terms of an artist and his moods. One of the outstanding characteristics of both good comparison and simile is that the picture evoked can be immediately deflected onto the actual fact, that is the reflection, the transposition, takes place during our actual reading.

A comparison or simile is, then, most convincing when it is evident that the image introduced expresses a fact much better and clearer than a mere statement would do. And often we recognize the real function of an image when we try to express the same thing without using any metaphorical language. Thus, when James wants to express how difficult it was for Roderick's companions to talk with him, how difficult not to touch upon any subject that might cause one of the artist's wild emotional outbursts, he finds a more artistic, concise and meaningful way of conveying such an impression than by a mere dry description: "talking with him was like skating on thin ice, and his companions had a constant mental vision of spots designated 'dangerous'[6]." Shortly before Ralph's death James wants to emphasize the "strange tranquillity in his face", and does it with a short, but effective simile: "it was as still as the lid of a box[7]." With this picture of the stiff and motionless lid of a box James achieves to foreshadow Ralph's similar state in his imminent death. This imminence is also conveyed shortly afterwards, when a transcendental element is introduced in the way Isabel is affected by Ralph's look: "when he opened his eyes to greet her, it was as if she were looking into immeasurable space[8]." Something lying above the grasp of human experience seems to be expressed with this picture. Already in *The Portrait* it is difficult to separate merely rhetorical comparisons and images from those of a greater functional significance, as the last two examples amply show. The same difficulties are encountered in *The Old Things*, and particularly in the three late novels. Is the following comparison, for instance, merely rhetorical or is it intended as one of the repeated battle images introduced to describe Mrs. Gereth? "She trod the place like a reigning queen or a proud usurper; full as it was of splendid pieces, it could show, in these days, no ornament so effective as its menaced mistress[9]." The question may be raised because, in comparison with the other battle images used iteratively to denote a certain quality of Mrs. Gereth's character, the present one is more ambiguous as to this particular function, especially as it is coupled with the majestic "reigning queen". Only the "proud usurper" conveys the notion of fierce battles and treacherous deeds. Other images, however, in the same novel, show themselves clearly as rhetorical, though again particularly Jamesian in the effort to create new, more effective pictures[10].

The functional importance with which James invests his imagery, especially in his later novels, leads him to frequent comparisons with pagodas, Hindu goddesses, figures from Greek mythology and all sorts of historical and fictional characters. This, of course, demands a high intelligence of his readers and wide reading. On the other hand it is very noticeable in his late works that he avoids difficult comparisons when using the rhetorical image. On the contrary, he chooses the simplest matters, known to everyone, and at once creates the intended picture in any reader's mind. In the opening pages of *The Ambassadors* we read of Strether: "What had come as straight to him as a ball in a well-played game—and caught, moreover, not less neatly—was just the air, in the person of his friend, of having seen and chosen[11]." As in this case, it is mostly abstract matters, feelings, impressions, problems, that are thus rendered comprehensible by a simple and straightforward image. This effect becomes apparent in another example from the same novel, when it is said of Strether that "he was able, however, to drop his problem at the door very much as if it had been the copper piece that he deposited, on the threshold, in the receptacle of the inveterate blind beggar[12]". Without this picture we would not be able to realize how completely Strether was able to get rid of this particular problem that had occupied his mind. This image also shows how deliberately James chose his pictures so that they were appropriate where they are introduced. This particular one stands at the point of Strether's entrance into Notre-Dame in Paris and is therefore remarkably adapted to the external action.

If in his early novels James occasionally introduced unconvincing images[13], his complicated late style now and then obscures their clarity, depriving them of their immediate effect. This lack of clarity is caused by putting too much into a single sentence. Although the images themselves are simple and well chosen, they lose their power because of the many subordinate clauses, appositions, and so on, involved. In a long sentence in *The Golden Bowl* there occur three images which, reduced to their essential words, read as follows: "He crossed the hotel court ... to the due amputation or extraction of excrescences and redundancies of barbarism", and: "with the general exotic accent and presence suspended, as with wings folded or feebly fluttering, in the superior ... Parisian medium", and: "the hotel court ... resembled some critical apartment of large capacity." But these three images are part of a long involved sentence which, quoted in its entirety, shows how difficult it is to grasp the full meaning at the first reading:

> He crossed the hotel court, which, overarched and glazed, muffled against loud sounds and guarded against crude sight, heated, gilded, draped, almost carpeted, with exotic trees in tubs, exotic ladies in chairs, the general exotic accent and presence suspended, as with wings folded or feebly fluttering, in the superior, the supreme, the inexorably enveloping Parisian medium, resembled some critical apartment of large capacity, some "dental", medical, surgical waiting-room, a scene of mixed anxiety and desire, preparatory, for gathered barbarians, to the due amputation or extraction of excrescences and redundancies of barbarism[14].

Such sentences are certainly an effect of James's late habit of dictation. It is a typically "spoken" sentence, emerging only in its clear meaning after its essentially Latin form of construction has been noticed and when read with appropriate stresses and correct raising and lowering of the voice.

James, in his late style, also shows a strong tendency to use complex images, to compare a picture with another one, enhancing its power by adding yet another characteristic detail. He also avoids more and more the words "like" and "as ... as", which are usually connected with comparisons and similes. In the above quotation he uses "resembles" instead of "like", in the following example he avoids it by the subtle "the suggestion as of": "The mere fine pulse of passion" in Maggie's remark, the suggestion as of a creature consciously floating and shining in a warm summer sea, some element of dazzling sapphire and silver, a creature cradled upon depths, buoyant among dangers, in which fear or folly, or sinking otherwise than in play, was impossible—something of all this might have been making once more present to him [Adam], with his discreet, his half shy assent to it, her probable enjoyment of a rapture that he, in his day, had presumably convinced no great number of persons either of his giving or his receiving [15].

The main difference from earlier examples is that the picture which serves as a comparison is no longer part of the main sentence, being now merely a clause. Another development is evident here in James's continued exploitation of the same image. It appears here like a theme with variations; first the creature is seen floating and shining in the summer sea, then the impression of the expanse of water is transformed into "some element of dazzling sapphire and silver", and finally the image of the creature is taken up again in three variants. This is the utmost achievement in the field of the rhetorical comparison and simile. We are here in the region of transition into more significant forms of imagery.

B. METAPHOR

James was well aware that metaphor was a much more powerful and significant form of imagery than either comparison or simile. Therefore most of his metaphors are carefully chosen, although the early novels show a frequent use of common, everyday types. About half the metaphors in *Roderick Hudson* belong to this category [16]. In their merely decorative function, they contribute to a flowery style not unlike that, for instance, of Maria Edgeworth, and are often affected and superfluous. A comparison of some such metaphors in *Roderick Hudson* with Edgeworth's *Castle Rackrent* and *Belinda* makes it obvious that there is hardly any development to be noticed in the imagery between this early Victorian novelist and James's first novel [17]. Dickens or Thackeray or many novelists before James could serve for a like comparison. With them all metaphors do in most cases seem to be not more than mere decoration. James, in his first novels at least, followed them on this path to a certain extent. But then he lifted his images to a level only reached in a much smaller degree by George Eliot. The change from the use of common to more significant metaphors comes between *The Portrait* and *The Old Things,* and it is very likely that James's experiments with the drama had a decisive influence on his more careful choice of his metaphors.

The Golden Bowl shows two distinct developments of the rhetorical metaphor which are particularly Jamesian. The first lies in the taking up of a common metaphor, the second in its alteration. Adam Verver says to his daughter: "'You've got something up your sleeve.' She had a silence that made him right. 'Well, when I tell you you'll understand. It's only up my sleeve in the sense of being in a letter I got this morning.'[18]" "To have something up one's sleeve" is an everyday expression, but in taking this metaphor up and altering it slightly, its triteness is almost completely transformed. Moreover Mr. Verver's challenge and Maggie's answer are thus closely related to one another. This simple example exhibits one of James's late devices which he used frequently, and often more elaborately, with significant images. It takes its maturest form when the image originally introduced is employed much later, and sometimes more than once. This arrangement is often made use of when James gives us a person's train of thoughts, stretching over many pages.

The other form of development is the more expressive one. To say that "some one's cup is full" is a common metaphor indeed. But there is one example in *The Golden Bowl* where its introduction initiates a most significant sequel, transforming the common into a typically Jamesian and highly significant image. The stale and lifeless cup-metaphor thus gains new life and a particular meaning. Charlotte and the prince are alone together, and, "while the minute lasted, it passed between them that their cup was full; which cup their very eyes, holding it fast, carried and steadied and began, as they tasted it, to praise[19]". By thus adding to the common metaphor this passage has lost its merely rhetorical character; it shows the transition into one with a great functional significance[20].

In *Roderick Hudson* and *The Portrait* also some of the rhetorical metaphors show a tendency to artificiality, as for instance when Roderick says: "If I'm to fizzle out, the sooner I know it the better. Sometimes I half suspect it. But let me at least go out and reconnoitre for the enemy, and not sit here waiting for him, cudgeling my brains for ideas that won't come![21]" This enemy image is not clear. Why should Roderick go out in order to reconnoitre for his enemy, as he is within himself? It is an inner destruction of which he is the victim. And he is certainly the person who can and must realize this fact best of all. The only interpretation which makes sense is that by the "enemy" he means the moral laws of society which prevent him from having his imagination properly fed. Or has he reached a point in his development at which he tries to avoid his outward enemy and surrenders to his inward one, which is idleness coupled with passion? Roderick's image appears neither convincing in its choice nor clear in its meaning.

James did, surprisingly, not merely retain an unconvincing metaphor in *The Portrait* in the revised version but even added a clause. Henrietta Stackpole "fixed her eyes upon" Ralph, "and there was something in their character that reminded him of large, polished buttons; he seemed to see the reflection of surrounding objects upon the pupil[22]." The main fault with this image is that something completely dead, as buttons are, is compared with the human eye, which is perhaps fuller of life than any other object.

On the whole, then, common metaphors play a less prominent part in James's novels than rhetorical comparisons and similes. Taken together and put into the scale against the remaining images, we find that in the early novels rhetorical images hold the balance with the others, but from *The Old Things* onwards there is a steady and considerable decrease in their application. Their place is taken by images which have greater functional significance.

CHAPTER 3

The Expanding Image

The function of expanding images is to emphasize important facts, to illustrate certain statements, thus rendering their meaning clearer, and also—to a lesser degree—to bring about comic effects. Expanding images are, therefore, afterthoughts, illustrating or emphasizing a statement by a following image. They are mostly comparisons or similes, and their significance is often but slightly higher than that of the rhetorical image. The main difference between the two groups of imagery lies in the fact that in the expanding image, with some exceptions among the revised and added images, we always meet James's own creations.

A. REVISED IMAGES

When James revised *Roderick Hudson* he felt that he had especially failed in the presentation of Mary Garland. The reader was not prepared by the story "to take more closely home the impression made by Mary Garland[1]". He tried to correct this defect in his revision as far as that was still possible, and to lay "the ground" which "had not been laid" in the earlier version by altering already existing images or even adding some which were completely new. With these James on the one hand enhanced Mary's beauty, and on the other emphasized the importance of her smile. Both are essential for the understanding of Rowland Mallet's relation to her. The effect of her beauty on Rowland is, in the first version, given only in simple terms, as a straightforward statement. Only the final version adds a much stronger emotional note, thus stressing Rowland's affection for Mary, who strikes him as having "more expression, facial and other, and it was beautifully as if this expression had been accumulating all the while, lacking on the scene of her life any channel to waste itself. It was like something she had been working at in the long days of home, an exquisite embroidery or a careful compilation, and she now presented the whole wealth of it as a kind of pious offering[2]." This is a subjective and emotional judgment of which we find nothing in the first version. Other revisions in this novel mostly concern imprecise images[3]. To this group belong those images in the dialogue which James altered in order to adapt them to the character using them. Giving his opinion on Roderick's statuette of the water-drinker, Gloriani says in the first edition: "This sort of thing is like a man trying to lift himself up by the seat of his trousers. He may stand on tip-toe, but he can't do more[4]." Gloriani is a prototype of intelligence and cleverness. This very common image which he uses here is inappropriate to the general impression he makes. The New

York Edition, therefore, reads much more convincingly: "Your beauty, as you call it, is the effort of a man to quit the earth by flapping his arms very hard. He may jump about or stand on tiptoe, but he can't do more. Here you jump about very gracefully, I admit; but you can't fly; there's no use trying[5]."

Roderick Hudson is the novel least altered of the three written before 1882, whereas *The American* received the most extensive revision. But even in *The Portrait,* more than a sixth of all existing images were altered, and we find about as many added images. The revisions make Isabel Archer's development, her relation to the world surrounding her, and her reactions to it, more plausible than in the first version. At the point of Goodwood's final attack on Isabel at Gardencourt, James made the most important alteration of the whole revised version. After Goodwood's kiss the first version reads merely: "His kiss was like a flash of lightning; when it was dark again she was free[6]." Although powerful, this comparison does not convey more than a fraction of Isabel's feelings at that particular moment. The same passage in the final version is very pregnant, full of hidden meanings, giving us not only Isabel's reaction at that moment but a retrospective view of her life and her whole state of mind (notice also the accumulation of the vowel 'i' in monophthongs and diphthongs):

> "His kiss was like white lightning, a flash that spread, and spread again, and stayed; and it was extraordinarily as if, while she took it, she felt each thing in his hard manhood that had least pleased her, each aggressive fact of his face, his figure, his presence, justified of its intense identity and made one with this act of possession. So had she heard of those wrecked and under water following a train of images before they sink. But when darkness returned she was free[7]."

Isabel realizes during this wild attack that giving herself up to Goodwood would mean her "death", her sinking slowly like those "wrecked". If she has to choose between mental suffering (Osmond) and moral suffering (Goodwood), she will decide for the former without hesitation. The final edition brings out this aspect quite clearly and helps considerably to an understanding of Isabel's final decision to go back to Rome, to a life of unhappiness and suffering. Her sense of duty and her pride are the foremost reasons for her return to Osmond and Pansy.

B. ADDED IMAGES

Whereas there is a perceptible decrease of revised images after *The Portrait,* there is, on the other hand, an increase in additional images. The main additions in *Roderick Hudson* again concern Mary Garland and Rowland Mallet's relation to her. "She always had a smile, she was always eager, alert, responsive[8]"; so reads a brief characterization of Mary in the original version.

Revising this passage, James felt that Mary's smile, with the importance attached to it, was insufficiently described. Hence the passage reads in the final edition: "She was always eager, alert, responsive; she had always her large settled smile, which reminded him of some clear ample 'spare-room', some expectant guest-chamber, as they said in New England, with its window up for ventilation[9]." This comparison exemplifies the importance an image may have as emphasizing some special point. In the original version the four qualities of Mary's character stand equally side by side. But as her smile has a special import, James connected with it an image in the final edition. Thus it stands out as the most distinctive and essential of her qualities. Similarly, Rowland's uncertainty about Mary's feelings, the secret side of her character, into which he cannot penetrate, has to be brought out more clearly. In the first edition there is just a mention of Mary's beauty, as it impresses Rowland: "he would have called her beautiful[10]." This plain statement is not subtle enough for the mature James; he replaces it completely and adds an image which emphasizes Mary's mystery: "he would recklessly have pronounced it 'rich'. It was as if she had somehow put lights in her dim windows and you could hear somewhere behind them the tuning of mystic fiddles[11]." The change from "beautiful" to "rich" is a typical example of the change from clear to ambiguous style. At the moment the importance lies not in Mary's beauty, but in the mystery of her character, which Rowland cannot make out. The stress on this fact has a similar importance for the understanding of the happenings after Roderick's death as the lightning image has for the ending of *The Portrait*.

This novel contains a great number of added images. Most of them serve to stress one particular aspect of a person's character which had not been brought out clearly in the original version, as for instance Ralph's attitude towards his illness[12], or Osmond's relation to works of art[13]. The most revealing additions, however, concern Goodwood and Isabel's relation to him. His aggressive character had not been duly stressed in the first edition. Therefore James has added the following two images in the final version: "Caspar Goodwood raised his eyes to her own again; they seemed to shine through the vizard of a helmet[14]." and: "she saw the different fitted parts of him as she had seen, in museums and portraits, the different fitted parts of armoured warriors—in plates of steel handsomely inlaid with gold[15]." Not only is Goodwood's aggressiveness brought out much clearer by these images, but we recognize in them also a preparation for Isabel's final rejection of him, as it is always the heroine of the novel who is struck by such martial attributes in connection with him. They show her fear of the unknown in him, a quality emphasized very effectively in two further images which were missing in the first edition. One is introduced when Goodwood had left Isabel after their meeting in London. She "found herself now

humming like a smitten harp ... She intensely rejoiced that Caspar Goodwood was gone; there was something in having thus got rid of him that
was like the payment, for a stamped receipt, of some debt too long on her
mind[16]." The harp image, especially, can easily be conceived of as an intentional preparation of Isabel's brief surrender to him at the end of the novel.
Shortly before this happens we read in another added passage: "she had
never been loved before. She had believed it, but this was different; this was
the hot wind of the desert, at the approach of which the others dropped
dead, like mere sweet airs of the garden. It wrapped her about; it lifted her
off her feet, while the very taste of it, as of something potent, acrid and
strange, forced open her set teeth[17]." This is the temptation of the unknown,
the seducing element in Isabel's momentary weakness and Goodwood's
permanent strength. But the image of the "hot wind of the desert" is an
ample stress on the danger of such passion, the uncertainty of its origin and
its sudden and unpredictable change of direction. This part of the image also
points to the fact that in Goodwood's passionate attack Isabel is facing a
phenomenon furthest away from anything she has experienced in her past
life. The fear of the unknown makes her prefer the "cage" into which she is
prepared to go back rather than accept Goodwood's offer. If she had "not
known where to turn" when she came to Ralph's death-bed, she saw "a
very straight path" in front of her after the experience with Goodwood.

Some of the added images in *The Old Things* are remarkably colourless and
therefore remain ineffective[18]. There are, on the other hand, a few instances
where there is no doubt why James added these images, and no doubt about
their significance and effectiveness. They all concern Fleda, but fewer had
to be added than in any of the earlier novels. One point James had to render
more clearly was Fleda's strong affection for Owen. This he does in a very
simple, but nevertheless effective image: "At the sight of him two fresh
waves passed quickly across her heart, one at the heels of the other[19]." The
stress here lies on the fact that for Fleda the relation to Owen is a matter of
the heart, not of the mind. The image evokes the impression that she is
clearly excited at her surprising meeting with him in the streets of London.
Another significant image is added after her brief surrender to him. In her
case we are not confronted with an immediate rejection, as with Isabel and
Goodwood. Fleda still nourishes slight hopes that a union of happiness
between her and Owen can be brought about. Although she tries to conceal
her hopes in front of him she cannot help giving herself away with a question.
Her curiosity is stronger than her resolution: "As for the other [thought],
it had no sooner come into her head than she found it seated, in spite of her
resolution, on her lips[20]." The personification of thought indicates clearly
that this image is a creation of the mature James, just as the most significant
added image in this novel personifies Fleda's feelings. It occurs at the be-

ginning of the last chapter: "she had made up her mind that her feelings had no connection with the case. It was her claim that they had never yet emerged from the seclusion into which, after her friend's visit to her at her sister's, we saw them precipitately retire: if she should suddenly meet them in straggling procession on the road it would be time enough to deal with them. They were all bundled there together, likes with dislikes and memories with fears[21]." This subsequent touch to Fleda's picture helps towards a correct interpretation of the novel. Her heroic and highly moral behaviour has given external success to others. But her inner victory stands out in greater glory. She has been successful in conquering her feelings, her affection for Owen.

The Ambassadors, written only a few years before James began to revise his novels, was not much altered. The already existing images have been left unchanged. There are, however, two functionally very important metaphors added in the passages which James interpolated, or rather restored, in the final version[22]. The first passage follows Strether's long reflections over his "lost" years in Woollett, in which there occurs an image portraying the emptiness of his hometown to which the Paris that now surrounds him forms a considerable contrast. The function of the restored passage is above all to bring out this contrast more clearly. It reaches its climax in the added comparison in Strether's mind of Paris to a jewel. If we compare this image to others in earlier novels we discern a marked development in the combination of metaphor and comparison. Paris, at first, "hung" before Strether as "the vast bright Babylon", a very evident and convincing association which is a natural impression of the city's cosmopolitan character. The following comparison adds a new picture: "like some huge iridescent object, a jewel brilliant and hard in which parts were not to be discriminated nor differences comfortably marked. It twinkled and trembled and melted together, and what seemed all surface one moment seemed all depth the next[23]." Paris is, in other words, a tremendous temptation for Strether to give himself up to its charm, as Chad had done. In its contrast with the images used to characterize Woollett the present one marks the beginning of Strether's inner conflict between his duty and his surrender to the old world. The image of the "vast bright Babylon" has yet another function. It foreshadows the anticlimax which is soon to follow in Strether's mind, and which expresses itself in his warning to little Bilham on the occasion of Gloriani's garden party[24].

C. OBSCURING IMAGES

Artificial or too complicated images tend to become obscure in their meanings. We do not find many such images in the first versions of the early novels. Occasional obscurity in them is mostly brought about by James's revisions. An example from *The Portrait* may show that the image of the first version is much clearer than its revised form. At one point we get an indication of the position Ralph thinks to occupy in Isabel's life. "Ralph rendered perfect justice to her affection and knew that in her thoughts and her thoroughly arranged and servanted life his turn always came after the other nearest subjects of her solicitude, the various punctualities of performers of the workers of her will[25]." It is difficult to extract James's meaning from the second part of this sentence. The only point that emerges clearly is that Ralph, in his own mind, realized that he came after a few other things in Isabel's life. But what kind of things they are it is impossible to discern. The passage in the first edition reads: "Ralph rendered perfect justice to her affection, and knew that in her thoughts his turn always came after the care of her house and her conservatory (she was extremely fond of flowers)[26]." It is evident that this passage struck James as too ordinary and not poetical enough when he revised the novel.

Images which show a strong tendency to obscurity are more numerous in the novels after 1900. It is, of course, impossible to draw a distinct line between clear and obscure images. Therefore only one of the extreme examples of the latter kind shall be quoted here from *The Golden Bowl*. Maggie and her husband have just received a telegram from Charlotte announcing her and Adam's coming for tea: "what Charlotte's telegram announced was ... clear liberation. Just the point, however, was in its being clearer to herself than to him; her clearnesses, clearances—those she had so all but abjectly laboured for—threatened to crowd upon her in the form of one of the clusters of angelic heads, the peopled shafts of light beating down through iron bars, that regale, on occasion, precisely the fevered vision of those who are in chains[27]." Even if one knows from the context that just before this quoted passage Maggie had, in her thoughts, likened her husband to one of the aristocratic captives in the French Revolution during his last day of captivity, it does not help much towards an understanding of James's metaphor. Its origin must lie in one of James's own experiences. Maybe he had seen a painting which represented a similar scene to that which he describes by his metaphor[28].

There is yet another group of images which must be mentioned here, namely those which are based on literary allusions. With them it depends on each reader whether they are obscure or not. They are in most cases comparisons drawing a parallel between one of James's characters and one or several fictional ones. At the beginning of *The Ambassadors* Strether's thoughts, including Maria Gostrey and Waymarsh, run as follows: "There were moments when he himself felt shy of professing the full sweetness of the taste of leisure, and there were others when he found himself feeling as if his passages of interchange with the lady at his side might fall upon the third member of their party very much as Mr. Burchell, at Dr. Primrose's fireside, was influenced by the high flights of the visitors from London[29]." This, of course, presupposes that the reader is familiar with Goldsmith's *The Vicar of Wakefield*. It is equally doubtful that every reader can abstract the full meaning of the following literary allusion, when James says that Maria Gostrey had made Waymarsh fare "as Major Pendennis would have fared at the Megatherium[30]". Allusions to characters from Thackeray's novels are the most frequent. Others are from Shakespeare, Dickens, George Eliot, Goethe, to name only a few. It is true that James always chose his literary comparisons from well-known authors and novels so that he could expect his readers to be familiar with those works. This endeavour becomes all the more clear if we compare it with the tendency of a modern poet like T. S. Eliot, who very often does exactly the opposite, thus in many instances requiring footnotes in order to make the allusions in his texts comprehensible[31]!

D. COMIC EFFECTS THROUGH IMAGES

Plain humour is not an outstanding quality of James's novels. The nature of the subject he deals with does not allow an extensive development of the comic side. And it is single characters that strike us as comic rather than whole situations. In the early novels there is more room for comic effects, particularly in *Roderick Hudson*. But James never achieves them in the direct and outspoken manner of Shakespeare's fooling, for instance, but in an indirect and hidden way. This is the foremost reason why the comic element in his fiction has so often been overlooked. Another point is that he achieves his humour mostly not with plain but with metaphorical language. Barnaby Striker, a *petit bourgeois*, trying to make a favourable impression on the cosmopolitan Rowland, is one of the first comic types in James's novels. He uses many images in quick succession with the clear intention of impressing. Though many of his images are rhetorical we feel that he does not normally use them in his daily language. This device allows James to achieve comic effects within the dialogue, as Striker's images in his little speech before Rowland may illustrate: "I didn't go off to the Old World to learn my business; no one took me by the hand; I had to grease my wheels myself ... The crop we gather depends upon the seed we sow. He [Roderick] may be the biggest genius of his age: his potatoes won't come up without his hoeing them ... Take the word for it of a man who ... doesn't believe that we'll wake up to find our work done because we've lain all night a-dreaming of it: ... If your young protajay finds things easy ... you had better step round to the office and look at the books[32]." This is obvious caricature. But some of the images, though conventional, are very appropriately chosen. Twice Mr. Striker uses images drawn from agriculture, which is not surprising, as Massachusetts was at that time a typical farming community. Comedy is also to be found in mere descriptions: "Mr. Leavenworth was a tall, expansive, bland gentleman, with a carefully brushed whisker and a spacious, fair, well-favored face, which seemed, somehow, to have more room in it than was occupied by a smile of superior benevolence, so that (with his smooth, white forehead) it bore a certain resemblance to a large parlor with a very florid carpet, but no pictures on the walls[33]". We clearly *see* Mr. Leavenworth, through whom James is making fun of the self-made man, in front of us, not as the static, dead creation of the novelist, but as a living, dynamic person. Later the caricature of Mr. Leavenworth is heightened when James says of him that he "stood stirring his tea and silently opening and shutting his mouth ... like a large, drowsy dog snapping at flies[34]". This is the kind of comic effect through imagery which we also find frequently applied by novelists before James, as for instance when Dickens writes of Mr. Micawber that he had "no more hair on his head ... than there is upon an egg".

It has to be pointed out that only the minor characters are endowed with comic features (with the exception of Christina Light). Here we see one of the main functions of these "ficelles". They have to relieve the strict and heavy line of the main action. This function is still evident in James's last novels, although there it is even more remote and transformed into irony and sarcasm. In *The Portrait* it is above all Henrietta Stackpole and Edward Rosier and, to a lesser degree, the Countess Gemini, who contribute some comic effects by means of images. These effects are mostly of the same kind as in the earlier novel, but far less numerous[35]. James's interest in the psychological development of his characters had already become so predominant that there was hardly any room for comedy. External descriptions, which James frequently uses for comic effects in his first novel, are almost non-existent.

Whereas there is a certain consistency in the introduction of comic images in the early novels, especially in *Roderick Hudson,* there is none in the late works, where it is obvious that such images are used at random. The reason is that James concentrated his efforts on other and more important problems. And yet he contrived that even in the last three completed novels some characters stand out very clearly as comic. In *The Ambassadors* they are Miss Barrace, Waymarsh and the Pococks[36], in *The Wings* Mrs. Stringham[37], in *The Golden Bowl* Bob Assingham, who is by far the most comic of these persons. There is an element of stupidity, even, in him. He is the only character whom James endowed with consistently comic images, as for instance: "Her husband's exaggerated emphasis was *his* box of toy soldiers, his military game ... bad words, when sufficiently numerous and arrayed in their might, could represent battalions, squadrons, tremendous cannonades and glorious charges of cavalry. It was natural, it was delightful— the romance ... of camp life and of the perpetual booming of guns. It was fighting to the end, to the death, but no one was ever killed[38]." Or: "He was always lonely at great parties, the dear Colonel—it wasn't in such places that the seed he sowed at home was ever reaped by him[39]."; and finally: "he moved about less like one of the guests than like some quite presentable person in charge of the police arrangements or the electric light[40]."

In the late novels we also find comic images of a general nature in which we feel that James himself has ironically expressed his own opinion. The best example of this kind occurs in *The Golden Bowl:* "the tea of the English race was somehow their morality, 'made', with boiling water, in a little pot, so that the more of it one drank the more moral one would become[41]."

E. ILLUSTRATIVE IMAGES

Emphasis and illustration are the most frequent functions fulfilled by images in James's work. Both kinds are used for similar effects, namely to bring more weight to a particular passage, to single out one special and important point. In a writer like Jane Austen, in whose novels images occur very rarely, we might sometimes wish for some such accents brought about by appropriate metaphors. It is probably due to the lack of imagery in her work that, in comparison with James's or George Eliot's, her novels convey a rather colourless impression. In James's novels the illustrative image helps to clarify an idea, a thought, an action or a reaction by either a preceding or a following picture. Picture and thought are set parallel to each other so that the result is more often a comparison or a simile than a metaphor. Even if the words "like" or "as ... as" do not appear, illustrative images are comparative in essence.

1. General

In *Roderick Hudson* the illustrative images are always of a very simple nature. The parallelism between image and reality is obvious, because one is always immediately followed by the other. In one of his emotional outbursts Roderick uses two such images. In the first example the picture precedes the "reality": "A mother can't nurse her child unless she follows a certain diet; an artist can't bring his vision to maturity unless he has a certain experience[42]." The introduction of the mother image before the facts about an artist has the effect, and is done with the intention, that Rowland should see how important and necessary experience is for any great and creative artist. With the second example the order of picture and fact is reversed: "If you want them [the artists] to produce, you must let them conceive. If you want a bird to sing, you must not cover up its cage[43]." Here, the image is an afterthought and serves as an illustration of the preceding sentence. Occasionally the subsequent illustrative image enlarges the meaning. When Roderick says: "I've seen enough for the present", we are inclined to assume that he does not *want* to see any more at that moment. But the following image makes it quite clear that it is not a voluntary matter; he is just not able to do so. He has had so many new experiences during his short stay in Rome that he first has to digest his impressions before he takes in any more. In order to express this thought his previously quoted sentence is followed by: "I've reached the top of the hill[44]."

The Portrait already adds a new and more elaborate way of pictorial illustration in so far as an image is not always immediately afterwards explained. In many instances three or more pages lie between image and illustration. When Isabel inherits the large sum after Mr. Touchett's death we are not told at once what effect this magnanimous deed has upon her. This James only reveals gradually, thus creating suspense in the minds of his readers. The first information about Isabel's reaction is given indirectly by Mrs. Touchett: "She doesn't know what to think about the matter at all. It has been as if a big gun were suddenly fired off behind her; she is feeling herself, to see if she be hurt[45]." And only towards the end, when Isabel herself recalls the events of the past few years, are we informed about her own feelings in this important matter: "At bottom, her money had been a burden,— had been on her mind, which was filled with the desire to transfer the weight of it to some other conscience[46]." In retrospect this image is of particular significance in so far as it throws much light on one aspect at least of Isabel's marrying Osmond, or rather of her marrying at all. The "burden" of her inheritance must have influenced her decision considerably and must particularly have sped it up.

In the same novel James also begins to make use of illustrative imagery for his indirect method, that is to say, he does not always describe the actual events, but uses some outsiders to comment on particular situations. One of these points is the beginning of Isabel's marriage, which Ralph sees as "only the first act of the drama, and he was determined to sit out the performance[47]". And to Lord Warburton he says: "her going off with me would make the explosion[48]." By such metaphorical comments upon the marriage between Isabel and Osmond we are made to realize its tension and the state of unhappiness in which Isabel must live. Only much later do we hear it from her.

In the maturer novels we find a few examples of the simple form of illustration which occurs frequently in *Roderick Hudson*[49], and also some of the developed kind of *The Portrait*[50]. But James chooses his illustrations more carefully, thereby reducing their number considerably. One characteristic quality is their elaborateness of one kind or another. In *The Ambassadors,* for instance, he first tells us simply that Strether has been affected in a strange way by little Bilham. But we do not yet know what has been the reason for this affection. It is only after Maria Gostrey has met the artist herself that we are told that it "was by little Bilham's amazing serenity that he had at first been affected, but he had inevitably, in his circumspection, felt it as the train of the serpent, the corruption, as he might conveniently have said, of Europe[51]". By this image we know not only of Strether's first and immediate, positive reaction to little Bilham, but also of his subsequent doubts, his fear that the young artist might represent one form of European corruption. The achievement of such retrospective illustration lies in the linking of scenes which are otherwise far apart. A continuity of thought is reached, which, at the same time, means an insistence on an important thought or scene. James thus leads the attention of his readers back to such points in a most powerful and successful way.

Chapter eleven of *The Wings* contains the significant scene in which Lord Mark shows Milly the Bronzino picture which so much resembles Milly herself. Chapter twenty-four narrates Lord Mark's visit to her in Venice. By the introduction of an illustrative image James brings about an immediate connection between this visit and the Bronzino episode, revealing only now the importance it had for Milly herself: "She had not been so thoroughly alone with him since those moments of his showing her the great portrait at Matcham, the moments that had exactly made the high-water mark of her security, the moments during which her tears themselves, those she had been ashamed of, were the sign of her consciously rounding her protective promontory, quitting the blue gulf of comparative ignorance and reaching her view of the troubled sea[52]." Without this elaborate illustrative metaphor we would not be made to realize that Milly's confrontation with her image in the Bronzino picture had, for her, meant the most decisive turning-point in her life. It was then that knowledge of the existence of "the troubled sea" broke the peace of her "blue gulf" of ignorance. The picture of the "high-water mark" makes it obvious in how great and acute a danger Milly must then all of a sudden have seen herself. The image quoted above is one extremely rich in meanings. It is a masterly creation, and in its rather ambiguous formulation a typical product of the mature James.

In contrast to the early novels the illustrative images especially in *The Golden Bowl* are sometimes complicated and ambiguous. Of English society James says in regard to the prince that it "cut him ... in two", that his relation with it reminds him of "a man possessed of a shining star". James then elaborates this star image, leaving it more or less open what the prince's star may represent, although he makes a rather vague suggestion when he adds that the "Prince's shining star may, no doubt, having [sic] been nothing more precious than his private subtlety[53]". The main difference between this and earlier illustrative passages lies in the fact that James, after suggesting the equivalent of his image in reality, returns to the development of the star metaphor.

2. Path Images

These are considered under a special heading because they are extremely frequent in James's early work, and are also to be found in his later novels, although here they are far less numerous. As path images are nowadays often used in daily language, many of James's images strike us as common[54]. More interesting and significant, however, are the particularly Jamesian versions of such images. The earliest example of this kind occurs in *The Portrait*. Isabel describes her idea of happiness as "a swift carriage, of a dark night, rattling with four horses over roads that one cannot see[55]". For this very expressive image James is most certainly indebted to Goethe, whose *Dichtung und Wahrheit* ends with Egmont's famous words: "Kind, Kind! nicht weiter! Wie von unsichtbaren Geistern gepeitscht, gehen die Sonnenpferde der Zeit mit unsers Schicksals leichtem Wagen durch, und uns bleibt Nichts, als muthig gefaßt die Zügel fest zu halten und bald rechts, bald links, vom Steine hier, vom Sturze da die Räder abzulenken. Wohin es geht, wer weiß es? Erinnert er sich doch kaum, woher er kam!" It must be "dark night" when one cannot see where one is going. Isabel is not keen to see everything clearly before her eyes. She rather trusts Providence completely. It is represented by the "four horses" of which she hopes that they will lead her the right way without her watching the road and guiding them. In other words, she is afraid of making any decisions of great importance at present, for she chooses the smoothest, and apparently easiest, way quite blindly, with the hope that everything will turn out well. This image stresses her own responsibility for her subsequent unhappiness.

A very elaborate image occurs in *The Ambassadors,* one that is a typical example of James's late style. It sums up the result of the Pococks' stay in Paris, as Strether sees it. Chad has brought them "to the uttermost end of the passage accepted by them perforce as pleasant". He lives in the very centre of Parisian life; nothing leads further. He had guided them into a "brave blind alley, where to pass was impossible and where, unless they stuck fast, they would have ... publicly to back out[56]". If one has accepted Chad's guidance one either accepts this end, this life—as Strether himself has done—or one has "to back out", which is what the Pococks will necessarily have to do. The image also dramatizes the crucial scene—at the beginning of which it is introduced—describing the invitation of the Pococks, together with many other guests, to Chad's apartment. Arriving there is a symbolic expression of the fact that the decisive point in any relationship with him has been reached. For any non-Parisian—especially for Americans—it means taking the vital decision of either accepting or refusing Chad's life and society. If the whole scene, in Strether's mind, "represented the terminus of the cul-de-sac", we are prepared for the fact that the Pococks' decision must be at hand, and thus the element of suspense hangs over this whole chapter.

By means of such images James lifts the general and slight significance of common pictorial expressions onto a higher plane. They start the reader thinking and pondering over the specific meaning, and this ought always to be the function of any significant image. Another of these particularly Jamesian path images occurs in his last completed novel, immediately after Maggie has told Fanny Assingham of her discovery about the golden bowl. Maggie is afraid that she might "meet" more surprising things of this kind. "Though ignorant still of what she *had* definitely met Fanny yearned, within, over her spirit; and so, no word about it said, passed, through mere pitying eyes, a vow to walk ahead and, at cross-roads, with a lantern for the darkness and wavings away for unadvised traffic, look out for alarms[57]." In contrast with the image from *The Ambassadors,* the implicit meaning of this metaphor is more obvious. Fanny's mute promise is to render her the great service of removing any possible dangers from Maggie's road to happiness. Thus Fanny is clearly taking her side, because she wants to keep up appearances.

3. Light Images

James handles light images more or less in the same way as path images. In all of his novels we find light images of a less significant kind[58]. When used more suggestively they denote contrasts, light and dark, security and uncertainty, knowledge and doubt. As such they fulfil significant functions. To this category belongs an image which has the function of illustrating Christina Light's beauty: "the perfection of her features and of her person and the mysterious depth of her expression seemed to glow with the white light of a splendid pearl[59]." As we know that James always chose the names of his characters very carefully we may even see in the choice of Christina Light with its bright vowels and Roderick Hudson with its dark ones an intentional contrast of light and dark.

In *The Portrait* significant light images occur only in the second half of the novel. They are mainly used to contrast Isabel's former felicity with her misery after her marriage. Shortly before that event Caspar Goodwood's visit seems to her to impair her state of complete contentment. "He had come to her with his unhappiness when her own bliss was so perfect; he had done his best to darken the brightness of these pure rays[60]." After her marriage James introduces a few significant and contrasting light images which stress the darkness, the unhappiness now characterizing Isabel's married life. "Pansy had a sufficient illumination of her own, and Isabel felt that she herself just now had no light to spare from her small stock[61]." And when Ralph Touchett comes to see her in Rome she feels that his "visit was a lamp in the darkness[62]". When Isabel journeys from Rome to England in order to see Ralph for the last time, she thinks, again, over her past and the prospects of her future. "Isabel recognised ... the quick vague shadow of a long future. She should not escape; she should last[63]." The "shadow of a long future" is the acceptance of her unhappiness as the result of her sense of duty. The organic relation of such a series of images in as early a novel as *The Portrait* is a remarkable achievement. As one of this particular group of images it has not been surpassed in any of the novels here considered.

The three late novels show a use of light images mainly on the lines of those in *The Portrait*. What is missing in most instances, however, is the close relation of several images. They stand by themselves, but as such they serve a distinct function. There is one point in *The Ambassadors* where Strether feels himself in a very dangerous and awkward position between Woollett and Paris. He is in danger of losing the old world altogether. But what will he gain in the new one? He has come to a point where he cannot help being afraid. This fear is expressed by the image of Strether's whistling in the dark. And as the dark presses more sharply on him it creates the need "for a louder and livelier whistle". After his sending a message to Mrs. Newsome he "whistled long and hard". And on hearing that Chad had some news from his mother "he whistled again". But the fact that he himself "was hearing almost nothing" led to an "increase of his darkness" and "the quickening ... of his tune[64]". Light images are more frequent in the last two novels than in any other. What distinguishes many of them from examples in the early novels is the more frequent avoidance of the conventional. James has again tried to give these pictorial creations new life. They are mostly introduced to stress the fact that a person has realized something. But only occasionally are they significant[65].

In *The Golden Bowl* a development can be discerned; the light images have, generally, gained in pictorial content. This is apparent in a sequence of three significant images introduced after Maggie's suspicion about Charlotte's and Amerigos's intimacy has almost become a certainty. "Then it was that she knew how hugely expert she had been made, for judging it quickly by that vision of it, indelibly registered for reference, that had flashed a light into her troubled soul the night of his late return from Matcham[66]." And a few pages later we read that "the flame" with which the idea of Charlotte's and Amerigo's intimacy at Matcham "burned afresh during these particular days, the way it held up the torch to anything, to everything that *might* have occurred as the climax of revels springing from traditions so vivified—this by itself justified her private motive and reconsecrated her diplomacy[67]".

When Maggie had gained certainty "there glowed upon her from afar, yet straight and strong, a deep explanatory light which covered the last inch of the ground[68]". As in *The Portrait* these images seem to have been introduced with a certain consistency, and they contribute to emphasize the development of Maggie's knowledge about Amerigo and Charlotte.

4. Theatre Images

Most of the theatre images in the early novels—and surprisingly even those in *The Old Things*—are undistinguished[69]; but, as a result of James's years as a dramatist, they are more significant in his later novels. They can stand for various things, as for instance falsity and unnatural behaviour. One image introduced in regard to Christina stresses this aspect of her character, and it is in its conception as powerful as many similar images in later novels. "Madame Grandoni had insisted on the fact that Christina was an actress, though a sincere one, and this little speech seemed a glimpse of the cloven foot. She had played her great scene, she had made her point, and now she had her eye at the hole in the curtain and she was watching the house[70]." Christina is seen playing a part, which differs from her own natural self. In society she never behaves naturally, but pretends to be a kind of person she is fundamentally unlike.

An interesting image is introduced towards the end of *The Old Things*. "Fleda's eyes rested, in the great hard street, on passing figures that struck her as puppets pulled by strings[71]." The whole world around her seems to her to be false, unnatural. She alone appears to be aloft, with the achievement of inner victory over outward defeat. The remarkable thing about this image is, however, that it is entirely unlike any theatre metaphor in ordinary use, and the first one of its kind in the novels considered. It indicates a change towards the introduction of more original, and therefore functionally more significant images.

In *The Ambassadors* James has heightened the impression of a drama being acted before our eyes by the introduction of several theatre images. On the occasion of the Pococks' visit to Chad's apartment Miss Barrace "had quitted the other room, forsaken the music, dropped out of the play, abandoned, in a word, the stage itself, that she might stand a minute behind the scenes with Strether and so perhaps figure as one of the famous augurs replying, behind the oracle, to the wink of the other[72]". A little later she says to Strether: "We know you as the hero of the drama, and we're gathered to see what you'll do." To which he answers: "I think that must be why the hero has taken refuge in this corner. He's scared at his heroism—he shrinks from his part." And her reply takes the form: "Ah, but we nevertheless believe he'll play it.[73]" From this point onwards the remainder of the novel is seen as a drama of which Strether is the hero. The important point, however, which is stressed in the first image, is that he has gained a superiority by his transformation which allows him to abandon the stage and place himself in a position from which he can direct the development of the action. On the other hand he has not yet reached the summit of his transformation; he still feels inferior to Chad and his friends. The second image particularly stresses, too, that Strether has not yet completed his task, and that it is still for him to make important decisions and to take decisive action. The mastery of such late images lies above all in the realization of more than one function. Images like those just quoted do not merely illustrate or emphasize, they also convey an atmosphere—here it is that of dramatic tension and suspense. Earlier images occasionally possess the same quality, but what is still mainly lacking there is the consistency, the restatement of an atmosphere once created by the introduction of similar images at a later point. In *The Ambassadors* James returns to the theatre image five chapters later. Strether, having left Paris for a short while and finding himself alone at an inn in the country, realizes that "he had never yet so struck himself as engaged with others and in midstream of his drama. It might have passed for finished, his drama, with its catastrophe all but reached; it had, however, none the less been vivid again for him as he thus gave it its fullest chance. He had only had to be at last well out of it to feel it, oddly enough, still going on[74]". This initial restatement of the dramatic theme is powerfully continued in one of James's most elaborate theatre images. Strether sees the surroundings as "a scene and a stage" and "the very air of the play was in the rustle of the willows and the tone of the sky. The play and the characters had ... peopled all his space for him." Everything strikes Strether as part of the drama. "Not a breath of the cooler evening that wasn't somehow a syllable of the text." And finally the picture and the play seem to him "to melt together in the good woman's broad sketch of what she could do for her visitor's appetite[75]". The description continues, in the same peculiar mingling together of "picture" and "play". It is as if James, as a dramatist, were working out instructions for a producer about the scenery in front of which the drama has to be enacted. Thus the description leads smoothly over into reality with the appearance, in this picture, of the boat with its two occupants: Chad and Madame de Vionnet. The passage, in its combination of imagery and reality, is one of James's most masterly achievements in working up to a climax.

The theatre images in *The Ambassadors* all act as a reinforcement of the dramatic structure of the whole novel. In *The Wings* James wants to emphasize the falsity and wickedness of Mrs. Lowder and Kate Croy, and also the dependence of the latter on the former. It is Densher who realizes "what Kate was to do for the character she had undertaken, under her aunt's roof, to represent". He sees her as "the poor actress in the glare of the footlights" who has "to look, to speak, in every way to express the part" with Mrs. Lowder as the "watchful manager" in the "depth of a box". Densher pictures himself "as in his purchased stall". These images contrast with the activity of Mrs. Lowder and Kate and Merton's passivity, his relegation to "mere spectatorship". James now elaborates and achieves a similar swift change-over from the image back to reality, as in the theatre metaphor from *The Ambassadors*: "The drama ... meanwhile went on—amplified soon enough by the advent of two other guests ... who visibly presented themselves to Kate ... as subjects for a like impersonal treatment[76]." At a much later point two other theatre images occur. One shows Densher's change from passive "spectatorship" to an active part in the "drama" after his intercourse with Kate[77]; the other pictures the development of Kate's false play into a treacherous double game. She now not only pretends to the world around her in general but particularly as far as Milly is concerned. The close friendship between the two young women had led to "intimate confessions, private, frank ironies that made up for their public grimaces and amid which, face to face, they wearily put off the mask". James, however, stresses the fact that they are not on equal terms. It is Kate who has a considerable advantage over her innocent American friend; and she exploits it to the full. Without their masks it was "that what they were keeping back was most in the air". The difference was that Milly "didn't quite see what her friend could keep back ... that would be so subject to retention; whereas it was comparatively plain sailing for Kate that poor Milly had a treasure to hide[78]".

In *The Golden Bowl* there is one example of clearly intentional repetition of theatre images. They concern Maggie and occur when she changes from passivity to activity. What the images illustrate is her rising to supreme control over the others. Maggie "reminded herself of an actress who had been studying a part and rehearsing it, but who suddenly, on the stage, before the footlights, had begun to improvise, to speak lines not in the text. It was this very sense of the stage and the footlights that kept her up, made her rise higher: just as it was the sense of action ... quite positively for the first time in her life[79]." The second image, nine chapters later, shows her already on a much higher level: "she felt not unlike some young woman of the theatre who, engaged for a minor part in the play and having mastered her cues with anxious effort, should find herself suddenly promoted to leading lady and expected to appear in every act of the five[80]." The culmination is reached soon afterwards in the crucial scene at Fawns where Maggie watches the others playing bridge from her dominating place outside on the terrace. They strike her as "figures rehearsing some play of which she herself was the author". She has the notion of a drama to come, a "scene she might people, by the press of her spring, either with serenities and dignities and decencies, or with terrors and shames and ruins[81]". In contrast to this series stands another theatre image which occurs much earlier in the novel and is attributed to Adam Verver. All his relations are "a matter of the back of the stage, of an almost visibly conscious want of affinity with the footlights. He would have figured less than anything the stage-manager or the author of the play, who most occupy the foreground, he might be at the best, the financial 'backer', watching his interests from the wing[82]." His whole attitude towards life differs widely from Maggie's; if he has any influence, and a kind of passive key position, it is merely because of his enormous wealth. This theatre image is part of the picture we receive of Adam as a man of social perversity. Together with the stress on the unnatural (also strongly implicit in the three images in regard to Maggie) and the falsity, theatre images here reach their highest and most intense function. At the same time it often becomes difficult to distinguish clearly between illustrative and emphasizing functions. In many of the examples quoted from the later novels illustration falls together with emphasis, and the latter function of the image gains more importance.

F. EMPHASIZING IMAGES

The function of emphasizing images is not so much a pictorial explanation or clarification of a thought as the stressing of a particular point which is of importance for the understanding of things that have happened or are going to happen; they can also contribute to dramatic intensity; they can create suspense, elucidate hidden relationships, and so on.

If one were not to distinguish too closely, one might regard the emphasizing function as common to all images. They all, in a general way, emphasize one thing or another. And even if one sets out to distinguish between several groups of imagery in James's works, the emphasizing images far outnumber any other group.

1. General

The Portrait is the first novel where significant emphasizing images are introduced with consistency. Questions like: is Isabel herself responsible for her own unhappiness?—did she really suspect the relation between Osmond and Madame Merle before the Countess Gemini's revelation?—was Ralph Touchett in love with Isabel? and others can easily and unequivocally be answered by the interpretation of certain images. In her unhappiness Isabel admits to herself at least that Osmond "had not disguised himself, during the years of his courtship, any more than she. But she had seen only half his nature then, as one saw the disk of the moon when it was partly masked by the shadow of the earth. She saw the full moon now,—she saw the whole man[83]." Sadly but freely she admits that then "she had mistaken a part for the whole". Osmond's helplessness had charmed her, had put her under a spell from which she could not escape. She saw him as "a sceptical voyager, strolling on the beach while he waited for the tide; looking seaward, yet not putting to sea [84]". This view of him aroused pity in her tender heart and she decided to give him the necessary impulse to "launch his boat for him". She married him out of compassion; "there was no charitable institution in which she was as much interested as in Gilbert Osmond [85]". And what could be more welcome to her than a "charitable institution"—which was at the same time a human being—which allowed her to get rid of the burden of her money in the form of a charitable deed!

A further image stresses clearly enough that Isabel must have had a strong suspicion of a dreadful relationship between Osmond and Pansy on the one hand, and Madame Merle on the other. This becomes evident when the Countess Gemini begins her revelation and expects a tremendous reaction from Isabel. But in that hope she is disappointed: "she had expected to kindle a conflagration, and as yet she had barely extracted a flash. Isabel seemed more awe-stricken than anything else [86]."

Ralph's strong affection for her is emphasized from the very beginning of their friendship, and here again it is an image which helps considerably to convey the impression of his cheering up after her coming to Gardencourt: "At a time when his thoughts had been a good deal of a burden to him, her sudden arrival, which had promised nothing and was an open-handed gift of fate, had refreshed and quickened them, given them wings and something to fly for [87]."

On the whole the emphasizing images in *The Portrait* are plain in their meaning, but not yet of particular strength [88].

Those in *The Old Things* are of a great dramatic intensity and leave the impression that they have been very carefully selected in order to bring out the intended meaning as clearly as possible. Wanting to stress that Mona Brigstock is Fleda's exact contrary, that she is stupid, aggressive, "all will", James emphasizes this blind aggressiveness by saying that "She was not so stupid as not to see that something, though she scarcely knew what, was expected of her that she couldn't give; and the only mode her intelligence suggested of meeting the expectation was to plant her big feet and pull another way [89]." Stupidity and an animal-like instinct are here emphasized as the characteristic qualities of Mona's nature. Although she could not give any reasons, this instinct told her that she had to oppose Mrs. Gereth's plans and ideas, just as it told her later on that she was to work against Fleda in order not to lose Poynton and Owen.

When confronted with Mrs. Gereth after Owen's visit to Ricks, Fleda feels that the crisis "put forth big encircling arms,—arms that squeezed till they hurt and she must cry out". She is afraid that she might give Mrs. Gereth a hint as to Owen's confession of his love for her and the condition Mona has laid down before she would marry him. But the continuation of the above image makes it obvious that these were the two secrets which Fleda manages to keep to herself. "It was as if everything at Ricks had been poured into a common receptacle, a public ferment of emotion and zeal, out of which it was ladled up to be tasted and talked about; everything, at least, but the one little treasure of knowledge that she kept back[90]." Before Mrs. Gereth's fatal action of sending her treasures back to Poynton, James introduces two successive images which help to make this move plausible. The first emphasizes Mona's perseverance and her stubbornness, the second the questionability of Mrs. Gereth's victory over Mona and Fleda's disbelief that it will last. Fleda's "eyes grew wan as she discerned in the impenetrable air that Mona's thick outline never wavered an inch. She wondered fitfully what Mrs. Gereth had by this time made of it, and reflected with a strange elation that the sand on which the mistress of Ricks had built a momentary triumph was quaking beneath the surface[91]."

The emphasizing images in *The Ambassadors* are generally of a plain kind[92], though many of them are not so obvious as those in the preceding novels. They require more careful analysis if one wants to grasp their full meaning. When Strether watches a play at a Parisian theatre James says that he had stuck in the box "like a schoolboy wishing not to miss a minute of the show![93]" This comparison seems to be very insignificant. But it is a strong emphasis on the new and unfamiliar world surrounding Strether everywhere in Paris. Even the worst show captures his whole attention. He is completely taken in by the smallest detail and is not willing to miss anything. This simple image then emphasizes his falling under the spell of the life and atmosphere of Paris. When he meets Chad there for the first time "Strether didn't, as he talked, absolutely follow himself; he only knew he was clutching his thread and that he held it, from moment to moment, a little tighter[94]." His "thread" is his errand, what he has come to Paris for. But it is already emphasized in this metaphor how uncertain he has become of whether he is doing the right thing, now that Chad presented himself so differently from what he had expected. Strether has not yet quite the courage to admit that Chad seems to have improved, although he is asked this very question. He is so perplexed and confused because "everything was so totally different. But in spite of that he had put the flag at the window. That was what he had done, and there was a minute during which he affected himself as having shaken it hard, flapped it with a mighty flutter, straight in front of his companion's nose[95]." This putting up of "the flag at the window" was Strether's duty, which now appears to him as an awkward burden. It is typical that, after having shaken the flag, he has the relieving sense of "having already acted his part". But this means nothing less than a shrinking back from his duty. These two images emphasize Strether's conviction of

Chad's improvement and mark the beginning of his inner struggle between his duty and his own transformation.

After the first brief meeting with Marie de Vionnet, James emphasizes that Strether "had not yet had so quiet a surrender[96]". But nevertheless it is a surrender; he has ceased to struggle, he has accepted a world of which Madame de Vionnet appears as the prototype. The emphasis on his surrender to her is like an overture to his warning given to little Bilham which, characteristically enough, opens with a metaphor which gains significance by its elaboration: "You don't strike me as in danger of missing the train", because, "with the clock of their freedom ticking as loud" as it does in Paris, people can be pretty well trusted "to keep an eye on the fleeting hour". In Woollett there is no such clock which would serve as a stimulus to make use of every possible fraction of time in order to lose as little as possible. There one is bound to lead such a remote life that one never becomes aware of how quickly time passes. Living the provincial life of Woollett means not living at all. In the second part of the image Strether refers back to a passage towards the end of book two, when we find him thinking of the time when he was still "helplessly young". At least thirty years have elapsed since then, and now, being back in Paris at the age of fifty-five, he has to make the sad discovery that it is "too late" that he has "missed the train". But at the same time he admits that it is largely his own fault, for "the train had fairly waited at the station for me without my having had the gumption to know it was there. Now I hear its faint receding whistle miles and miles down the line[97]." Why does James emphasize this particular realization of Strether's in such a significant way? It gives us again an essential clue to his subsequent actions and behaviour. All his efforts now are to prevent the same thing happening to Chad, to prevent his return to Woollett. This attitude of Strether's is caused by two discoveries he has made during his short stay in Paris. The first is that of Chad's considerable improvement, the second that of his own failure in life.

The function of most emphasizing images in *The Wings* is to draw a sharp contrast between Milly's innocent world and that of the corruption and wickedness in which Mrs. Lowder moves, gradually drawing Kate and Merton into it as well. Mrs. Lowder "sat somehow in the midst of her money, founded on it and surrounded by it, even if with a clever high manner about it, her manner of looking, hard and bright, as if it weren't there". Milly's attitude about hers is quite different. She was "far away on the edge of it, and you hadn't, ... in order to get at her nature, to traverse, by whatever avenue, any piece of her property[98]". Money, for Mrs. Lowder, is everything; for Milly, on the other hand, it is of no particular importance. The young American girl is, in fact, so innocent that she cannot even conceive of the idea that someone may show an interest in her just for the sake of her wealth. This is exactly where Mrs. Lowder takes a hold, and it is only after a certain time that Milly begins to suspect. "Susie's overture to Mrs. Lowder had been their joke, but they had pressed in that gaiety an electric bell that continued to sound. Positively, while she sat there, she had the loud rattle in her ears, and she wondered, during these moments, why the others didn't hear it[99]." This suspicion of Milly's grows stronger and stronger until it gains certainty when Lord Mark shows her the Bronzino picture at Matcham.

The major development in the application of emphasizing images since *The Ambassadors* lies in James's attitude of not only stressing one particular fact by the introduction of a single image, but by repeating it and therewith insisting on the importance of that particular fact. Milly's innocence and love of complications are emphasized in such a series of images. When Mrs. Stringham remarks that they "move in a labyrinth", Milly replies: "Of course we do. That's just the fun of it! ... Don't tell me that—in this for instance—there are no abysses. I want abysses[100]." The second image, although introduced much later, is clearly connected to the initial metaphor: "It would have taken but another free moment to make her see abysses— since abysses were what she wanted—in the mere circumstance of his [Densher's] own silence, in New York, about his English friends[101]." The third image follows almost on the heels of the second: "It was to be added at the same time that even if his silence had been labyrinthine—which was absurd in view of all the other things too he couldn't possibly have spoken of—this was exactly what must suit her, since it fell under the head of the plea she had just uttered to Susie[102]." The theme in the passages quoted is that of the relationship between Kate and Merton, which Milly approaches with a thoughtlessness and light-heartedness which again puts a strong emphasis on her innocence. She perceives as little as Merton Densher himself that he is caught "in a wondrous silken web" which is Mrs. Lowder's and Kate's work, a web which he, in his stupidity, finds to be "amusing". But Milly, in contrast to Densher, is not stupid. She is capable of seeing more things than any one would believe, if only she wanted to. "Susan Shepherd perceived ... such signs of an appetite for motive as would have sat gracefully even on one of her own New England heroines. It was seeing round several corners; but that was what New England heroines did, and it was moreover interesting for the moment to make out how many really her young friend had undertaken to see round[103]." In that quality of her character she reminds us strongly of Isabel Archer.

In *The Golden Bowl* emphasizing images largely serve to underline Maggie Verver's dawning awareness of the real relationship between Charlotte and Amerigo. When we come to the first image in this series we make the surprising discovery that Maggie, too, shows the characteristic common to Isabel and Milly, namely the shrinking back from essential knowledge, the fear to light dark corners. And in Maggie's case it is clearly because she has a suspicion that finding out too much about her dear friend Charlotte Stant might ruin the good impression she has of her, might even ruin their friendship. This is clearly implied when Maggie says to her father about Charlotte: "I don't think I want even for myself to put names and times, to pull away any veil. I've an idea there has been, more than once, somebody I'm not acquainted with—and needn't be or want to be[104]." This image suggests that Maggie, even at this stage, has a vague notion that Amerigo might be involved in the question of Charlotte's former lovers. But she cannot base her suspicions on any evidence but merely on her feeling. The image also stresses the fact that Maggie belongs to the group of James's innocent Americans, characterized by their belief in the goodness and virtue of human beings, trusting them blindly and beginning to doubt only when there are strong reasons for it. When we have reached this point of the story James emphasizes the possibility of Maggie's knowledge in an indirect way, so as still to leave a small doubt whether she really knows. He gives us only Fanny Assingham's conviction that Maggie must have "seen", when she says to her husband: "She couldn't keep it from me—though she left her post on purpose: came home with me to throw dust in my eyes. I took it all—her dust; but it was what showed me[105]." Only during a discussion five chapters later does Fanny get the proof that her suspicion as to Maggie's knowledge was justified. The princess says there: "And if I'm both helpless *and* tormented I stuff my pocket-handkerchief into my mouth, I keep it there, for the most part, night and day, so as not to be heard too indecently moaning. Only now, with you, at last, I can't keep it longer; I've pulled it out, and here I am fairly screaming at you[106]." The maturity and significance of this image shows itself in the variety of functions it fulfils. Long before its introduction the reader knows of Maggie's knowledge[107]. Therefore this image is firstly a restatement of this fact. Secondly, it stresses that Fanny is now certain that Maggie knows. Its third and most significant function is that of stressing the fact that Maggie is silently suffering because of her knowledge. She is tormented but does not show it to anyone but Fanny. The reason for her silent suffering is her conviction that she will gain final happiness not by a rash action but only by patiently waiting for the right moment to act. When this point is reached it is emphasized by a powerful metaphorical creation: "It was as if she had come out ... of a dark tunnel, a dense wood, or even simply a smoky room, and had thereby at least for going on the advantage of air in her lungs ... the change brought about by itself as great a difference of view as the shift of an inch in the position of a telescope. It was her telescope in fact that had gained in range[108]."

The last three novels have one particular form of the emphasizing image in common. This is the direct comment upon a person's inner reaction to a remark. At the same time our attention is directed to the importance of the remark in question. *The Golden Bowl* yields the maturest example of an emphasizing image used for this particular purpose[109]. It occurs during a talk between Adam and Maggie. At the crucial point the discussion is interrupted for the sake of a long passage, giving Maggie's soliloquy:

> This was the moment, in the whole process of their mutual vigilence in which it decidedly *most* hung by a hair that their thin wall might be pierced by the lightest wrong touch. It shook between them, this transparency, with their very breath; it was an exquisite tissue, but stretched on a frame, and would give way the next instant if either so much as breathed too hard. She held her breath, for she knew by his eyes, the light at the heart of which he couldn't blind, that he was, by his intention, making sure—sure whether or no her certainty was like his. The intensity of his dependence on it at that moment—this itself was what absolutely convinced her so that, as if perched up before him on her vertiginous point and in the very glare of his observation, she balanced for thirty seconds, she almost rocked: she might have been for the time, in all her conscious person, the very form of the equilibrium they were, in their different ways, equally trying to save[110].

The most remarkable feature of this elaborate image—or rather series of images—is the interrelation of image and reality. There is a constant swift oscillation between the two. The passage of Maggie's soliloquy is about three times as long as the one quoted above, and James's main achievement lies in the creation of an immense tension between Adam's wish to know what it is that she is sacrificing him to—the question which causes her reflections—and Maggie's final answer which stands at the end of her thoughts. The contribution of the images in this passage is that of dramatic intensity. They emphasize the importance of Maggie's answer, and create suspense by deferring it.

It becomes evident, especially in *The Golden Bowl,* that every image stands exactly in its proper place in the development of the plot, and particularly that the emphasizing images are always introduced at essential points. Whereas images in novels written before James took to writing plays occasionally leave an impression of fortuitousness, those in novels written after that period do not. If the emphasizing images in the early novels point back to the lesser kinds of imagery, those in the late works rather point forward to the higher forms. But before dealing with these we have yet to consider two special groups of emphasizing images.

2. Key Images

Key images are as common in James's work as path and light metaphors. Frequently, moreover, they are not more than rhetorical and hence of no particular significance[111]. Their general function is also one of emphasis, be it that of a mystery about a certain person, the nature of a relation between two or more characters, or even the helplessness of some one in a particular situation or in regard to another person. The possession of the key to something or somebody appears, then, like the discovery of the solution to a riddle, or, as James put it in one of his short stories, the figure in the carpet.

As early as *Roderick Hudson* there are two related key images which are Jamesian in their conception and formulation. One of them emphasizes the possibility of Roderick's inevitable failure: "One morning ... Roderick delivered himself of a tissue of lugubrious speculations as to the possible mischances of one's genius. What if the watch should run down ... and you should lose the key? 'What if you should wake up one morning and find it stopped, inexorably, appallingly stopped?'[112]" At a much later point James refers to this speculation of Roderick's and achieves a direct relation in taking up the key image, when Rowland says: "I suppose there is some key or other to his character, but I try in vain to find it; and yet I can't believe that Providence is so cruel as to have turned the lock and thrown the key away[113]." Both examples have gained new life, because James has succeeded in conveying a lively picture. In the first example he achieves it by relating the key image to the preceding watch metaphor; in the second by turning it into vivid action.

Significant key images in *The Portrait* are restricted to the relationship between Ralph and Isabel. Two of these are very important, and one is, again, directly linked with the other. The first is introduced in one of Ralph's soliloquies: "Suddenly I receive a Titian ... to hang on my wall,—a Greek bas-relief to stick over my chimney-piece. The key of a beautiful edifice is thrust into my hand, and I am told to walk in and admire." By the "Titian" and so on, James obviously means Isabel. It is characteristic of his early method that he first has Ralph deliver his soliloquy, and then he himself interpolates a few remarks, warning the reader that "it was not exactly true that Ralph had had a key put into his hand[114]". Somewhat later Ralph himself realizes that "the door was fastened, and though he had keys in his pocket, he had a conviction that none of them would fit[115]". This second key image has the greater functional significance. If Ralph himself comes to the conclusion that none of his keys would fit for Isabel it means nothing else but that he cannot fully understand her character. But in spite of this knowledge he persuades his father to bequeath a large sum to Isabel, hereby instigating her subsequent unhappiness. Although his action shows great generosity and magnanimity it does at the same time show irresponsibility and short-sightedness, because he cannot possibly judge the effect of his generous deed upon her.

In *The Old Things* there occur no significant key images[116], and even *The Ambassadors* contains very few and none of them is particularly noteworthy[117]. If we look forward to the two following novels we find a probable reason for the decline in the application of key images in the late works. It is James's realization that they must always be less significant than any of his entirely new creations because they are basically part of our daily language. And even if he succeeded in bringing new life to such key images by altering them—as we shall see presently—there still remains the latent danger that they might be overlooked.

In *The Wings* James's efforts to actualize, even to dramatize, the key images are obvious. Moreover we perceive a development from the earlier novels. It is the consistency with which he attributes key images to one particular person, namely Mrs. Stringham. Her thirst for knowledge and her shortcomings in these efforts, because of her restricted intelligence, are emphasized in this way: "Yet in respect to this relation at least it was what did prove the key of knowledge; it lighted up as nothing else could do the poor young woman's history[118]." This image remains completely within the frame of the conventional. "The key of knowledge was felt to click in the lock from the moment it flashed upon Mrs. Stringham that her friend had been starved for culture[119]." This is more Jamesian and thus breathes new life, as do the following examples: "there were special keys she had not yet added to her bunch, impressions that, of a sudden, were apt to affect her as new[120]." The following example, though introduced ten chapters later, shows a direct connection to the image just quoted: "yet when once the key had been offered Susie slipped it on her bunch, and her young friend could again feel her lovely imagination operate[121]." It seems that a wholly satisfactory application of a key image can only be reached when it is made part of a wider pictorial conception. One such example occurs in *The Wings,* when Densher says to Kate: "You keep the key of the cupboard, and I foresee that when we're married you'll dole me out my sugar by lumps[122]." Although only the starting point of a more widely conceived metaphor, the key image remains the most significant part, stressing the fact that Kate has complete control over Merton, degrading him to a mere tool in her hands, a useful instrument of her will and intentions. This bondage compels him to do everything she asks of him, even if it is against his own will.

In *The Golden Bowl* key images have disappeared almost completely. Two which do occur are, however, of special interest. The first is introduced at the very beginning of the novel. Its power is the latent ambiguity with which it conveys a fact in a metaphorical way, without giving any reasons or any further explanations for the time being. Here again James's mature method of gradual revelation shows itself. The image is introduced when Amerigo is thinking over his past and comes to the point of his recent engagement to Maggie, which has actually taken place only a few hours before we follow the prince's meditations. His reaction to the event is not a happy one, but on the contrary, "the moment had something of the grimness of a crunched key in the strongest lock that could be made[123]". Hereby James emphasizes the possibility of difficulties and complications caused by an element yet unknown to the reader; but this gradually turns out to be the prince's former intimacy with Charlotte. The second one is introduced during that crucial scene at Fawns. "They might in short have represented any mystery they would; the point being predominantly that the key to the mystery, the key that could wind and unwind it without a snap of the spring, was there in her pocket—or rather, no doubt, clasped at this crisis in her hand and pressed, as she walked back and forth, to her breast[124]." Maggie is here pictured as the holder of the vital key to the mystery, and so this metaphor belongs to those other images which serve to emphasize the fact that Maggie has by that point of the novel gained complete command over the others.

3. Images Based on Games

The main purpose of images based on games is the indication of risks, of luck or difficulties; or they may emphasize the grouping of various characters who are working together, or oppose each other. They can also stress triumph or loss or several qualities of a character, such as secrecy, wickedness, and so on.

In *Roderick Hudson* all such images are introduced in the dialogue. This fact justifies their being simple and common. But at the same time their functional significance is, of course, restricted[125]. The most characteristic example may illustrate the quality of such an early image. Rowland says to the Cavaliere Giacosa: "I don't understand double people, Cavaliere, ... and I don't pretend to understand you. But I have guessed you are going to play some secret card." To which the Cavaliere answers: "That card is Mrs. Light's, not mine." This image gains its particular significance by its relation to another which follows immediately afterwards, giving this whole passage a dramatic intensity. After Rowland's question whether Mrs. Light's "card" is a menace, the Cavaliere answers: "The sword of Damocles! It hangs by a hair! Christina is to be given ten minutes to recant, under penalty of having it fall. On the blade there is something written, in strange characters[126]." The card image emphasizes the fact that the decisive secret lies with Mrs. Light, and it helps to create a feeling of suspense.

In *The Portrait* images drawn from games, when introduced in actual talk, are still conventional[127]. Quite different is the effect of one such image which forms part of Isabel's reflections after the true relation between her husband and Madame Merle has been revealed to her: "Now that she was in the secret, now that she knew something that so much concerned her, and the eclipse of which had made life resemble an attempt to play whist with an imperfect pack of cards, the truth of things, their mutual relations, their meaning, and for the most part, their horror rose before her with a kind of architectural vastness [128]." This image emphasizes Isabel's realization of the inferior position to which the wickedness of Osmond and Madame Merle has relegated her. It is the first example of a really significant card image.

The Old Things shows the first consistent application for one particular purpose of images based on games. They emphasize the relation between Mrs. Gereth and Fleda. Both play their own games, play their cards. The first game image is introduced when Fleda, after Owen's visit to Ricks, has made up her mind how she is going to act in the future, especially during the meeting with her hostess, which is soon to take place. "If she should now repeat his words, this wouldn't at all play the game of her definite vow; it would only play the game of her little gagged and blinded desire [129]." Mrs. Gereth, however, succeeds in drawing one secret from Fleda, and then thinks she has found out everything. Fleda even warns her when she says: "You smooth it down because you see more in it than there can ever be; but after my hideous double game how will you be able to believe in me again? [130]" Both these images stress the fact that Mrs. Gereth might misjudge Fleda's character, especially her honesty. The game image which is introduced after she has sent all her treasures back to Poynton is therefore immediately based upon the earlier two: "To have played such a card was therefore, practically, for Mrs. Gereth, to have won the game. Fleda had certainly to recognize that, so far as the theory of the matter went, the game had been won [131]." This image powerfully stresses the fact of Mrs. Gereth's miscalculation. When she sent the treasures back to Poynton she did it with the conviction that Fleda had really done what she had expected of her, namely drawn Owen away from Mona. Therefore she played the last card which should in theory have won the game. These game images are very significant in so far as they provide the reason for Mrs. Gereth's final defeat and loss of her treasures. And it is a considerable achievement that James was thus able to characterize the deeper relationship, or rather, opposition, between the two major characters of the novel. In that endeavour he was the more successful, in that he intentionally restricted the application of such metaphors to Fleda and Mrs. Gereth.

In *The Ambassadors* James introduces game images as an effective means of illustrating Strether's development. At the beginning of the novel, he feels himself completely left out of the game which the others are playing, but slowly moves into their circle and becomes an active participant. When, in his box at the theatre, he is wondering why little Bilham and Chad have not yet turned up, he needs Maria Gostrey's help to realize that "they *had* arranged ... every move in the game", that "they've been arranging ever since[132]". The "they" is intentionally left somewhat ambiguous, although it is clear that at least little Bilham and Chad belong to it. But here it is just a matter of sides; "they" means anyone of Chad's circle whom Strether might have to face as somebody working against him. Two chapters later he is still incapable of understanding Chad's behaviour and actions, when he asks little Bilham: "What game, under the sun, is he playing?[133]" Soon afterwards Chad tells Strether that he should like him to meet two of his best friends, mother and daughter. With this information Strether at once "sees": "It seems to give away, now, [Chad's] game. This is what he has been doing—keeping me along for. He has been waiting for them[134]." When he hears that Jeanne is going to be married he realizes that he has been grossly misled by believing that *Chad* would marry her: and therefore Marie de Vionnet's announcement "affected him on the spot as a move in a game[135]". All these images stress the working together of the persons around Chad, who do this in such a subtle way that Strether is not able to predict their moves. Again and again he is shown to be at a loss and to be taken by surprise by certain events. Contrasted with these Europeans are the Pococks who, coming to Paris, are seen playing their own game. "It's Mamie ... who'll be their great card[136]", says Maria Gostrey to Strether before the arrival of the Pococks. At his first sight of Sarah his sense of a respite "had come in the smile with which Sarah ... rustled down to them a moment later ... It was only a sign, but enough: she was going to be gracious and unallusive, she was going to play the larger game[137]." Here an allusion seems to be implied of Strether's notion that he may encounter even greater difficulties to discern Sarah's policy and tactics. He knows exactly that her friendly behaviour is only a mask behind which deeper motives must be hidden. Strether, so far, has always been excluded from the games which all the others played. He has maintained a neutral position, first towards Chad's and his friends' game, later, after the arrival of the Pococks, between the two sides. But a final game image emphasizes that he has chosen one side, namely Chad's. This is above all brought out by the change from the "they" to the "we", with which is meant Chad and himself: "We've both been good then—we've played the game[138]."

If we judge the game images in *The Ambassadors* as a whole we notice that they are all of a rather conventional nature. The consistency with which they are introduced, however, in order to describe the opposed sides and Strether's finally choosing one of them gives these rather common images a significance as a group which puts them on a higher level than any in an earlier novel.

In *The Wings* there is also one series of images based on games which is used consistently, namely for the relationship between Merton Densher and Kate Croy[139]. The nature of their actions is characterized by the kind of game they are said to be playing. None of these images is of a particular significance. Only the frequency of their occurrence has the effect of putting a strong emphasis on the successful co-operation between them in reaching their egotistic goal.

In *The Golden Bowl* very few game images are introduced, but at the same time they have a much greater functional significance, and are more elaborate. They emphasize an important fact in understanding Maggie's behaviour. After she has found out about the intimacy between Amerigo and Charlotte one may indeed wonder why she never even makes the slightest allusion to this discovery when speaking to her father. The answer is that she knew "there was a card she could play, but there was only one, and to play it would be to end the game". This card which she was not allowed to play, was "to ask a question, to raise a doubt, to reflect in any degree on the play of the others", who, of course, are Charlotte and Amerigo. She must, in fine, refrain from showing her father that she was jealous and to tell him the reason of her jealousy; "and she could, in her private hours, but stare long, with suffused eyes, at that impossibility[140]". James does not yet reveal at this point why Adam should not know of his daughter's jealousy. Only four chapters later does he give us another piece of evidence which helps us to complete the puzzle. He takes up Maggie's thoughts again where he had left them at the end of the first passage. She could, of course, tell her father what she knew of the relation between Charlotte and Amerigo. "That hideous card she might in mere logic play—being by this time ... intimately familiar with all the fingered pasteboard in her pack." If she were to play the card it would mean sacrificing her father which "involved even a horror of finding out if he would really have consented to be sacrificed. What she must do she must do by keeping her hands off him[141]". Thus playing her card would not necessarily mean winning the game for Maggie, but rather losing it. In contrast to many earlier images of the same kind, the two just quoted are fully exploited, showing a development like that of a musical theme after its first introduction. They are woven into the text and not easily to be separated from it. They show above all one remarkable step forward in method when compared with the earlier novels by being more organically related to one another. The principal function of the game image here is the connection of the two passages, to bring the reader's mind back to the earlier when he comes to read the latter. Both images contribute to emphasize Maggie's high moral behaviour. Her final goal is to reach happiness; not only for herself and Amerigo but also for her father and Charlotte. Any wrong move might bring her happiness, but would destroy her father's for ever[142]. The two examples show the culmination of James's method of gradual revelation, of slowly adding one touch to the other until the complete picture emerges before our eyes. There is a strong element of suspense, created by the interest we take in seeing the completed picture, with all its touches, all its colours.

On the whole, the expanding images in James's work leave the impression that he still stands in the tradition of the novelists immediately preceding him. Many of his expanding images show a direct dependence upon the rhetorical image out of which they directly grow. It is for this reason that the significance of many such images is very restricted, not outstanding. There are, however, a few exceptions showing James's realization that imagery can be successfully used for other means than mere decoration. This impression is particularly conveyed by the examples in the later novels, where the expanding images also share in the significance of James's metaphorical language, forming an organic part of the whole work. This transformation from the common to the particular and meaningful shows itself above all in the more frequent change of conventional images into typically Jamesian ones, into new creations with life and meaning, and it is moreover evident in their more careful and appropriate choice.

CHAPTER 4

The Characterizing Image

For the full understanding of James's characters it is essential to examine with what kind of images he surrounds each of them and how, in this way, certain qualities stand out more clearly than others. He developed various techniques in order to characterize his persons. The simplest and most direct way of doing so is to let them speak frequently in images. Thus, by a proper choice of spoken images, each of them can be endowed with a special colour which is particularly his own, distinguishing him from any of his companions. The development of this device is indeed essential in James's works, as the only direct judgment we can form of most of the characters is through their talk. The greater part of the picture is given us as the reflection of the central consciousness. And therefore we are inclined to be influenced in our evaluation of persons like Caspar Goodwood, little Bilham, Mrs. Lowder, Fanny Assingham and others by Isabel's, Strether's, Merton's or Maggie's judgments. It is only in the dialogue that we get a neutral, uninfluenced picture of all the characters in a Jamesian novel. A second way is the external characterization. This is a device which James used only rarely, as this method tends to remain rather superficial, giving no hints as to the deeper motives of a person's actions. The most significant characterizing images are those which emphasize particular qualities of a person's mind by relating them to special kinds of images, as for instance animal or war metaphors.

A. SPOKEN IMAGES

About half the images James introduces form part of the dialogue. But it is obvious that they are the less significant half of James's, or for that matter, of any other writer's, imagery. The reason for this fact is clearly that they must be such as a person would use in conversation. If they are too elaborate they strike us as artificial and unnatural. The spoken images in James's novels are carefully chosen. This is shown first of all by the fact that they are not evenly distributed among the characters. The more sensitive persons frequently use images in their talk, and they are also inclined to speak in elaborate metaphors.

In *Roderick Hudson* James developed the device of using the spoken image as a means of contrasting certain characters. The two persons most differentiated in this way are the hero himself and Mrs. Light. The latter's low mentality is shown by the many common images she uses, especially when she is excited: "If this goes on we may both as well turn scarecrows ... To have nourished a serpent, sir, all these years! to have lavished one's self upon a viper that turns and stings her own poor mother! ... to have eaten the bread of bitterness, and all the rest of it ... I would have lain down in the dust and let her walk over me; I would have given her the eyes out of my head if she had taken a fancy to them[1]." This is purely rhetorical imagery, giving Mrs. Light's talk a prosaic note. Roderick's images are different: "Nothing is more common than for an artist who has set out on his journey on a high-stepping horse to find himself all of a sudden dismounted and invited to go his way on foot. You can number them by the thousand—the people of two or three successes; the poor fellows whose candle burnt out in a night. Some of them groped their way along without it, some of them gave themselves up for blind and sat down by the wayside to beg." His words have a great beauty which is completely lacking in those of Mrs. Light. The whole conception and formulation of the artist's ideas move on a higher level and are the expression of a sensitive mind. But in spite of this, Roderick's thoughts are as clearly expressed as Mrs. Light's. His ideas are even easier to follow, just because of the images he uses in order to illustrate what he means. One image grows out of the other and so they form an organic whole. Mrs. Light's speech is largely incoherent because she just utters whatever crops up in her mind. Her images, then, are an expression of the vulgarity of her mind. On the other hand we find a reference to the bible ("it bloweth where it listeth", St. John, iii, 8) and two literary allusions in the course of Roderick's talk, one when he says that genius is "dealt out in different doses, in big cups and little, and when you have consumed your portion it's as naïf to ask for more as it was for Oliver Twist to ask for more porridge". With the other he concludes his argument: "My mind is like a dead calm in the tropics, and my imagination as motionless as the phantom ship in the Ancient Mariner![2]" These passages show much that is characteristic of James's early handling of imagery in the dialogue. If we think of earlier Victorian novelists, we perceive a great step forward when we read James's imagery. His characters do not all use the same kind of imagery— unlike, for instance, Becky Sharp and Amelia Sedley in *Vanity Fair,* who, although they are so different from each other, are not differentiated by the images they use. Mrs. Light uses images similar to those of Thackeray's characters. Roderick's, on the other hand, are adjusted to his genius. They are wonderfully singular, and we have the feeling that only he could think of them in the connection in which they are used. They have become an essential and untransposable part of himself.

What we have tried to show, using the examples of Roderick and Mrs. Light, repeats itself on a smaller scale with many other characters in this early novel[3]. These examples show us James's strong tendency to get away from the conventional, to let his characters create new pictorial conceptions.

It is Ralph Touchett who uses more significant images than any other character in *The Portrait*. "You use too many metaphors[4]", his mother says once, reproaching him, but all his images are carefully chosen and very appropriate to the respective situations. His bitter reaction after his discovery that Isabel did not even mention Goodwood's existence to him is aptly expressed when he says: "What is the use of being ill and disabled, and restricted to mere spectatorship at the game of life, if I really can't see the show when I have paid so much for my ticket[5]." This image tells us that his only pleasure in life, after the advent of Isabel, was really living her life, partaking of it as much as he could. He had hoped that some such privilege at least would be granted to him. In contrast to her son's images Mrs. Touchett's are conventional[6]. There is nothing particular, nothing very significant about them. We notice a similar difference in intellectual level as between Roderick and Mrs. Light.

One device that is not yet to be found in *Roderick Hudson* is that of self-characterization by means of imagery. Henrietta Stackpole has come to ask a favour of Ralph: "I shall enjoy that immensely!" he exclaims. "I will be Caliban, and you shall be Ariel." She is clever enough to take up his allusion: "You are not at all like Caliban, because you are sophisticated, and Caliban was not. But I am not talking about imaginary characters; I am talking about Isabel. Isabel is intensely real. What I wish to tell you is that I find her fearfully changed." And now she asks Ralph to help her to change Isabel back again, which gives him a chance to take up his metaphor again: "I am only Caliban; I am not Prospero." "You were Prospero enough to make her what she has become. You have acted on Isabel Archer since she came here, Mr. Touchett[7]." The literary allusions in this passage cause the whole meaning to be enlarged. The image emphasizes that Ralph realizes well enough that his command over Isabel is incomplete. This passage also points to a new function which can be fulfilled by certain images introduced in the dialogue. It is that of connecting different parts of it by referring to an originally introduced image. The images, then, are like the red thread that goes through the whole and keeps the different parts together. Shortly before his death Mr. Touchett has a talk with his son, during which Ralph says of Isabel: "I should like to put a little wind in her sails[8]." At first this image stands alone, and only about six hundred words later does Ralph's father refer to it when he says: "You say you want to put wind in her sails; but aren't you afraid of putting too much?"; and Ralph's immediate answer is: "I should like to see her going before the breeze![9]"

The major function of the spoken image in *The Old Things* is to denote the various levels of intelligence. An analysis of these images allows us a clear classification of the major characters. We realize that Owen's imagination must be of the poorest nature when we hear him say: "Oh yes, I told her exactly, and that you had been most awfully kind, and that I had placed the whole thing in your hands[10]." or: "You haven't lifted a finger! It's I who have taken possession[11]." All his other images are of a similar kind, common and conventional. Simply as images they have no significance at all, but in so far as they throw light on his mind they are of great importance. They suit his stupid character perfectly. More elaborate pictorial language from him would affect us as unnatural, inconsistent with the general impression he conveys[12].

The images used by Fleda are on a much higher level. They still show a tendency to the simple and common, but in most of them we perceive an element of her own creation, a realization of the pictorial conception which is totally lacking in Owen's images. She says to him about Mrs. Gereth: "You must remember that to have to withdraw from the ground she has taken, to make a public surrender of what she has publicly appropriated, will go uncommonly hard with her pride[13]." At another point she takes up one of Owen's images, so that we are again confronted with the method of pushing the dialogue forward by referring to a previously introduced image and by slightly altering it. He has reproached her for behaving like a stone: "'Perhaps, after all', she risked, 'there may be, even in a stone, still some little help for you.'[14]" The strength of the following example lies in its astonishing and effective simplicity. To Mrs. Gereth Fleda says about Mona: "It was fortunate for you ... that she's apparently not aware of the manner in which, almost under her nose, you advertised me to him at Poynton[15]." The function of this simple image is to bring the reader's mind back to that early scene at Poynton, where Mrs. Gereth had made it plain, in front of Mona, that she should infinitely prefer Fleda as a future daughter-in-law. By the pictorial contents of the verb "advertised" the connection with that early scene is at once and unmistakably established.

Mrs. Gereth's images are more significant and more elaborate than either Owen's or Fleda's. And they never leave the impression of being inappropriate to her character. "I've literally come, ... with a band-box and a kitchen-maid; I've crossed the Rubicon. I've taken possession. It has been like plumping into cold water: I saw the only thing was to do it, not to stand shivering. I shall have warmed the place a little by simply being here for a week; when I come back the ice will have been broken[16]." Although this passage forms part of a letter we can be sure that Mrs. Gereth is writing as she would have spoken. To Fleda she says: "I pricked up my ears, and all that this might mean dawned upon me when you said you had asked nothing about Mona. It put me on the scent ... I felt it was *in* you, deep down, and that I must draw it out. Well, I *have* drawn it, and it's a blessing[17]." And referring to her discussion with Mrs. Brigstock: "I said to her that my hands were spotlessly clean of any attempt to make him make up to you ... I was determined that if I had bit my tongue off to oblige you I would at least have the righteousness that my sacrifice gave me[18]." In *The Old Things* especially, with its very few characters, James's achievement in differentiating them by the spoken word is obvious enough. The kind of images persons use when talking is a considerable help in assessing their mental level, not absolutely but relative to one another.

Before dealing with the remaining novels we have yet to consider one particular form of the spoken image which is common only to the first three novels. It is a well-known fact that excited, sensitive persons show a tendency to use more images in their talk than usual, and above all they use them in quick succession. Most emotional images have the characteristic in common that they are dynamic. They serve to express all kinds of emotional states, as for instance complaint, suffering, passionate wishes or curses. They are particularly frequent in *Roderick Hudson*. Roderick's fits are shown both by his actions and his words. An example of the former is when he seizes a hammer and destroys a bust of his lawyer, so that a dozen pieces topple with a great crash upon the floor. His account of the hated Mr. Striker and the farewell he gives him is well suited to show how frequently he uses images when excited:

> Mr. Striker ... is not simply a good-natured attorney, who lets me dog's-ear his law books ... He looks after my mother's property and kindly consents to regard me as part of it ... I freely forgive him his zealous attempts to unscrew my head-piece and set it on hind part before ... We speak a different language—we're made of a different clay. I had a fit of rage yesterday when I smashed his bust, at the thought of all the bad blood he had stirred up in me; ... This morning I grasped the bull by the horns ... 'I'm going to be a sculptor ... I won't bid you good-by just yet ... But I bid good-by here with rapture to these four detested walls—to this living tomb!'[19]

He is very excited about his new prospects of being able to go to Rome, of giving up the lawyer's office, which he hated as much as its proprietor, and while telling Rowland how he parted from Mr. Striker, he lives through his whole fit of rage again. Without the images Roderick's emotional state would not be rendered half as clearly. Only by the accumulation of several images in quick succession does James achieve the purpose of bringing home to the reader the artist's excited state at such moments as is well exemplified in another of his emotional outbursts[20].

In *The Portrait* James had already found a new device for characterizing persons in an excited state. He lets them use very short sentences, with many repetitions. One involuntarily reads such passages at a much greater speed, and the same effect is achieved as with the many images which accompanied Roderick's outbursts. But James still uses images when he comes to a climax in such speeches, as for instance when Goodwood is alone together with Isabel in Rome, and in his despair, at the possibility of never seeing her again, says: "It's the last time—let me pluck a single flower![21]" It is obvious what he means by this image, and yet he could not have expressed this meaning in plain words. There is a passage in a discussion between Madame Merle and Osmond towards the end of the novel which, in its technique of applying images to characterize her passion, comes nearest to the method of the earlier novel: "Then she went on, with a sudden outbreak of passion, a burst of summer thunder in a clear sky, 'The matter is that I would give my right hand to be able to weep, and that I can't! ... Oh, I believe you'll make me cry still. (I mean make me howl like a wolf) ... You've not only dried up my tears; you've dried up my soul[22].'" As the images do not follow each other immediately, and as there are not as many as in Roderick's outbursts, James is compelled to emphasize Madame Merle's passion by prefacing it with an image.

In *The Old Things* two remarks are uttered with a passion that is clearly emphasized by the two images which are used in them. The first one is a curse which Mrs. Gereth throws at Fleda after she has learned how stupidly, in her eyes, Owen had behaved in her company: "Any one but a jackass would have tucked you under his arm and marched you off to the Registrar![23]" Soon after this remark Fleda shoots back when she reproaches Mrs. Gereth: "'The tangle of life is much more intricate than you've ever, I think, felt it to be. You slash into it', cried Fleda finely, 'with a great pair of shears you nip at it as if you were one of the Fates! If Owen's at Waterbath, he's there to wind everything up.'[24]" From the examples in this novel and in *The Portrait* we can see that this method of introducing a rapid succession of images in order to represent his characters in states of excitement leads on to other methods of portraying emotions.

So far as the spoken images are concerned *The Ambassadors* marks a clear turning-point. James's interest and his whole emphasis lie on the presentation of the inner development of his characters: the external happenings are but of secondary importance. He analyses the motives which lead to these actions. The characters, therefore, are no longer contrasted by what they say, but by what they think and feel, and to a lesser extent by how they act and react. One characteristic of the spoken images of the earlier novels, however, is retained. It is that the more sensitive persons use many more images. But most of them are conventional and rhetorical and no longer allow us to distinguish the characters intellectually[25]; the few more significant images that occur in the dialogue have primarily other functions than that of differentiating. When, for instance, Maria Gostrey says to Strether: "You've got your momentum, and you can toddle alone[26]", the main function is to emphasize that by that time he is familiar enough with the life and society of Paris to make out things for himself, without the help of someone like Maria.

One of James's great achievements is that of applying images in order to impel the dialogue, or for that matter the action, onward. Here we perceive a development since *The Portrait* where they rather only held it together. In *The Ambassadors* the image in the dialogue is used to greater effect. The initial image is taken up by another person, but considerably altered, thus leading smoothly over to a new thought and bringing other essential elements into the discussion. Towards the end of the novel Strether says to Chad, summarizing their attitude to the Pococks: "We gave them ... their chance to be delighted, and they've walked up to it, and looked all round it, and not taken it." Chad then expresses his view of the matter by suggesting: "You can bring a horse to water—!" Strether promptly takes up this metaphor: "Precisely. And the tune to which this morning Sarah wasn't delighted—the tune to which ... she refused to drink—leaves us on that side nothing more to hope." Chad brings a new thought into the discussion: "It was never of course really the least on the cards that they would be 'delighted'." This remark urges Strether to state his own position in the matter. "Well, I don't know, after all ... I've had to come as far round. However ... it's doubtless *my* performance that's absurd[27]."

In *The Wings* this device has come to a greater maturity, for James applies it with more economy. Usually one single image at a time suffices to impel the action onward in this thoroughly dramatic way. It is, first of all, Lionel Croy who, at the beginning of the novel, convinces his daughter that it would be advantageous for both of them if she left him in order to live with and be under the influence of Mrs. Lowder. "You can describe yourself—*to* yourself—as, in a fine flight, giving up your aunt for me; but what good, I should like to know, would your fine flight do me?" If Kate were to go on living with him it would be a disadvantage for both of them because they are not "possessed of so much, at this charming pass, please to remember, as that we can afford not to take hold of any perch held out to us". And Mr. Croy strengthens his argument by saying: "One doesn't give up the use of a spoon because one's reduced to living on broth. And your spoon, that is your aunt, please consider, is partly mine as well[28]." On the other hand he knows the consequences which Kate's living with her aunt must have for himself: "You must do me the justice to see that I don't do things, that I've never done them, by halves—that if I offer you to efface myself, it's for the final, fatal sponge that I ask, well saturated and well applied[29]." There is no immediate connection between these images. Each stands for itself; each stresses one important fact for the understanding of Kate's subsequent living with her aunt and letting herself be guided by her. Considered as a whole these images appear, nevertheless, like the red thread in Mr. Croy's arguments that have to convince Kate. They hold his speech together and impel it onward at the same time.

In *The Wings* the action is occasionally impelled onward by means of an image in a discussion. In *The Ambassadors* it was not so much the action as the dialogue itself which was carried forward. Referring to Milly Densher says to Kate: "She affects one ... as a creature saved from a shipwreck. Such a creature may surely, in these days, on the doctrine of chances, go to sea again with confidence. She has *had* her wreck—she has met her adventure." Kate agrees with Merton on the point that Milly's incurable illness is her "wreck", but she differs as to whether it should also be looked upon as an adventure. "Do let her have still her adventure. There are wrecks that are not adventures", is Kate's strong point, and his response to this remark is nothing else than a giving in, an assent to her plan about Milly. "Well—if there be also adventures that are not wrecks![30]" He already knows at this point that he himself should be Milly's "adventure", but is not strong enough to refuse; he can only wonder whether he shall not be a "wreck" himself as an "adventure".

The majority of the spoken images in *The Golden Bowl* serve the same purpose of impelling the action onward. But in contrast to any earlier novel most of them are much more elaborate. James, on the other hand, was very careful in choosing the right characters to use these images so that they never have the effect of artificiality. There is a passage in a discussion between the prince and Fanny in the early stages of the novel, during which he urges her to assist him and to lead him. There is, however, a new element in Amerigo's images, one that has not yet been exploited in any earlier novel. It is that of referring to the past, stressing an important fact that has occurred before the novel actually begins[31].

Compared with Amerigo's images those used by Bob and Fanny Assingham are plain. But even in these examples we feel James's endeavour to avoid the conventional. In a discussion with her husband Fanny stresses Maggie's behaviour after her discovery of the intimacy between Charlotte and Amerigo: "our understanding's signed and sealed ... It's a grand, high compact. She has solemnly promised[32]." What this compact consists of is revealed only gradually, namely that it is Maggie's pretence that she believes in Charlotte's and Amerigo's innocence. This is a necessary clue for the understanding of Maggie's behaviour throughout the second part of the novel. The image has the effect of drawing the reader's attention to this particular passage. It also creates suspense, because it is not self-explanatory.

B. EXTERNAL CHARACTERIZATION

Descriptions of the appearance of his characters are very rare in James's novels, and the use of images for this purpose even less frequent. But if we take the few examples which occur throughout the novels together we perceive a difference between the early and late method. In *Roderick Hudson* James gives us full and compact character descriptions at once, *en bloc*[33], and they still occur in *The Portrait*, where we encounter an excellent example, when the Countess Gemini is pictured in the following way:

> She was thin and dark, and not at all pretty, having features that suggested some tropical bird, —a long, beak-like nose, a small, quickly moving eye and a mouth and chin that receded extremely ... The soft brilliancy of her toilet had the look of shimmering plumage, and her attitudes were light and sudden, like those of a creature that perched upon twigs ... (Her demonstrations suggested the violent waving of some flag of general truce—white silk with fluttering streamers.)[34]

In his later novels James never describes his characters in this traditional manner, which is common to most of the Victorian novelists. The external appearance of a person is seldom fully described, not even gradually, and indeed it happens very often that our mental picture of the outward appearance of James's characters remains vague and obscure. We recognize characters like Strether, Milly or Maggie rather by their feelings, thoughts or actions. If James gives an external description, it is always only one particular part that is described and emphasized; and here it is mostly part of a person's face, the eyes, the smile, or the general impression which a face leaves on another character. Strether's helplessness in front of Gloriani is made more apparent when the effect of the artist's face on him is described as: "Gloriani showed him, in such perfect confidence, on Chad's introduction of him, a fine, worn handsome face, a face that was like an open letter in a foreign tongue[35]." He strikes Strether as some one utterly different, having nothing in common with him. Gloriani is entirely rooted in Europe, in a culture with which Strether has lost every contact, if ever he had any. It is because of this fact that Gloriani affects him like a riddle, like something in a foreign language which he cannot understand. He is for him "a dazzling prodigy of type", something he has never met with in his "old geography". Strether is similarly impressed by Madame de Vionnet's head, which,

> extremely fair and exquisitely festal, was like a happy fancy, a notion of the antique, on an old, precious medal, some silver coin of the Renaissance; while her slim lightness and brightness, her gayety, her expression, her decision, contributed to an effect that might have been felt by a poet as half mythological and half conventional. He could have compared her to a goddess still partly engaged in a morning cloud, or a sea-nymph waist-high in the summer surge. Above all she suggested to him the reflection that the *femme du monde*—in these finest developments of the type—was, like Cleopatra in the play, indeed various and multifold[36].

The image, then, is not only a characterization of Madame de Vionnet, but serves also to show that her roots are in European culture, shows her as an outstanding representative of everything that is different from the American way of life.

In *The Wings* it is Sir Luke Strett's face which makes the decisive impression on Milly when she first meets him: "His large, settled face, though firm, was not ... hard; he looked ... half like a general and half like a bishop, and she was soon sure that ... what it would show her would be what was good, what was best for her. She had established, in other words ... a relation with it." It is the expression on the great doctor's face which inspires Milly with confidence. The relation to the face is for her "like an absolute possession, ... something done up in the softest silk and tucked away under the arm of memory. She hadn't had it when she went in, and she had it when she came out; she had it there under her cloak, but dissimulated, invisibly carried[37]."

The most elaborate, and at the same time most significant, facial descriptions are to be found in *The Golden Bowl*. Characteristically enough, two of these are related to architectural images. When we read them we are strongly reminded of the passage in James's preface to *The Portrait*, in which he compares fiction to a house with a million windows, at each of which stands a figure with a pair of eyes. Next to the whole impression made by the face, it is always the eyes whereby a person can best be judged. "The Prince's dark blue eyes were of the finest, and, on occasion, precisely, resembled nothing so much as the high windows of a Roman palace, of an historic front by one of the great old designers, thrown open on a feast-day to the golden air." The first general impression evoked by the description of Adam's face is quite different. "His neat, colourless face, provided with the merely indispensable features, suggested immediately, for a description, that it was *clear,* and in this manner somewhat resembled a small decent room, clean-swept and unencumbered with furniture, but drawing a particular advantage, as might presently be noted, from the outlook of a pair of ample and uncurtained windows." The similarity lies in the pictorial conception, Amerigo's face being compared to a palace, Adam's to a small room. He is a man of privacy and intimacy, retiring in his habits. These two comparisons are extended to the description of the eyes. If the prince's were "high windows", it is said of Adam Verver's that they "both admitted the morning and the evening in unusual quantities and gave the modest area the outward extension of a view that was 'big' even when restricted to the stars". The further development of the image describing the prince's face shows him quite distinctly as a public figure, "a ruler, warrior, patron". It is his look which is the most remarkable feature of his face, and it suggests an image "of some very noble personage who, expected, acclaimed by the crowd in the street and with old precious stuffs falling over the sill for his support, had gaily and gallantly come to show himself: always moreover less in his own interest than in that of spectators and subjects whose need to admire, even to gape, was periodically to be considered". With Adam's face the eyes themselves are the most prominent feature "with their ambiguity of your scarce knowing if they most carried their possessor's vision out or most opened themselves to your own". This makes any person confronted with him feel uneasy and uncertain. But whatever one might feel about his eyes "they stamped the place with their importance ... so that, on one side or the other, you were never out of their range, were moving about, for possible community, opportunity, the sight of you scarce knew what, either before them or behind them[38]". Everything in Amerigo's face, on the other hand, is plain and outspoken. It conveys rather the sense of emptiness, for he gives the impression of a "great frame" in which there appears "the ghost of some proudest ancestor[39]". His main aim is to please, not in his own interest but in that of others, and it is, therefore, much easier to deal with him than with Adam Verver. This assumption is confirmed during the second half of the novel, when Maggie encounters more difficulties in coping successfully with her father than with her husband. A blow dealt to Amerigo can at the utmost destroy one room of his huge palace, but he will still be able to live comfortably in those remaining. He has grown up in a tradition which has known treachery and corruption. In Adam's case there is only one small room, and the slightest harm done can be fatal to the whole existence of the person who inhabits it. These facts explain why Maggie does not hesitate at all to let her husband realize that she knows of his intimacy with Charlotte, whereas she is most anxious not to disturb the harmony and peace of her father's "room". Adam is too innocent, and any knowledge of the treachery in question could harm him fatally. The two metaphorical passages, then, stress also a difference in sensibility. If Adam's is very delicate, Amerigo's is extremely tough. The face of a person is, for James, the expression of his whole character. Therefore he takes so much pains to paint his characters' faces with the richest palette possible, with nuances that give us the most intimate details. But it is only in *The Golden Bowl* that he made full use of this possibility.

In the same novel he describes a very different type, standing, in every respect, on a much lower level than either the prince or Mr. Verver. The description of Bob Assingham's face gives the impression of a narrow-minded, almost stupid, but kind and gentle person, brave and honest within his limits: "His smooth round head, with the particular shade of its white hair, was like a silver pot reversed; his cheekbones and the bristles of his moustache were worthy of Attila the Hun. The hollows of his eyes were deep and darksome, but the eyes within them were like little blue flowers plucked that morning[40]." Thus the architectural vastness of Amerigo's or Adam's face has, in Bob's case, shrunk to a "silver pot reversed"; his eyes are no longer big windows but have become "little blue flowers". The description of his face is nearer to James's early method in that it does not penetrate, but remains essentially an external characterization; whereas when we read the descriptions of Amerigo's or Adam's face we feel that they open up the persons described, and let us see a large portion of their soul and spirit.

C. GENERAL CHARACTERIZATION

The most frequent function of characterizing images is to contrast different types of persons, and in many cases we find them applied when the difference between innocence and experience, or between Americans and Europeans, has to be emphasized.

1. General

On the whole the characters in *Roderick Hudson* are colourless—to a certain extent even lifeless. Occasional characterizations are of a general kind, as for instance when we read of Roderick: "Here and there, doubtless, as he went, he took in a reef in his sail; but he was too adventurous a spirit to be successfully tamed[41]." This image stresses one side of his character, which certainly contributes largely to his final destruction in the heavy storm in the Swiss Alps. But James had not yet developed the device of making consistent use of images to throw light upon character. The only notable exception is a lengthy pictorial characterization of Mary Garland, by which he stresses her thirst for knowledge, for "facts that she might noiselessly lay away, piece by piece, in the perfumed darkness of her serious mind". Her way of acquiring knowledge was to let things go, at the moment, "but she watched them on their way, over the crest of the hill, and when her fancy seemed not likely to be missed it went hurrying after them, and ran breathless at their side, as it were, and begged them for the secret". She did it because she wanted to know "where she was going", because she had "a temper of mind that had not lived with its door ajar ... upon the high-road of thought, for passing ideas to drop in and out at their pleasure; but had made much of a few long visits from guests cherished and honored—guests whose presence was a solemnity[42]". These images give us a good picture of various aspects of Mary's character. Though she was keen to obtain full knowledge of everything that captured her interest, hers was too shy and modest a nature as that she would have pursued these interests publicly and obtrusively. She seems to be content with that which life has granted her, and she never tries to strive after values beyond her limits. On the other hand she is capable of leading a full and felicitous life by extracting the utmost from her possessions and the few new experiences she may have.

In *The Portrait* a few images stress important qualities of Isabel's character. Her conceit is pointed to in an image which likens her nature to a garden, "a suggestion of perfume and murmuring boughs, of shady bowers

66

and lengthening vistas, which made her feel that introspection was after all an exercise in the open air, and that a visit to the recesses of one's mind was harmless when one returned from it with a lapful of roses[43]". In this image her conceit appears almost as a weapon against the danger of inhibitions. She enlarges her innocent American soul, trying to adapt it to the largeness of the new world which seems so much richer, bigger and more promising than the one she came from. The garden image also gives us an idea of the richness and beauty of her soul; on the other hand, the "shady bowers and lengthening vistas" already indicate the possible shadows that might darken her "virginal soul" and her life; they point to the dangers lying hidden in her own nature; she is uncertain about her ways, that is, she has not an absolute command over herself. This results in a fear of most things around her, and of taking any vital decision. This quality of her character is stressed in two further images. She is afraid to "touch the cup of experience", as she says to her cousin, because "it's a poisoned drink![44]" She is guided by a belief that nothing and nobody will ever harm her if she does not look too much into the matter and does not establish any intimate relations. "With all her love of knowledge, Isabel had a natural shrinking from raising curtains and looking into unlighted corners[45]." Had she not possessed such a "natural shrinking" she could perhaps have seen through the sinister Madame Merle before it was too late[46].

One of the outstanding qualities of Henrietta Stackpole's character is her extreme inquisitiveness. Two related images are introduced to emphasize this particular quality. The first occurs in the part that appeared in the September issue of *The Atlantic Monthly*. It reads: "He [Goodwood] was the most reserved, the least colloquial, of men, and this inquiring authoress was constantly flashing her lantern into the quiet darkness of his soul[47]." James expected of this lively pictorial creation that it would leave a lasting impression on his readers, because he takes it up again in the October issue, where we read: "Moreover, since her arrival in Rome she had been much on her guard; she had ceased to flash her lantern at him[48]." There can be no doubt that the similarity of these two images is intentional. The main function of the second one is that of recalling to the minds of his readers the earlier scene at Florence and the discussion there between Goodwood and Henrietta[49].

In *The Old Things* we encounter the first case of a character systematically being identified with *objets d'art*. Mrs. Gereth's treasures are seen not so much as something to which she has a relation but as something forming part of her body, and James indeed once introduces the picture of an amputation when referring to her and the spoils. Her identification with the *objets d'art* at Poynton is emphasized by two images: "'Things' were of course the sum of the world; only, for Mrs. Gereth, the sum of the world was rare French furniture and oriental china[50]." And: "Wherever she was, she was

67

herself the great piece in the gallery[51]." The function of such images is to provide us with the reasons for Mrs. Gereth's fighting so hard to retain possession of the treasures, or at any rate not to let them slip into the hands of an unworthy and detested person, such as Mona Brigstock is, in her opinion. Apart from these characterizing images, there are hardly any others of a general nature in this novel, because James was beginning to develop the device of applying group images to characterize certain types of persons.

In any of James's novels in which Americans and Europeans confront one another, one can generally distinguish three groups of characters. It is interesting to notice how he uses images in *The Ambassadors* to contrast the different groups. There are, of course, the genuinely European characters like Gloriani and Madame de Vionnet. At the other end we find the unadulterated Americans, represented by Waymarsh, Mrs. Newsome and the Pococks. Between these two groups we discover the type of the transformed American, such as we meet in Chad, Maria Gostrey or little Bilham. Madame de Vionnet, rooted deeply in the history of her country, affects Strether "dressed as for thunderous times, and it fell in with the kind of imagination we have just attributed to him that she should be in simplest, coolest white, of a character so old-fashioned, if he were not mistaken, that Madame Roland, on the scaffold, must have worn something like it[52]". There could have scarcely been a better way of emphasizing the truly European character of Madame de Vionnet than comparing her to a character of the French Revolution. Of Waymarsh, the typical American, we read at the beginning of the novel that Europe "had as yet, then, for him, rather failed of its message; he had not got into tune with it, and had almost, at the end of three months, renounced any such expectation[53]". And shortly afterwards he says to Strether: "the trouble is that I don't seem to feel anywhere in tune[54]." The prototype of the transformed American, Chad Newsome, is no longer the young man Strether used to know at Woollett, "For that he *was* smooth was as marked as in the taste of a sauce or in the rub of a hand[55]." He strikes Strether "as if, in short, he had really, copious perhaps, but shapeless, been put into a firm mould and turned successfully out[56]". The difference between the various groups of characters comes out even better when they are confronted with one another, as for instance when Waymarsh's and Strether's differing attitudes towards Europe are emphasized by two related images. Although not very evident, an intentional likeness in the two pictorial conceptions seems to have been established by James. This assumption is strengthened by the fact that the first image, in the serialized version of the novel, appeared in the January issue, the second in that of the following month. The first passage reads: "Alas, nothing so little resembled floating as the rigor with which, on the edge of his bed, he hugged his posture of prolonged impermanence. It suggested to his comrade something that always, when kept up, worried him—a person established in a railway coach with a forward inclination. It represented the angle at which poor Waymarsh was to sit through the ordeal of Europe[57]." The second image makes it obvious that Strether is determined not to "sit through the ordeal of Europe" in such an uncomfortable angle as Waymarsh's. Little Bilham and Miss Barrace commend Chad's munificence and approve his taste, "and in doing so sat down, as it seemed to Strether, in the very soil out of which these things flowered. Our friend's final predicament was that he himself was sitting down, for the time, with them, and there was a supreme moment at which, compared with his collapse, Waymarsh's erectness affected him as really high[58]." Shortly before the arrival of the Pococks another image emphasizes the extent to which Strether and Waymarsh have grown away from each other: "Waymarsh had always more or less the air of sitting at the door of his tent, and silence, after so many weeks, had come to play its part in their concert. This note indeed, to Strether's sense, had lately taken a fuller tone, and it was his fancy to-night that they had never quite so drawn it out. Yet it befell, none the less, that he closed the door to confidence when his companion finally asked him if there were anything particular the matter with him[59]." If Strether's "tune" is different from Waymarsh's, a fact which is stressed by the image, Strether himself must be "in tune" with Europe. And if silence between them was the main note in "their concert", it means nothing else than their having reached a point of complete disagreement and of mistrust. The estrangement between them is one indication of Strether's attitude towards his new surroundings. Apart from such contrasting images, *The Ambassadors* contains many which contribute to the result that each of the characters leaves an individual picture in our minds at the end of the novel[60].

In *The Wings* Mrs. Lowder's wicked, dangerous and mysterious character is, above all, stressed by images. "It was an oddity of Mrs. Lowder's that her face in speech was like a lighted window at night, but that silence immediately drew the curtain. The occasion for reply allowed by her silence was never easy to take; yet she was still less easy to interrupt. The great glaze of her surface, at all events, gave her visitor no present help[61]." This image makes it quite clear that her presence must have exercised an enormous power over people, and she was not a person who would ever make the slightest concession in anything that concerned her. It is in this novel that James makes, for the first time, an extensive use of images drawn from the east, using comparisons with Indian and Hindu gods or mythology. Any images drawn from this field suggest the unknown, the mysterious, the dangerous. Therefore two such images are attributed to Mrs. Lowder. Densher says of her that "she's on the scale, altogether, of the car of Juggernaut—which was a kind of image that came to me yesterday while I waited for her at Lancaster Gate. The things in your drawing-room there were like the forms of the strange idols, the mystic excrescences, with which one may suppose the front of the car to bristle[62]." Judged from the war and animal images Mrs. Lowder's deceptive character is stressed when we read that she "loved everyone within range, down ... to Milly herself, who was, while she talked, really conscious of the enveloping flap of a protective mantle, a shelter with the weight of an eastern carpet. An eastern carpet, for wishing-purposes of one's own, was a thing to be on rather than under[63]." It is characteristic of Milly's innocence and her belief in the goodness of people that, listening to Mrs. Lowder, she feels herself enveloped by a "protective mantle". The image fulfils, therefore, a double function. On the one hand it throws much light on Mrs. Lowder's way of deceiving and exploiting other persons who are primarily good-natured and, in one way or another, weak, especially Milly and Merton. On the other hand it shows us that Milly, at that point, still blindly trusts the persons around her[64].

Probably because James had hoped that he could first publish *The Wings* in serialized form, he has retained the method of recalling earlier scenes by means of related images. Densher once characterizes Kate by saying: "'The women one meets—what are they but books one has already read? You're a whole library of the unknown, the uncut.' He almost moaned, he ached, from the depth of his content. 'Upon my word, I've a subscription!'[65]" When James introduces the second image after about forty thousand words, he begins it by recalling the earlier one: "He had compared her once, we know, to a 'new book', an uncut volume of the highest, the rarest quality; and his emotion, to justify that, was again and again like the thrill of turning the page[66]." These two images emphasize clearly enough that, for Merton at least, Kate's character has a strong quality of mystery that attracts him most of all. He seems to be constantly marvelling at her beautiful way of managing everything, always at the same time demonstrating new and unexpected aspects of her being.

There is a group of characterizing images in *The Golden Bowl* which is applied to both Maggie and Adam Verver, in order to stress their innocence. In several instances James introduces images which show them as children, innocent, without any problems, enjoying life. Three such children-images are used of Adam:

> thus had shaped itself the innocent trick of occasionally making-believe that he had no conscience ... a small game to which the few persons near enough to have caught him playing it ... attached indulgently that idea of quaintness, quite in fact that charm of the pathetic, involved in the preservation by an adult of one of childhood's toys. When he took a rare moment "off" he did so with the touching, confessing eyes of a man of forty-seven caught in the act of handling a relic of infancy—sticking on the head of a broken soldier or trying the lock of a wooden gun[67].

70

Fanny Assingham "disputed with him so little, agreed with him so much, surrounded him with such systematic consideration, such predetermined tenderness, that it was almost—which he had once told her in irritation—as if she were nursing a sick baby[68]". To Amerigo "he looked, at the top of his table, so nearly like a little boy shyly entertaining in virtue of some imposed rank, that he *could* only be one of the powers, the representation of a force—quite as an infant king is the representative of a dynasty[69]". One image is introduced in connection with Maggie, who, before Fanny's eyes, "built ... on this affectionate interest ... —very much as a wise, or even a mischievous, child, playing on the floor, might pile up blocks, skilfully and dizzily, with an eye on the face of the covertly-watching elder[70]". In addition there is one image in which Adam and Maggie are seen as children together. "There was nothing in the world they liked better than these snatched felicities, little parties, long talks, with 'I'll come to you tomorrow', and 'No, I'll come to *you*', make-belief renewals of their old life. They were fairly, at times, the dear things, like children playing at paying visits, playing at 'Mr. Thompson' and 'Mrs. Fane', each hoping that the other would really stay to tea[71]." James had never before used child images to such an extent; the emphasis he puts on this side of Adam's and Maggie's characters cannot be overlooked. It puts all their actions into a specific light. Whatever they do, they have no bad intentions, and if their actions affect others as wicked, horrid, or disgusting, they themselves believe that their deeds are perfectly justified, that they are doing right and harming no one.

2. War Images

The general function of war images can be described as indicating active, aggressive, courageous characters. But they can also point to certain dangers in which a character may find himself, or, on the other hand, they may indicate that he has reached safety, is on his guard, protected against possible attacks. In *Roderick Hudson* the few war images are all of a rather common nature[72]. Only in *The Portrait* do we come across two which are clearly James's own creations. The first was probably suggested to him by the Prussian military drill which had a decisive influence on the surprising and rapid victory over France in the 1870–71 war. Isabel is meditating upon the nature of her mind which, lately, appeared to her "a good deal of a vagabond, and she had spent much ingenuity in training it to a military step, and teaching it to advance, to halt, to retreat, to perform even more complicated manœuvres, at the word of command. Just now she had given it marching orders, and it had been trudging over the sandy plains of a philosophic history of German poetry[73]". If her mind affected her as a "vagabond" it means that she had no control over it, that she lacked the necessary will-power—until she herself became aware of this defect. The image suggests very clearly that it came much more naturally and easily to her to let herself go, not to think matters through to the end. We can take this early passage as a clue to Isabel's close friendship and her marriage to Osmond without her realizing, until it is too late, what has been happening to her all the time since the beginning of her acquaintance with Madame Merle. In connection with this image the wonderfully smooth shift from the image back to reality is worth noticing. The passage quoted above is continued: "Suddenly she became aware of a step very different from her own intellectual pace; she listened a little, and perceived that some one was walking about the library, which communicated with the office." This change-over is a further emphasis on Isabel's lack of absolute concentration in her thoughts. The other significant war image emphasizes the wide experience which Madame Merle has had in her past life, seen in contrast to Isabel, who wonders and marvels at it. "Madame Merle was armed at all points; it was a pleasure to see a person so completely equipped for the social battle. She carried her flag discreetly, but her weapons were polished steel, and she used them with a skill which struck Isabel as more and more that of a veteran[74]." This image also implies the subsidiary meaning that Madame Merle hides herself behind an outward armour, and does not show her real, wicked self. Isabel, in her innocence, sees Madame Merle's external shell only; she cannot make out her hidden nature.

The Old Things is the first novel in the selection in which war images are consistently introduced as a group. They are obviously applied with the intention of dramatizing the actions which are taken about the spoils. Such images are therefore not introduced in the second half of the novel. The war images mark various stages in the removal of the *objets d'art*. Mrs. Gereth's determination not to let Mona Brigstock become the mistress of Poynton and gain possession of all the treasures initiates a first image: "Fleda was struck, was even a little startled, with the way Mrs. Gereth had turned this over,—had faced, if indeed only to recognize its futility, the notion of a battle with her only son[75]." It starts when Mrs. Gereth decides to remove certain treasures from Poynton: "Fleda asked Mrs. Gereth whether she literally meant to shut herself up and stand a siege, or whether it was her idea to expose herself, more informally, to be dragged out of the house by constables. 'Oh, I prefer the constables and the dragging!' the heroine of Poynton had answered. 'I want to make Owen and Mona do everything that will be most publicly odious'[76]." When Fleda pays her first visit to Ricks, and finds most of the *objets d'art* there, she thinks that it "had come, indeed, to a question of 'sides', ... for the whole place was in battle array[77]". And when she wonders how Mrs. Gereth managed to get the treasures away from Poynton, the description she receives is in the terms of a strategic manœuvre: "By calculating, by choosing my time. I *was* quiet, and I *was* quick. I manœuvred; then at last I rushed." And referring to her servants she continues: "I know the three persons you have in mind: I had them in mind myself. Well, I took a line with them,—I settled them ... I took hold of them hard,—I put them in the forefront. I made them work[78]." The images strengthen the significance of the action for the following development of the story. Mrs. Gereth's "side" has made a move. What is the other "side" going to do? But the function of the war images is also to bring out this extremely active and aggressive side of Mrs. Gereth's character—she knows no compromise.

Two other images concern Fleda Vetch. Both indicate that she is taking an active part in the struggle between mother and son; the second, moreover, points to the weak spot in her character, her lack of determination. The first image, although not highly significant, still makes us aware that she has not enough strength to oppose Mrs. Gereth: "the fight made a demand upon her, and her pugnacity had become one with her constant habit of using such weapons as she could pick up[79]." The second image is more significant: "Owen Gereth was looking to her for a struggle, and it wasn't a bit of a struggle to be disgusted and dumb. She was on too strange a footing,—that of having presented an ultimatum and having had it torn up in her face. In such a case as that the envoy always departed; he never sat gaping and dawdling before the city[80]." The "ultimatum", to which the image alludes, is Fleda's request that Mrs. Gereth should send the treasures back to Poynton. But upon that lady's refusal Fleda remains inactive. The reason for her passivity after a first fruitless attempt to convince Mrs. Gereth lies in her own love for Owen and her conviction that the return of the spoils would be followed immediately by the marriage of Owen and Mona.

The Ambassadors has, of all James's novels, the least amount of action. It is a novel of discrimination. Therefore, no war images of any significance are introduced[81]. In the last two novels James uses them powerfully to make a clear distinction between active and passive characters. Mrs. Lowder has a strong affinity with Mrs. Gereth in her extreme aggressiveness and activity, in her unscrupulous and uncompromising behaviour. Kate lives in her room as in a "refuge", and her aunt's presence in the same house affects her "like the rumble of a far-off siege heard in the provisioned citadel". She is afraid of a "general surrender ... to aunt Maud's looming 'personality'". Then another picture for Mrs. Lowder crops up in her mind, that of "Britannia of the Market Place" who should not be happy "till she might on some occasion add to the rest of her panoply a helmet, a shield, a trident and a ledger". For Kate she carried on, "behind her aggressive and defensive front, operations determined by her wisdom. It was ... as a besieger that our young lady ... had for the present most to think of her[82]". By means of the metaphorical conception of Mrs. Lowder as Britannia we get, from the very beginning, a very clear, decisive and lasting picture of this woman and of this essential side of her character. Two chapters later Merton feels that "Her arms of aggression, her weapons of defence, were presumably close at hand, but she left them untouched and unmentioned, and was in fact so bland that he properly perceived only afterwards how adroit she had been ... who knew what might happen should he take to liking *her?* Well, it was a risk he naturally must face. She fought him, at any rate, but with one hand, with a few loose grains of stray powder[83]." This image emphasizes another quality of Mrs. Lowder's, her power and strength. She needs only one hand to fight Merton Densher who wasn't "dangerous enough for policy[84]". A few chapters later, the original Britannia image is enlarged and carried into detail when the potential largeness, the danger and unpredictability of Mrs. Lowder's actions are emphasized. "Susan Shepherd's word for her, again and again, was that she was 'large'"; when Mrs. Stringham in America "had handsomely figured her friends as not small ... there was a certain implication that they were spacious because they were empty. Mrs. Lowder, by a different law, was spacious because she was full, because she had something in common, even in repose, with a projectile, of great size, loaded and ready for use[85]."

Describing Mrs. Lowder, James starts off with an initial picture, that of Britannia, and all the subsequent war images accumulate on this basis, are additions to this original conception. It is a gradual revelation of detail after detail until the whole picture is complete. The war images in *The Old Things* still lack this inner organic integration which distinguishes the later image sequel. We recognize a similar achievement in the organic harmony of the war images introduced for Milly. They are all completely different in nature from those attributed to Mrs. Lowder, and are only introduced from the moment of Milly's meeting with Sir Luke Strett and her learning of the limited time she has yet to live. It is through the physician's advice to be active and to "live" that Milly has got a new impulse:

> It was as if she had had to pluck off her breast, to throw away, some friendly ornament, a familiar flower, a little old jewel, that was part of her daily dress; and to take up and shoulder as a substitute some queer defensive weapon, a musket, a spear, a battle-axe—conducive possibly in a higher degree to a striking appearance, but demanding all the effort of the military posture.
> She felt this instrument, for that matter, already on her back, so that she proceeded now in very truth as a soldier on a march—proceeded as if, for her initiation, the first charge had been sounded ... she might, from the curiosity she clearly excited in by-ways ... literally have had her musket on her shoulder, have announced herself as freshly on the warpath[86].

If this passage denotes action, it is clearly action against her own self. Before

74

her interview with Sir Luke Strett, she had been in an extremely depressed state. Milly, coming from the great doctor, is going away with the resolution to live as intensely as she can, to have as many great adventures as possible. But the image makes it quite clear that with Milly a different kind of action is involved from that of Aunt Maud. There is nothing unscrupulous or immoral about Milly's intentions. They cannot even be called aggressive, as her actions are not directed against any one but herself. In contrast to Mrs. Lowder's activity we might call Milly's defensive action or active defense. This defensive character of her "warfare" is again stressed much later when we read about her and Kate: "The relief of getting out of harness—that was the moral of their meetings; but the moral of this, in turn, was that they couldn't so much as ask each other why harness need be worn. Milly wore it as a general armour. She was out of it at present, for some reason, as she had not yet been for weeks; she was always out of it, that is, when alone[87]." We come across yet another image associated with warfare when we read of Kate that she was, as "a wondering, pitying sister condemned wistfully to look at [Milly] from the far side of the moat she had dug round her tower[88]". These further war images are perfectly in harmony with the defensive struggle which Milly's activities assume from a certain point onwards. It is the struggle of a human being who defends herself against any possible exploitation. If we compare this picture of Milly, as it is evoked by these images, with that which she leaves on us at the beginning, we notice a clear change in her attitude. At first she is free, full of life and vitality, even careless to a certain extent[89]. In the second part of the novel she makes a much more reserved impression; she is more careful, less free in her contact with her many friends and admirers; in fine, she is on guard ever since the revelation at Matcham.

With Maggie Verver we find a similar change between the first and second parts of the novel. Here again war images are introduced to establish and emphasize the transition which, in her case, is from passivity to activity. The first image is introduced at the very beginning of the second part. She has performed an action which would strike Amerigo as unusual: "She had put her thought to the proof, and the proof had shown its edge; this was what was before her, that she was no longer playing with blunt and idle tools, with weapons that didn't cut. There passed across her vision ten times a day the gleam of a bare blade, and at this it was that she most shut her eyes, most knew the impulse to cheat herself with motion and sound[90]." This image is connected with one small but decisive action which Maggie takes on the grounds of her suspicion, an action which she saw in retrospect as the one which "had made the abrupt bend in her life[91]". Maggie is only just beginning to collect proof. When the next war image is introduced she is, theoretically, in possession of sufficient evidence to start the fight, but for various reasons the time for it has not yet come: "There were hours, truly, when the Princess saw herself as not unarmed for battle if battle might only take place without spectators[92]." The "spectator", to whom this image alludes, is certainly Maggie's father whom she wants to spare under all circumstances. The third and decisive stage of her efforts to attain final happiness is reached when she is convinced that Amerigo will never tell Charlotte that he is aware of Maggie's realization: "She stood there, in her full uniform, like some small erect commander of a siege, an anxious captain who has suddenly got news, replete with importance for him, of agitation, of division within the place[93]." These three related images show three stages in Maggie's growing activity; firstly she acts only under a suspicion; then she waits, with enough proof in hand, for the appropriate occasion; finally she dominates the whole scene. Because they thus depict stages of action, they are, in their method, more nearly related to the war images in *The Old Things* than those in *The Wings*. But as far as the pictorial conception of the images is concerned, those of *The Golden Bowl* are of a finer and maturer quality than those used for Mrs. Gereth's actions[94].

3. Animal Images

It is the group of animal images which James most used and developed as a means of contrasting Europeans and Americans, power and weakness, slyness and straightforwardness. When the clear distinction is made, those animal images which relate to Europeans are always associated with evil, and they depict either strong and powerful, or cunning, insidious animals, such as lions, panthers, cats, snakes and so on. In addition to their strength or cunning these animals are always free and superior. Wherever James uses the word "beast" in one of his animal images he refers to this first category of unpleasant and dangerous human beings. On the other hand, Americans of the innocent type are always characterized by weak and, very often, caged animals.

Roderick Hudson contains only one animal image of any significance with a characterizing purpose; but it is not yet used to contrast Europe and America. Looking at Roderick "as he lay stretched in the shade, Rowland vaguely likened him to some beautiful, supple, restless, bright-eyed animal, whose motions should have no deeper warrant than the tremulous delicacy of its structure, and be graceful even when they were most inconvenient[95]". It is not specified what kind of an animal Rowland has in mind. What matters here is the implication of the image. Its function is to emphasize Rowland's uncertainty as to what will become of Roderick; it implies even more the hidden dangers one has to reckon with when confronted with certain kinds of animals. Rowland has a presentiment that he will never be able to understand Roderick completely. The element of the unknown, the unexpected, the unpredictable, will always play a large part in the relationship between the two men in particular, but also in that between Roderick and any other person[96].

Of the many common animal images in *The Portrait*[97] only one is of particular interest because it shows the first diffident use of a device which James developed in his last novels. The image is introduced when Isabel herself begins to realize slowly that she has been "caught" by Osmond (and indirectly by Madame Merle), that he only married her for the sake of her money. Ralph warns her that she is "going to be put in a cage", to which she answers: "If I like my cage that needn't trouble you[98]." No explicit reference is made to any animal, but the indirect allusion qualifies the image as the first example of an innocent American pictured as caged by some experienced and corrupt European.

The two significant animal images which are to be found in *The Old Things* are introduced after Mrs. Gereth has lost all her *objets d'art* and they have the function of stressing the fact that her treasures were an organic part of her being, without which she is a ruined person: "Mrs. Gereth's three minutes with Owen had been a blow to all talk of travel, and after her woeful hour at Maggie's she had, like some great, moaning, wounded bird, made her way, with wings of anguish, back to the nest she knew she should find empty[99]." This picture of a broken, helpless woman is further emphasized by one shortly afterwards. Fleda "had had a vision of her now lying prone on some unmade bed, now pacing a bare floor like a lioness deprived of her cubs. There had been moments when the mind's ear was strained to listen for some sound of grief wild enough to be wafted from afar[100]." Both images express the same idea, that of an animal which has lost its young, something that was a product of its own body, of the utmost pride and joy. The loss of Mrs. Gereth's *objets d'art* is thus pictured as something cruel, fatal and irredeemable[101].

The outstanding example of a person characterized by a series of animal images is Mrs. Lowder. They complete the picture of her painted by the war images. Again, the first of them is the most elaborate of all, creating, as it were, the basis for the following ones which are related to the original picture. It is introduced in the same context as the first war image. Kate has the notion that she may be "devoured", and she likens herself to "a trembling kid, kept apart a day or two till her turn should come, but sure sooner or later to be introduced into the cage of the lioness". This cage is identical with Mrs. Lowder's room on the ground-floor, which affects Kate "as a guard-house or toll-gate. The lioness waited—the kid had at least that consciousness; was aware of the neighbourhood of a morsel she had reason to suppose tender. She would have been meanwhile a wonderful lioness for a show, an extraordinary figure in a cage or anywhere; majestic, magnificent, high-coloured, all brilliant gloss ... with a lustre of agate eyes, a sheen of raven hair[102]." We are again confronted with a lioness, but this time not one deprived of her cubs but in full possession of power and strength, ready to devour anyone who should venture to enter her cage. At the beginning of the novel, Kate ist very much afraid of Mrs. Lowder. She is not yet on her side, is not yet a tool in her hands. But she is at the mercy of Aunt Maud, as much as Merton is. "She was in fine quite the largest possible quantity to deal with; and he was in the cage of the lioness without his whip—the whip, in a word, of a supply of proper retorts[103]." The allusion to the original image is obvious, and the relation is again established when, in the course of the ensuing discussion between Merton and Mrs. Lowder, the latter says: "I can bite your head off any day, any day I really open my mouth; and I'm dealing with you now, see—and successfully judge—without opening it[104]."

Apart from the lioness images which emphasize Mrs. Lowder's power and strength, James has stressed other wicked qualities in her character by means of different animal images. Her mental superiority and great gift for spying a chance, seizing it, and not letting it slip out of her hands, again find expression when Kate initiates an extended image by saying to Merton: "She fixed upon me herself, settled on me with her wonderful gilded claws." Densher renders the allusion more obvious: "You speak ... as if she were a vulture." And Kate completes the picture with: "Call it an eagle—with a gilded beak as well, and with wings for great flights[105]." Mrs. Lowder is not only seen as queen of all beasts but also as queen of the birds. Her being likened to a vulture and an eagle gives her a new dimension; she is able to pick out her prey from a towering height, and to swoop down upon it immediately; nor, like the vulture, will she release it until she has gained all that she desires. Her slyness and quickness are stressed by a cat image: "The way the cat would jump was always, in presence of anything that moved her, interesting to see; visibly enough, moreover, for a long time, it hadn't jumped anything like so far[106]." What caused Mrs. Lowder to jump "so far" was simply the advent of Milly, and Aunt Maud's immediate perception of her great chance.

An animal image used of Kate occurs after she has been introduced into Mrs. Lowder's "cage", and, like Merton Densher, has come out of it as a changed person. Milly "recalled, with all the rest of it, the next day, piecing things together in the dawn, that she had felt herself alone with a creature who paced like a panther. That was a violent image, but it made her a little less ashamed of having been scared[107]." Just as Kate was afraid of Mrs. Lowder, so is Milly now afraid of Kate: the original situation has repeated itself in a different form. The main function of the image, however, is to convey that Kate is now completely on her aunt's side, being friendly to

Milly but with the ultimate intention of exploiting her good-hearted nature and her fabulous wealth. It is evident that all these images are related to evil, wickedness, corruption. It is only Mrs. Lowder, Kate and Merton who are compared to beasts, birds and cats[108].

The situation and question of "sides" is much more complex in *The Golden Bowl*. Although two Americans and two Europeans appear among the principal characters, there is not the same distinction between innocence and experience as we find, for instance, in *The Wings*. It is no longer true that the American characters appear as weaker, as inferior to the Europeans. On the contrary, to judge from the animal images we find in this novel, the prototype of European history and tradition, Amerigo, is not at all aggressive and evil in the sense of Mrs. Lowder, for instance. If one excepts Adam Verver who, as a result of Maggie's strategy, remains an outsider in the struggle between Charlotte and the prince and Maggie, it is Amerigo himself who appears as the weakest character of the trio. Therefore he is likened to a "domesticated lamb" when we read that Fanny "was there to keep him quiet ... Fanny herself limited indeed, she minimised, her office; you didn't need a jailor, she contended, for a domesticated lamb tied up with pink ribbon. This was not an animal to be controlled—it was an animal to be, at the most, educated[109]." What James does, however, stress in a unique pictorial creation is the contrast of innocence and experience in the case of Adam and Amerigo. It is the latter who likens himself to "a chicken, at best, chopped up and smothered in sauce; cooked down as a *crême de volaille,* with half the parts left out". In contrast to himself he sees Maggie's father as "the natural fowl running about the *bassecour*. His feathers, movements, his sounds—those are the parts that, with me, are left out[110]." The prince, as a result of long tradition and experience, has gone through a process which turned him into a *"crême de volaille"*, with all the indigestible parts removed. But, nevertheless, he represents the best, the *"crême"* of the original. Adam, on the other hand, is still in an uncorrupted, unspoilt condition. But the interpretation of this image makes it evident that it is Adam, the American, who has the greater power, who is superior to the European. Whereas the prince is "dead", he is very much alive. This animal image, then, seems, in its conception, to be a parallel to the many *objet d'art* images in this novel where Amerigo is treated by Adam very much as dead matter, as a most valuable piece for an art collector. Charlotte is shown as a much stronger and more powerful character. She is not aggressive by nature, however, but only when attacked. Maggie sees her as in a cage with "the sight of gilt wires and bruised wings, the spacious but suspended cage ... The cage was the deluded condition, and Maggie ... understood the nature of cages." But although her stepmother is in a cage she is afraid. Maggie "walked round Charlotte's—cautiously and in a very wide circle". At the end of the image there is a hint that Charlotte might have the strength to free herself. She finally strikes Maggie "as making a grim attempt; from which, at first, the Princess drew back as instinctively as if the door of the cage had suddenly been opened from within[111]". This image, occurring in the final stages of the novel, pictures Charlotte in a much inferior position compared to Maggie, who has gained this great advantage and command over her stepmother because Amerigo has concealed from her his awareness that Maggie knows everything. Soon afterwards, when Charlotte is seen leaving the bridge-party in order to join Maggie on the terrace, the above image is taken up again and continued. Her move affects Maggie "as a breaking of bars. The splendid shining supple creature was out of the cage, was at large; and the question now almost grotesquely rose of whether she mightn't by some art ... be hemmed in and secured." A moment later Charlotte's "face was fixed on her, through the night; she was the creature who had escaped by force from her cage ... She had escaped with an intention, but with an intention the more definite that it could so accord with quiet measures[112]." These metaphorical passages provide drama by means of metaphor—an achievement seen at its greatest in *The Golden Bowl*. The images in the passage quoted last reveal that Charlotte's escape from her prison signifies nothing less than that she has come to the point where she suspects Maggie's knowledge. And the princess can save herself only by a lie and a treacherous kiss[113].

Although the animal images in *The Golden Bowl* do not quite reach the level of those in *The Wings* they are clearly more remarkable than those in any of the earlier novels, and mark a considerable development from the early, weak beginnings in *Roderick Hudson* and *The Portrait,* as well as being superior to the first outstanding examples in *The Old Things*.

CHAPTER 5

Images Expressing the Abstract in Terms of the Concrete

The present chapter deals with images that are introduced to express thoughts, ideas and feelings for which there exists no literal term that is their precise equivalent. They are the result of an inner urge, for they do not refer to external actions but mental processes. With their help the novelist allows his readers to penetrate most deeply into his characters, and their innermost problems are revealed and laid bare. The application of such images is a psychological device. It is, therefore, not surprising that no English novelist before James made use of imagery for this purpose to an extent that might be called systematic or consistent. Although Charlotte Brontë may be called the first English novelist who revealed the inner life of her characters, she did not analyse their consciousness as James does. Nor are her heroines' feelings rendered by means of imagery. This device, which James developed to maturity, can be found in its beginnings in George Eliot's novels. (The most striking example of a novel which is the exact opposite of James's in so far as it does not reveal any psychological details of its characters is to be found outside English literature, namely in Adalbert Stifter's *Witiko,* a novel in which images on the whole are extremely scarce.) From the point of view of the characters themselves their thinking in images appears as a help to their own reflections, as a crystallization of their thoughts.

We are here confronted with one of the highest and most significant forms of imagery, and it is therefore not surprising that we shall hardly find any comparisons and similes. Only the metaphor, the highest form of imagery, will suffice here, and when a comparison is included in a person's thinking, it is only for the sake of clarity. With this group of imagery James has developed yet another device. This is the expression of the relationship which exists between two or more persons. He gradually developed it into a most powerful and successful instrument with the help of which he emphasized every now and then in what relation his main characters stand to one another, and how far they are dependent on each other.

A. THE POETIC METAPHOR

There are, fundamentally, two kinds of metaphor. One of them may be called consciously introduced metaphors. Those belonging to the second group may be called poetic. In contrast to the other kind they are used spontaneously in order to objectify the world of feeling, of a writer's inner visions. Such metaphors, then, are the result of an urge which is particularly evident in the case of poets. Most novelists, on the other hand, make little use of the poetic metaphor.

Hardy and Meredith were, perhaps, the first English novelists who consistently introduced poetic metaphors into their works of fiction. As they were both poets as well, this fact is not surprising. But their main concern was not yet the revelation of thoughts and feelings.

With James it is different. His interest in the psychology of his characters confronts him with problems which every poet has to face and to solve. James does it frequently by the introduction of spontaneous, poetic metaphors. In this particular respect he stands at the beginning of a development which leads directly to James Joyce, in whose works metaphors are carried to their extreme limits[1].

James's early novels do not yet anticipate his achievement in the field of the poetic metaphor. Here he still follows the tradition of the Victorian novel in applying images for purely aesthetic reasons, with the result that they often render his style flowery. An example from *Roderick Hudson* may exemplify this point: "The monotonous days of the two women seemed to Rowland's fancy to follow each other like the tick-tick of a great time-piece, marking off the hours which separated them from the supreme felicity of clasping the far-away son and lover to lips sealed with the excess of joy[2]." It is not so much the first part of this image which sounds artificial and flowery. The "time-piece" is well chosen as a comparison indicating the monotony of the lives of Mrs. Hudson and Mary Garland in Northampton. But the "lips sealed with joy" cannot be regarded as a satisfactory pictorial creation. Rowland's becoming aware of the rising storm which brings about Roderick's death contains a more spontaneous metaphor. "At last he was startled by an extraordinary sound; it took him a moment to perceive that it was a portentous growl of thunder. He roused himself and saw that the whole face of the sky had altered. The clouds that had hung motionless all day were moving from their stations, and getting into position, as it were, for a battle. The wind was rising—the sallow vapors were turning dark and consolidating their masses. It was a striking spectacle[3]." Indirectly, this image also throws light upon Rowland's state of mind. It is certainly no coincidence that a storm follows the severe argument between the two men and that James mirrors the rising storm in Rowland's consciousness. One of his frequent manners of objectifying is by means of a personifying metaphor. In his first novel he concretizes in this way the idea of Rowland's finding a compensation in Mary Garland for the time he has lost through Roderick: "It seemed to him that he saw the idea from the outside, that he judged it and condemned it; yet it stood there before him, distinct, and in a certain way imperious. During the day he tried to banish it and forget it; but it fascinated, haunted, at moments frightened him ... His idea persisted;

it clung to him like a sturdy beggar[4]." The inward battle which Rowland is fighting out during his days of meditation at Florence is intensified and rendered comprehensible. This example also makes it evident that poetic metaphors, in most cases, are not only the result of an urge, but that they also fulfil a function, in this case that of illustrating the secondary theme of the novel, viz. Rowland's struggle for Mary Garland, his affection for her and his fruitless attempts to quell it.

In *The Portrait* the number of traditional images of a merely aesthetic intention has decreased considerably, but at the same time James's mostly successful endeavour to create new pictorial conceptions is very marked. The same tendency can be witnessed in *The Old Things*[5]. We also realize that there are no spontaneous metaphors which do not fulfil a distinct function at the same time. And it is often difficult to decide whether urge or purpose has been the major factor for the introduction of the metaphor. This may be exemplified by the personification of the dead front of a Florentine villa: "this ancient, solid, weather-worn, yet imposing front had a somewhat incommunicative character. It was the mask of the house; it was not its face. It had heavy lids, but no eyes; the house in reality looked another way— looked off behind, into splendid openness and the range of the afternoon light[6]." The particular achievement of this image lies in its giving life and significance to something dead and static. But it also indirectly foreshadows the nature of Osmond's character. The necessity of this pictorial creation was, then, the fulfilment of this double function.

The most successful and impressive poetic images are those relating to nature. There is an early and simple one which nevertheless beautifully conveys the whole atmosphere of Gardencourt, the place where all the decisive scenes in the novel, with one exception, take place. Without the metaphorical elements James could not have created this particular atmosphere in an equally impressive manner. "Real dusk would not arrive for many hours; but the flood of summer light had begun to ebb, the air had grown mellow, the shadows were long upon the smooth dense turf. They lengthened slowly, however, and the scene expressed that sense of leisure still to come which is perhaps the chief source of one's enjoyment of such a scene at such an hour." A little later James continues the description of Gardencourt: "Privacy here reigned supreme, and the wide carpet of turf that covered the level hill-top seemed but the extension of a luxurious interior. The great still oaks and beeches flung down a shade as dense as that of velvet curtains; and the place was furnished, like a room, with cushioned seats, with rich colored rugs, with the books and papers that lay upon the grass[7]." Hardy was, perhaps, the only English novelist who has given us equally impressive nature descriptions for which he has largely drawn upon imagery. His bond with nature is even more intense than James's, in whose novels nature only plays a secondary part[8]. *Wuthering Heights,* on the other hand, where nature plays a dominant part, contains almost no images—and these few are mostly conventional.

In *The Ambassadors* one particular form of the poetic metaphor is extremely frequent. It is, at the same time, the simplest kind, namely that of relating concrete to abstract terms by means of images. With other novelists such metaphors tend to be merely rhetorical, but James maintains a high standard of originality even with this simple form of the spontaneous metaphor. "It was absolutely true of him that—even after the close of the period of conscious detachment occupying the centre of his life, the gray middle desert of the two deaths, that of his wife and that, ten years later, of his boy—he had never taken any one anywhere[9]." The words "the gray middle desert of the two deaths" read like a line from a poem, but only through this picture are we told what effects these two deaths had upon Strether. The image also forms an immense contrast to the life with which Strether is confronted at the point of its introduction, that of Europe. Another example confirms the richness of James's creative mind. A general statement about relations among people in Strether's mind is rendered in the following way: "A personal relation was a relation only so long as people either perfectly understood or, better still, didn't care if they didn't. From the moment they cared if they didn't it was living by the sweat of one's brow; and the sweat of one's brow was just what one might buy one's self off from by keeping the ground free of the wild weed of delusion[10]." This example shows, too, that James's style has by now grown much more complex. His accumulation of negatives in particular requires sharp and logical thinking. A further example shows us the spontaneity of a Jamesian metaphor and his endeavour to turn a "dead" metaphorical expression into an original pictorial conception. "It must be added, however, that, thanks to his constant habit of shaking the bottle in which life handed him the wine of experience, he presently found the taste of the lees rising, as usual, into his draught[11]." The conventional expression "the wine of experience" forms only a minor part in the totality of the image, which is not very easy to comprehend. James must have felt that himself, for he continues: "His imagination had in other words already dealt with his young friend's assertion." We have here a reciprocal procedure whereby an image is illustrated afterwards by a plain statement. This fact strengthens the assumption that the metaphor has been introduced spontaneously. When Strether is alone with Mamie Pocock we read: "There had been at first, as he sat there with her, a moment during which he wondered if she meant to break ground in respect to his prime undertaking. That door stood so strangely ajar that he was half prepared to be conscious, at any juncture, of her having, of any one's having, quite bounced in. But, ... she exquisitely stayed out[12]." The sudden introduction of "that door", with its concrete associations, comes almost as a surprise. And yet, if we look at the preceding sentence, this turn has been carefully prepared by the slightly metaphorical, though conventional, expression "to break ground". The picture of the door that stands ajar while Strether wonders whether Mamie will suddenly bounce into the room (metaphorically speaking) makes the particular juncture tense and dramatic. A particular achievement in *The Ambassadors* are the many spontaneous metaphors which show a combination of psychological analysis and metaphorical language. One such example occurs when Strether walks to the "old arches of the Odeon" where he looks at the many books arrayed in the open air:

> He was there on some chance of feeling the brush of the wing of the stray spirit of youth. He felt it in fact, he had it beside him; the old arcade indeed, as his inner sense listened, gave out the faint sound, as from far-off, of the wild waving of wings. They were folded now over the breasts of buried generations; but a flutter or two lived again in the turned page of the shock-headed, slouch-hatted loiterers whose young intensity of type, in the direction of pale acuteness, deepened his vision, and even his appreciation, of racial differences, and whose manipulation of the uncut volume was too often, however, but a listening at closed doors [13].

These images evoke clear and lasting impressions in our minds, while there is also a continuity throughout the imagery of the whole passage, the wings being the central metaphorical symbol. This renders the whole passage vigorous and dynamic. The effect of movement is enhanced by the activity that is attributed to the "old arcade" which is described as giving out a sound, and also by the personification of Strether's "inner sense" which is listening to the sound emitted by it. We are not reading a colourless description but are seeing a picture develop in front of our eyes. The same is true when Strether makes a general statement about life, and it is unimaginable how his thought could be expressed equally well without the help of imagery: "The affair—I mean the affair of life—couldn't, no doubt, have been different for me; for it's, at the best, a tin mould, either fluted or embossed, with ornamental excrescences, or else smooth and dreadfully plain, into which, a helpless jelly, one's consciousness, is poured—so that one 'takes' the form, as the great cook says, and is more or less compactly held by it; one lives, in fine, as one can [14]." One's life is formed by the surroundings one is born into. The *milieu*—what Strether calls a "tin mould"—is the decisive factor. One has the illusion of freedom, especially if one lives in so remote and provincial a place as Woollett. Only now does Strether realize how "smooth and dreadfully plain" he and everyone at Woollett is in comparison with the people—wonderfully "fluted or embossed"—he meets in Paris.

The Ambassadors is full of small but delicate descriptions which are conceived in the spirit of poetry. They often lead us to think of little drawings or paintings, an effect which suggests the influence of the Italian masters with whose paintings and drawings James was so familiar. Of Maria Gostrey's room in Paris it is said that "the lust of the eyes and the pride of life had indeed thus their temple. It was the innermost nook of the shrine— as brown as a pirate's cave. In the brownness were glints of gold; patches of purple were in the gloom[15]." This image shows James's extraordinary feeling for colours and light effects. There is a fine vein of poetry in the following short passage: "The occupants had not come in, for the room looked empty as only a room can look in Paris of a fine afternoon, when the faint murmur of the huge collective life, carried on out-of-doors, strays among scattered objects even as a summer air idles in a lonely garden[16]." James spontaneously gives life to dead things, bestows activity upon motionless objects, and imparts variety of expression to what would otherwise be colourless facts. This intention is quite obvious in the following two examples: "A thousand unuttered thoughts hummed for him in the air of these observations[17]", and "Women were thus endlessly absorbent, and to deal with them was to walk on water ... if to deal with them was to walk on water, what wonder that the water rose? And it had never, surely, risen higher than in this woman[18]", namely Marie de Vionnet.

As the most purely poetic images in *The Wings* the many descriptions of Venice at once come to mind. The "Palazzo Leporelli held its history still in its great lap, even like a painted idol, a solemn puppet hung about with decorations. Hung about with pictures and relics, the rich Venetian past, the ineffaceable character, was here the presence revered and served[19]." At various points in the second part of the novel we encounter short descriptions of typical spots in Venice which, taken together, constitute a wonderful poetic image of the city[20]. We must see this "painting" of Venice primarily as an effort to create the atmosphere in which the whole drama moving about Milly takes place. Compare with those examples some of Trollope's rather wooden and lifeless renderings of places and buildings which remain mere descriptions, whereas James's imagination has clearly been at work to give us more than that—a colourful and singular picture, impressive and lasting. But not only does James provide the scenic background, he also accompanies the emotional development of the story in this part of the novel by light effects in his weather descriptions. It is not mere chance that the weather in Venice changes into rain and storm, or that the lightness and brightness of the sunshine changes into darkness when the novel reaches its sad climax, when Milly "turns her face to the wall".

The Wings, even more than *The Ambassadors,* is pervaded by imagery which serves the purpose of enriching the texture and adding colour and significance, as well as stimulating the reader's imagination. Merton's "idea of a series of letters from the United States from the strictly social point of view had for some time been nursed in the inner sanctuary at whose door he sat, and the moment was now deemed happy for letting it loose. The imprisoned thought had, in a word, on the opening of the door, flown straight out into Densher's face, or perched at least on his shoulder, making him look up in surprise from his mere inky office-table[21]." The images in this passage allow James to express infinite nuances of Densher's mental state. Such lines give us a chance to form valid judgments on the various characters in a Jamesian novel. The images here referring to Merton show him as a passive, irresolute character. Some of James's impressive personifications of lifeless things are again most convincing as spontaneous pictorial creations. They are presented in an active, dynamic way: "what Densher therefore would have struck at would be the root, in her [Milly's] soul, of a pure pleasure. It positively lifted its head and flowered, this pure pleasure, while the young man now sat with her[22]." With the help of such comparatively simple images James achieved his constant aim that his readers should not only be able to read what he had written, but also that they should "see", as his mind must have seen, everything in terms of vivid pictures. Such images also serve as indirect characterizations of the persons to whom they allude. A tendency to introduce them for this purpose can also be felt in some of George Eliot's examples, as for instance when Dorothea Casaubon's loneliness is rendered "in the kindly mornings when autumn and winter seemed to go hand in hand like a happy aged couple one of whom would presently survive in chiller loneliness". This image points forward to her spiritual condition after her husband's death.

On the whole, the maturest examples of poetic metaphors are to be found in James's last completed novel. The great majority of its images convey a strong sense of poetry, even if they are as plain as "She simply 'cleared them out'—those had been the three words, thrown off in reference to the golden peace that the Kentish October had gradually ushered in[23]", or: "What with the ... generous mood of the sunny, gusty, lusty English April, all panting and heaving with impatience, or kicking and crying, even, at moments, like some infant Hercules who wouldn't be dressed[24]." In both images we notice again James's early established device of personification, of which the most ingenious example occurs in the same novel. It is the plan for a journey:

There had been from far back ... a plan that the parent and the child should 'do something lovely' together, and they had recurred to it on occasion, nursed it and brought it up theoretically, though without as yet quite allowing it to put its feet on the ground. The most it had done was to try a few steps on the drawing-room carpet, with much attendance, on either side, much holding up and guarding, much anticipation, in fine, of awkwardness or accident. Their companions, by the same token, had constantly assisted at the performance, following the experiment with sympathy and gaiety, and never so full of applause ... as when the infant project had kicked its little legs most wildly—kicked them, for all the world, across the Channel and half the Continent, kicked them over the Pyrenees and innocently crowed out some rich Spanish name[25].

The interpretation of this metaphorical passage presents no difficulties. Its construction, however, calls for a few remarks. In the first place it is remarkable how appropriate the chosen picture is to the occasion, so much indeed that some readers may overlook the fact that the actual metaphor, starting at "nursed it ...", refers to the "plan", and then read the passage as alluding to "child"—until, with "when the infant project ...", any possible doubts are removed. The passage gives an excellent example of a metaphor that grows organically out of its context, because the "plan", pictured as a child, refers to a child.

The kiss of Isabel and Goodwood in *The Portrait* is described with great beauty and also with dramatic intensity, but that of Charlotte and Amerigo surpasses the earlier example in its poetic rendering: "Then of a sudden, through this tightened circle, as at the issue of a narrow strait into the sea beyond, everything broke up, broke down, gave way, melted and mingled. Their lips sought their lips, their pressure their response and their response their pressure; with a violence that had sighed itself the next moment to the longest and deepest of stillnesses they passionately sealed their pledge[26]." Images of such poetic beauty are frequent in *The Golden Bowl*. They also include most of the concretizing images, among which James, in his last novel, shows a strong preference for personification. These impressive metaphorical creations are all marked by a simplicity which heightens their power: "conviction ... budged no inch, only planting its feet the more firmly in the soil—but action began to hover like some lighter and larger, but easier form, excited by its very power to keep above ground[27]", or: "Pride, indeed, the next moment, had become the mantle caught up for protection and perversity; she flung it round her as a denial of any loss of her freedom[28]." It is evident that, although spontaneous, such images also fulfil essential purposes. Many of the metaphors dealt with in the subsequent chapters could, therefore, be regarded as the result of an urge. But the function which they have to fulfil stands out so clearly that it has to be considered in the first place.

B. THOUGHTS AND IDEAS

As early as *Roderick Hudson* a closer analysis of the metaphors expressing thoughts and ideas makes it evident that through them James gives us very important clues as to the relationship between Rowland and Roderick, and more especially to that between Rowland and Mary Garland. The importance of the latter is mostly overlooked in critical studies. And yet a true, correct understanding of this relationship is essential for the evaluation of the whole novel. We may indeed raise the question how far Rowland is responsible for Roderick's degeneration and death. Roderick, who "had caught, instinctively, the key-note of the old world[29]" is living very intensely in the culture of Europe, and Rowland must have realized that this is taking Roderick further and further away from Mary Garland. But he does nothing decisive to stop the process. On the contrary, "Rowland's theory of his own duty was to let him run his course and play his cards, only holding himself ready to point out shoals and pitfalls, and administer a friendly propulsion through tight places[30]". We are not explicitly told why Rowland looked upon his duty in the way described; but we may suspect that it is the result of his secret hopes for Mary which must, of course, favour Roderick's estrangement from his betrothed. This supposition is strengthened after the arrival of Mary and Mrs. Hudson. Rowland accompanies the two ladies and Roderick to Florence, but he goes only because he is interested in Mary and still has strong hopes: "he drank deep, only, of the satisfaction of not separating from Mary Garland. If the future was a blank to Roderick, it was hardly less so to himself[31]." And a little later, when Roderick tells him that he has had a "tremendous talk" with his cousin, Rowland's thoughts take the following course: "If their interview had been purely painful, he wished to ignore it for Miss Garland's sake, and if it had sown the seeds of reconciliation, he wished to close his eyes to it for his own—for the sake of that unshaped idea, forever dismissed, and yet forever present, which hovered in the background of his consciousness, with a hanging head, as it were, and yet an unashamed glance, and whose lightest motions were an effectual bribe to patience. Was the engagement broken?[32]" Rowland's thoughts are completely occupied with Mary. He, of course, cannot take any straightforward action that will bring about a break between Roderick and Mary, and for that reason the revelation of his thoughts is all the more important. The last image leaves no doubt as to Rowland's secret hopes and intentions, but at the end of the novel James speaks an even plainer language. When Roderick tells his friend that he has borrowed money from Mary "Rowland turned over and buried his face in his arms. He felt a movement of irrepressible elation, and he barely stifled a cry of joy. Now, surely, Roderick had shattered the last link in the chain that bound Mary to him, and after this she would be free![33]" His first reaction to Roderick's deed, then, is a feeling of elation and joy which he can hardly suppress, a joy which is the result of the conviction that Roderick has now definitely quelled Mary's affection for him. This certainty now makes him confess that he has been in love with Mary since he first knew her. Roderick reacts very calmly to this piece of news. But it is only his outward reaction that we see. His death in the Swiss mountains—melodramatic as it is—is certainly not suicide; the last spark of life in Roderick has been killed through Rowland's false play. These examples of images elucidating unuttered thoughts confirm the importance which imagery already plays in this first of James's novels as throwing light on hidden motives and thus rendering certain actions or events plausible.

The Portrait is James's first novel in which one character's consciousness is clearly the central reflector. All the images which are important for our discussion occur, therefore, in Isabel's thoughts. Some revealing metaphors are introduced before her marriage to Osmond. The first one gives us a clue to her final rejection of Caspar Goodwood and also a hint as to the character of her marriage with Osmond. "Deep in her soul—it was the deepest thing there—lay a belief that if a certain impulse were stirred she could give herself completely; but this image, on the whole, was too formidable to be attractive. Isabel's thoughts hovered about it, but they seldom rested on it long; after a little it ended by frightening her[34]." Even before her marriage, Isabel was already in doubts about Osmond's sincerity, and her reluctance to marry him was clearly the result of a vague fear that Osmond did not really love her, but wanted to marry her only for the sake of her money. "Her imagination stopped, ... there was a last vague space it could not cross—a dusky, uncertain tract, which looked ambiguous, and even slightly treacherous, like a moorland seen in the winter twilight[35]." This image forms the basis for Isabel's mistrust of her husband which she is able to repress at the beginning of her married life, but which flares up again after a short time. We are made aware of this in a long soliloquy during which Isabel's mind is completely opened up before us. Osmond "had had the evil eye", and they had reached a point where "a gulf had opened between them, over which they looked at each other with eyes that were on either side a declaration of the deception suffered". In her view this result of her married life was not her fault. "She had taken the first steps in the purest confidence, and then she had suddenly found the infinite vista of a multiplied life to be a dark, narrow alley, with a dead wall at the end." Instead of happiness, her feeling was one of depression and failure, brought about by her distrust of Osmond. At the end of the first year of marriage "the shadows began to gather; it was as if Osmond ... had put the lights out one by one". The "lights" here stand for Isabel's initial happiness. James now elaborates this image of light and dark: "The dusk at first was vague and thin, and she could still see her way in it. But it steadily increased, and ... there were certain corners of her life that were impenetrably black." Her house was one of darkness, of suffocation, with Osmond giving it neither light nor air. His mind "seemed to peep down from a small high window, and mock at her". Isabel was also aware that Osmond's egotism, which "lay hidden like a serpent in a bank of flowers", was a primary reason for her unhappiness. She was "shut up with an odor of mould and decay" and she had to "march to the stately music that floated down from unknown periods in her husband's past", and she had to live with his traditions, some of which "made her push back her skirts[36]". The images impart drama and intensity to the passage. Our foremost impression is that Isabel is compelled to lead, as it were, a life in prison. Some of the metaphors associate her thoughts with other passages earlier in the novel. When, for example, we read the image which pictures her life as a "dark, narrow alley, with a dead wall at the end", we recall the earlier one illustrating Isabel's idea of happiness[37]. And the picture of Osmond peeping down from a high window provides a powerful contrast to the many flying images attributed to Isabel and her freedom in the first part of the novel. The passage above is James's first great achievement in the field of psychological analysis, of his revelation of a character's inner life. And it shows unmistakably how great a part imagery plays in conveying a lively and lasting picture of Isabel's tormented soul. It is certainly largely due to the impressive images that such a passage remains vivid in our memory for a much longer time than, for instance, a similar description of the train of thoughts of one of Jane Austen's heroines, where we find virtually no images. Dorothea Casaubon, on the other hand, who shows many affinities with Isabel, is thrice characterized in her unhappiness with images strikingly similar to some used for Isabel: "Hence the mere chance of seeing Will occasionally was like a lunette opened in the wall of her prison, giving her a glimpse of the sunny air"; and: "now it appeared that she was to live more and more in a virtual tomb, where there was the apparatus of a ghostly labour producing what would never see the light. To-day she had stood at the door of the tomb and seen Will Ladislaw receding into the distant world of warm activity and fellowship", and: "How was it that in the weeks since her marriage, Dorothea had not distinctly observed but felt with a stifling depression, that the large vistas and wide fresh air which she had dreamed of finding in her husband's mind were replaced by anterooms and winding passages which seemed to lead nowhither?[38]"

In *The Old Things* the truly analytic images are again introduced only in the second part of the novel. The division between action and reaction is even more strongly felt than in *The Portrait*. If the first part deals mainly with Mrs. Gereth's actions, the interest in the second half is centred entirely on the inner development of Fleda Vetch. The main function of the analytic images in this part is to emphasize the nature of Fleda's intentions, the heroic and highly moral attitude which finally brings her to grief. What Fleda tried to conceal from everyone was her own passion for Owen, at first in front of him: "She had the real advantage, she considered, of having kept him from seeing that she had been overthrown. She had, moreover, at present, completely recovered her feet[39]." This image indicates clearly that she had been successful in her intentions at that particular meeting with Owen. At a later point in the novel, he asks her whether he should take any legal steps in order to restore the spoils to Poynton. Before Fleda answers, James gives a short passage of her thoughts in which we see her reaction to Owen's question. Fleda's reasoning is not easy to follow at first; the images, however, help much towards understanding the passage and with it the trend of her thoughts. Most readers would expect Fleda's answer to Owen's question to be a clear "yes", as the solicitor's action would seem the surest and safest way of having the spoils returned to Poynton. But Fleda's thoughts go further and penetrate deeply into the latent possibilities of the situation:

> She had at that moment turned away from this solution, precisely because she saw in it the great chance of her secret. If she should determine him to adopt it, she might put out her hand and take him. It would shut in Mrs. Gereth's face the open door of surrender: she would flare up and fight, flying the flag of a passionate, an heroic defense. The case would obviously go against her, but the proceedings would last longer than Mona's patience or Owen's propriety. With a formal rupture he would be at large, and she had only to tighten her fingers round the string that would raise the curtain on that scene [40].

With its many images this passage gives us the clue as to why Fleda fears that the solicitor's action would lead to a rupture between Mona and Owen, and would not, as one might expect, bring about their marriage. And yet it seems to leave one important question open. Why doesn't Fleda seize the great chance for herself? The passage quoted above does not give a direct answer to this question, but shortly before, we come across a significant flying image which provides the necessary explanation for Fleda's decision [41]. It is evident, therefore, that there exists an organic relation between many of the images, as they link the important parts together. Fleda's reasoning that Mrs. Gereth "would flare up and fight, flying the flag of a passionate, an heroic defense", for instance, relates this metaphor to the many war images introduced during the first part of the novel [42].

The next important stage in Fleda's inner development is her final breakdown in front of Owen by which she gives her last secret away, and Owen immediately becomes aware of her passion for him. This happens during their next meeting, when Fleda grows weaker and weaker until she bursts into sobs which mark the beginning of her surrender and her realization that Owen, "with the click of a spring, ... saw. He had cleared the high wall at a bound; they were together without a veil. She had not a shred of secret left; it was as if a whirlwind had come and gone, laying low the great false front that she had built up stone by stone [43]." It is this passage which emphasizes the moment at which Fleda's heroism and magnanimity come to grief; after this incident, indeed, she no longer acts for herself but is completely guided by Mrs. Gereth. And finally, after everything seems to be lost, her original heroism has turned into deep resignation. "Her emotion occupied some quarter of her soul that had closed its door for the day and shut out even her own sense of it; she might perhaps have heard something if she had pressed her ear to a partition. Instead of that she sat with her patience in a cold, still chamber." Not only resignation characterizes her state of mind, but also indifference, a feeling of not knowing what was happening to herself: "Her excitement was composed of pulses as swift and fine as the revolutions of a spinning top: she supposed she was going round, but she went round so fast that she couldn't even feel herself move." But she also sees the loss of Owen and the treasures as "a gain to memory and love". It was "in condonation of her treachery" that "the old things had crept back. She greeted them with open arms; she thought of them hour after hour; they made a company with which solitude was warm, and a picture that, at this crisis, overlaid poor Maggie's mahogany [44]." Through this exquisite metaphorical passage we enter into Fleda's mind and soul as into a house with its separate rooms, a house not empty but full of life. Nevertheless, she is the victim of a corrupt world, and her virtues are bound to fail in such surroundings. Judged from the outside, her fate is tragic; but within herself she has won a victory.

The Ambassadors is the one novel which does not show a division into two parts, one of action, the other of reaction. Throughout it deals with Strether's reactions, his attitude to Europe, to Chad's transformation, his friends and so on. The images introduced to reveal Strether's thoughts and ideas, taken together with those concerning his feelings, form a kind of skeleton for the whole novel. His fundamental inner transformation can be followed in its main outline simply by studying these images, for they mark and emphasize all the important stages of the process. The series of metaphors opens with three that contrast his new surroundings with those of his former life. They throw light on his reaction to a letter he has received from Mrs. Newsome: "Strether, however, could not at this point indeed have completed his thought by the image of what she might have to thank herself *for:* the image, at best, of his own likeness—Strether washed up on the sunny strand, thankful for breathing-time, stiffening himself while he gasped, by the waves of a single day." He begins to realize that the successful completion of his mission and his subsequent marriage to Mrs. Newsome as a reward might not, after all, be the true way to happiness. "It filled for him, this tone of hers, all the air; yet it struck him at the same time as the hum of vain things." And now he tries to comprehend why her tone strikes him in this way, and finally arrives at the conclusion that a fortnight ago he was still one of "the weariest of men", whereas now he feels a deep happiness and it "seemed to him somehow at these instants that, could he only maintain with sufficient firmness his grasp of this truth, it might become in a manner his compass and his helm[45]". Mrs. Newsome, as James pointed out, "is the reflection of his old self[46]". Strether's reactions to her letter are, therefore, to be taken as a reaction against a force within himself; his old outlook is slowly being superseded by a new attitude towards life.

The next stage in his evolution is characterized by his rapidly growing love for Paris. He had already spent some time in this city when he was young, and had always intended coming back. "As such plans as these had come to nothing, however, in respect to acquisitions still more precious, it was doubtless little enough of a marvel that he should have lost account of that handful of seed. Buried for long years in dark corners, at any rate, these few germs sprouted again under forty-eight hours of Paris[47]." Everything which Woollett had suppressed in him over the course of the years begins to live again in his mind, all the things that had been relegated to his sub-conscious mind "in the great desert of the years". This timeless "desert" of Woollett is again contrasted when Strether becomes aware that he "had not had for years so rich a consciousness of time—a bag of gold into which he constantly dipped for a handful[48]". The next important image in the series shows him already at a point where he is completely prepared to bear the consequences of his failure to fulfil his mission. He had "the sharp consciousness of wishing to prove to himself that he was not afraid to look his behaviour in the face. If he was by an inexorable logic to pay for it, he was literally impatient to know the cost, and he held himself ready to pay in instalments. The first instalment would be precisely this entertainment of Sarah[49]." Up to now Strether has been slowly getting away from Mrs. Newsome. But he even reaches a point where he openly works against her intentions by taking steps to keep Chad in Paris. "He took comfort, by the same stroke, in the swing of Chad's pendulum back from that other swing, the sharp jerk towards Woollett, so stayed by his own hand. He had the entertainment of thinking that if he had for that moment stopped the clock it was to promote the next minute this still livelier motion[50]."

The culmination of Strether's transformation is described in the scene which shows him alone in Chad's apartment, where he has to wait for his friend for an hour, one that he was to recall later "as the particular handful that most had counted[51]". During his long reflections he feels that "the freedom was what was most in the place and the hour; it ... brought him round again to the youth of his own that he had long ago missed ... everything represented the substance of his loss, put it within reach, within touch ... This was what it became for him at this singular time ... a queer concrete presence, full of mystery, yet full of reality, which he could handle, taste, smell, the deep breathing of which he could positively hear. It was in the outside air as well as within[52]." Strether has gone as far as he could; he has again established a communication with the happiness and freedom of his youth.

The fact that James, in *The Wings,* had not restricted himself to one central reflector has the effect that the metaphors throw light on at least three persons, namely Milly, Merton and Kate. In the first part analytic metaphors emphasize two facts. In the first place it is the strong affection between Merton and Kate. "It wasn't, in a word, simply that their eyes had met; other conscious organs, faculties, feelers had met as well, and when Kate afterwards imagined to herself the sharp, deep fact she saw it, in the oddest way, as a particular performance." And now James introduces a metaphor which probably has its origin in a real happening in his life[53]. "She had observed a ladder against a garden wall, and had trusted herself so to climb it as to be able to see over into the probable garden on the other side. On reaching the top she had found herself face to face with a gentleman engaged in a like calculation at the same moment, and the two inquirers had remained confronted on their ladders. The great point was that for the rest of that evening they had been perched—they had not climbed down; and indeed, during the time that followed, Kate at least had had the perched feeling—it was as if she were there aloft without a retreat[54]." We feel the tension that characterizes the first more intimate meeting between the two who later become lovers, and also get an idea of the secrecy which surrounds their friendship and love. The picture of a "ladder against a garden wall" indicates, too, the risks and dangers which accompany the first advances of each. We notice at the same time that the meaning of the metaphor is no longer so explicit and obvious as it had been with similar examples in earlier novels. A decided ambiguity is recognizable, which is the result of James's intention not to give everything away at once, but rather to reveal the facts gradually, piece by piece. This ambiguity is also to be felt when James stresses the second important point, namely that Merton's want of means could be a serious impediment to his marriage with Kate. "Only now, for the first time, had he to weigh his case in scales. The scales, as he sat with Kate, often dangled in the line of his vision; he saw them, large and black, while he talked or listened, take, in the bright air, singular positions. Sometimes the right was down and sometimes the left; never a happy equipose—one or the other always kicking the beam[55]." The meaning and full significance of this picture only becomes apparent when we read on and eventually realize that Kate's unfortunate family affairs might prove to be a grave drawback with her. It is characteristic that James, at this very early point of the novel, puts a strong emphasis on the fact of Merton's poverty, for the subsequent happenings are, to a great extent, the result of the effort to bring him into possession of a large sum of money.

Particularly in his last two completed novels did James develop the device of commenting on discussions in the consciousness of one of his characters. The outstanding example of this kind of imagery in *The Wings* is introduced during the scene which describes Merton's visit to Milly. It is a turning point in the whole novel because it shows his obliging her almost against his own will, though his behaviour, on the other hand, gives her the impression that he cares very much for her. It is the scene that leads straight up to the events in Venice. When Milly remarks that she would do anything for Kate, he feels that "she might for the moment have effectively laid a trap for whatever remains of the ideal straightness in him were still able to pull themselves together and operate". In other words he might give himself away with a wrong answer. When he finally says that he feels as if he didn't know Kate, it was "as if he had been at a corner ... so that it depended on him whether or no to turn it". Milly then asks him whether he would like to go for a drive with her, and to oblige her, Densher accepts. "If he had been drifting it settled itself in the manner of a bump, of considerable violence, against a firm object in the stream." The acceptance, moreover, affects him as if, with it, he was "turning his corner. He was quite round it, his corner, by the time the door had closed upon her and he stood there alone." During Milly's absence two things happen. Merton first becomes aware that his corner "was so turned that he felt himself to have lost even the option ... to retrace his steps. If he might have turned tail ... five minutes before, he couldn't turn tail now; he must simply wait there with his consciousness charged to the brim." Then Kate makes an unexpected and brief appearance. And when, upon Milly's return, he tells her that Kate had not known she would find him, he has the feeling that "his corner was so turned that it wasn't a question of a word more or less[56]". The central image of the turned corner is fairly common, but, as a result of its repeated introduction and its several modifications, it draws our attention to this passage and also dramatizes Merton's inner struggle between honesty and deception. When he slowly becomes aware of his treacherous behaviour, his foremost feeling is that of fear, fear lest his false play should be detected by Milly: "If he took off his hand, the hand that at least helped to hold it together, the whole queer fabric that built him in would fall away in a minute and admit the light ... He was walking ... on a high ridge, steep down on either side, where the properties ... reduced themselves to his keeping his head. It was Kate who had so perched him, and there came up for him at moments, as he found himself planting one foot exactly before another, a sensible sharpness of irony as to her management of him[57]." All these images make it abundantly clear that Merton is not the prime mover in the exploitation of Milly. Rather is he driven by powerful forces, one being his deep and true affection for Kate, the other his general weakness and lack of

96

determination. At the very end of the novel another significant metaphorical passage puts Densher even more emphatically in a favourable light. James first creates suspense by talking about one of Densher's thoughts without, however, telling us for the moment what it concerned. "The thought was all his own ... he kept it back like a favourite pang; left it behind him, so to say, when he went out, but came home again the sooner for the certainty of finding it there. Then he took it out of its sacred corner and its soft wrappings; he undid them one by one, handling them, handling *it,* as a father, baffled and tender, might handle a maimed child." Only now does James reveal that Densher's sacred thought was "that he should never, never know what had been in Milly's letter". And although he should probably know of the intention expressed in it, the part "missed for ever was the turn she would have given her act. That turn had possibilities", of which his imagination made "a revelation the loss of which was like the sight of a priceless pearl cast before his eyes—his pledge given not to save it—into the fathomless sea, or rather even it was like the sacrifice of something sentient and throbbing, something that, for the spiritual ear, might have been audible as a faint, far wail. This was the sound that he cherished, when alone, in the stillness of his rooms[58]." This passage makes it obvious that Merton is in love with Milly's memory, which makes it impossible for him to accept her money and to marry Kate.

Most of the analytic metaphors in *The Golden Bowl* show a strong tendency towards an intentional ambiguity. Because of their elaborateness some of them are not immediately effective and clear in their meaning. This is evident when we read, at the beginning of the novel, that Amerigo

> had kept no impression of the girl's [Maggie's] rejoinder. It had but sweetened the waters in which he now floated, tinted them as by the action of some essence, poured from a gold-topped phial, for making one's bath aromatic. No one before him ... had so sat up to his neck in such a bath ... the assurance of the enjoyment of more money ... was the element that bore him up and into which Maggie scattered, on occasion, her exquisite colouring drops. They were of the colour—of what on earth? of what but the extraordinary American good faith? They were of the colour of her innocence, and yet at the same time of her imagination[59].

If we attempt an interpretation of Amerigo's thoughts we have to make our start from the only straightforward hint that James supplies, namely "the assurance of the enjoyment of more money". His thoughts circle about his present pecuniary situation and his future prospects. If Amerigo sees himself floating in sweetened water, it confirms our impression that there is an abundance of money. The second half of the image stresses two other important facts. One is that Amerigo marries Maggie primarily for the sake of her money; it "was the element that bore him up". But he can do it only because she is an innocent American who cannot perceive his true intentions.

What happens to Maggie Verver is exactly, then, what happened to Isabel Archer. The difference lies in that Isabel becomes aware of it after her marriage, whereas Maggie never really does. If after her discovery of his adultery we wonder why Amerigo neither takes any action nor gives Charlotte the slightest hint as to what has happened, we know from the passage quoted above that he is too money-minded to take the risk of losing his wife. "The present order, as it spread about him, had somehow the ground under its feet, and a trumpet in its ears, and a bottomless bag of solid shining British sovereigns—which was much to the point—in its hand[60]." Amerigo does not want to lose "the ground" of his situation; he prefers to sacrifice Charlotte. Perhaps the initial metaphor is rather too ambiguous, so that many readers will overlook its essential function in the understanding of Amerigo's behaviour during the second half of the novel.

The most revealing analytic metaphors are attributed to Adam and Maggie. He is a self-made man. His eyes "showed him what he *had* done, showed him where he had come out; quite at the top of his hill of difficulty, the tall sharp spiral round which he had begun to wind his ascent at the age of twenty, and the apex of which was a platform looking down, if one would, on the kingdoms of the earth and with standing-room for but half-a-dozen others[61]". In *The Wings* James had already used "the kingdoms of the earth" as a symbol of Milly's wealth and unlimited freedom. And here it has the same purpose. The fundamental difference between Milly's fortune and Adam's is, of course, that hers is inherited, whereas he has made his way all by himself, earned every penny, as the image points out without any doubt. Adam Verver is a man who leads a life very much his own. He has no real friends. He does not want to have any. It is a form of egotism which is ultimately the result of his money-conscious character. His lack of human contact helps us to understand why he never has the slightest suspicion about the intimacy between Charlotte and Amerigo, and why Maggie is successful in keeping her father ignorant. His constant and sole occupation with his own self receives a further emphasis when we read that "*His* real friend ... was to have been his own mind ... He had knocked at the door of that essentially private house, and his call, in truth, had not been immediately answered; so that when, after waiting and coming back, he had at last got in, it was, twirling his hat, as an embarrassed stranger, or, trying his keys, as a thief at night. He had gained confidence only with time, but when he had taken real possession of the place it had been never again to come away[62]." Adam's egocentricity is a form of nihilism, a quality also to be noticed in Gilbert Osmond and Mrs. Gereth.

In regard to Maggie's thoughts James first has to throw some light on the reason why it took her such a long time to make her vital discovery. An elaborate metaphor, referring to this question, may exemplify how James's late style may render the understanding more difficult. Maggie's question "only went and lost itself in the thick air that had begun more and more to hang ... over her accumulations of the unanswered. They were *there,* these accumulations; they were like a roomful of confused objects, never as yet 'sorted,' which for some time now she had been passing and re-passing, along the corridor of her life." James has now introduced the basic elements for this metaphor. "The corridor of her life" is an adaptation of the more common "path of life" to suit the whole pictorial conception. The other element of the picture, the room full of "accumulations", stands for all Maggie's unsolved and discarded problems. If one understands the meaning of these elements it is comparatively easy to translate the following elaboration of the metaphor into the significance it has for Maggie's life:

> She passed it when she could without opening the door; then, on occasion, she turned the key to throw in a fresh contribution. So it was that she had been getting things out of the way. They rejoined the rest of the confusion; it was as if they found their place, by some instinct of affinity, in the heap. They knew, in short, where to go; and when she, at present, by a mental act, once more pushed the door open, she had practically a sense of method and experience. What she should never know about Charlotte's thought—she tossed *that* in. It would find itself in company, and she might at last have been standing there long enough to see it fall into its corner. The sight moreover would doubtless have made her stare, had her attention been more free— the sight of the mass of vain things, congruous, incongruous, that awaited every addition.

And now with a swift change that integrates the image within the whole, James turns back to reality: "It made her in fact, with a vague gasp, turn away, and what had further determined this was the final sharp extinction of the inward scene by the outward. The quite different door had opened and her husband was there[63]." The emphasis, then, is on Maggie's indifference in the past about every problem that either did not interest her or for which she did not possess the necessary energy to look more closely into. Had she but taken the trouble to sort out the "confused objects" of her "accumulations", her eyes would have been opened much earlier.

One aspect of the tragic happenings in *The Golden Bowl* is usually overlooked in critical works. It is Maggie's own guilt. She confesses it clearly at one point. Thinking over her past, when her father was not yet married to Charlotte, she realizes that "if their family coach lumbered and stuck the fault was in its lacking its complement of wheels. Having but three ... it had wanted another, and what had Charlotte done from the first but begin to act, on the spot, and ever so smoothly and beautifully, as a fourth?" After a further elaboration of this metaphor James shifts the emphasis of the picture in order to make Maggie's realization of her own guilt obvious. "She might have been watching the family coach pass and noting that, somehow, Amerigo and Charlotte were pulling it while she and her father were not so much as pushing. They were seated inside together, dandling the Principino and holding him up to the windows, to see and be seen, like an infant positively royal; so that the exertion was *all* with the others." And with dramatic intensity James then marks the moment of Maggie's realization of the relationship between Amerigo and Charlotte. "She had seen herself at last, in the picture she was studying, suddenly jump from the coach; whereupon, frankly, with the wonder of the sight, her eyes opened wider and her heart stood still for a moment. She looked at the person so acting as if this person were somebody else, waiting with intensity to see what would follow[64]." It had been largely because Adam and Maggie cared too much for each other that Charlotte and Amerigo had been driven together anew. Maggie has no right to make any severe reproaches to her husband, not even after the discovery of the story about the bowl. But we have to come back to the passage quoted above if we want to have a full understanding of her behaviour towards her husband in the later stages of the novel. Her guilt expresses itself later on in a decided fear that Amerigo might do or say something which could destroy her plans to restore their happiness, and, above all, to keep her father innocent. "She was keeping her head, for a reason, for a cause; and the labour of this detachment, with the labour of her forcing the pitch of it down, held them together in the steel hoop of an intimacy compared with which artless passion would have been but a beating of the air[65]." Maggie's foremost step to prevent her husband from taking any wrong actions is to devote herself completely to him, to bring back to their marriage the intimacy which had been lacking for a long time. "A single touch from him ... would hand her over to him bound hand and foot. Therefore to be free, to be free to act other than abjectly, for her father, she must conceal from him the validity that, like a microscopic insect pushing a grain of sand, she was taking on even for herself[66]." Both these images are introduced before Maggie's discovery of the story of the golden bowl, before Amerigo himself is aware of her knowledge. Therefore they emphasize that Maggie's position in relation to her husband is still weak. But it is different after the story of the bowl reveals to Amerigo that Maggie knows everything, for now he is completely in her hand, and she is only afraid that "to break the spell she had cast upon him and that the polished old ivory of her father's inattackable surface made so absolute, he would suddenly commit some mistake or some violence, smash some window-pane for air, fail even of one of his blest inveteracies of taste[67]". Maggie does not know that the prince is much too fond of her money for him to take a wrong step.

C. FEELINGS

In general it can be said that thoughts and ideas are prospective, whereas feelings are rather retrospective; their expression by means of imagery makes an event or events in a person's past coalesce with the emotional attitude taken towards them to form an imaginative interpretation. James also introduces such images in order to elucidate the emotional relation between two persons.

Most of the characters in *Roderick Hudson* are uncomplicated, and moreover, very outspoken. The best example is Roderick. If we think of his many emotional outbursts, we realize that a great deal of his feelings are expressed in his spoken words. The only relationship in the novel which is not outspoken is that between Rowland and Mary, and the only really significant metaphors concern his feelings for her. When Roderick tells his friend of his engagement to Mary Garland "Rowland listened to all this with a sort of feeling that fortune had played him an elaborately-devised trick. It had lured him into mid-ocean and smoothed the sea and stilled the winds and given him a singularly sympathetic comrade, and then it had turned and delivered him a thumping blow in mid-chest[68]." This image emphasizes yet another point besides Rowland's unrevealed passion for Mary. He had secretly hoped to have Roderick all to himself. Through his engagement, however, there was a second person who had even a greater right to take a share in Roderick's development. Rowland's passion for Mary has not diminished by the time of her arrival in Rome, although he thought that he had successfully conquered it, "but in her personal presence ... he seemed to face it and all that it might bring with it for the first time ... He felt like walking on tiptoe, not to arouse the sleeping shadows. He felt, indeed, almost like saying that they might have their own way later, if they would only allow to these first few days the clear light of ardent contemplation. For Rowland at last was ardent, and all the bells within his soul were ringing bravely in jubilee[69]." The "sleeping shadows" are obviously those of Rowland's passion. And his feeling that "they might have their own way later" puts a strong emphasis on his sincere hopes of marrying Mary. It is from the moment of her arrival in Rome that Rowland actively begins to play Roderick false. His constant endeavour in his strolls with her is to find out "whether the love-knot of which Mary Garland had the keeping still held firm", but he comes to the conclusion that "the young girl ... did not wear it on her sleeve[70]".

The whole interest of the images analysing feelings in *The Portrait* centres in Isabel Archer. Through them we witness her emotional reactions to some of the major happenings in the novel. When Isabel hears of Goodwood's arrival in Europe, she is uneasy and unhappy about his coming: "The feeling was oppressive; it made the air sultry, as if there were to be a change of weather; and the weather, socially speaking, had been so agreeable during Isabel's stay at Gardencourt that any change would be for the worse[71]." Here one feels that James has been striving to find an original image, but the fact that he has to make it clear that he is referring to the *social* weather points to the essential weakness of the metaphor. At the opening of Isabel's long meditations a short image marks the transition in her from vague feeling about her present situation into clear thinking: "Such a resolution, however, brought her this evening but little peace, for her soul was haunted with terrors which crowded to the foreground of thought as quickly as a place was made for them. What had suddenly set them into livelier motion she hardly knew[72]." Isabel is inclined to act upon her feelings and not to come to her conclusions by sharp reasoning. Only now that she suspects a closer relationship between her husband and Madame Merle does she really start thinking—and the result is that, for the first time since her marriage, she begins to realize her true position.

Isabel's feelings about her stepdaughter give us an important clue: "Pansy, who faced her stepmother, at first kept her eyes fixed on her lap; then she raised them and rested them on Isabel's. There shone out of each of them a little melancholy ray, a spark of timid passion which touched Isabel to the heart. At the same time a wave of envy passed over her soul, as she compared the tremulous longing, the definite ideal, of the young girl with her own dry despair[73]." She recognizes that part of her duty lies in preserving and watching over Pansy's "tremulous longing, the definite ideal" so that it will not be destroyed by Osmond or any of his kind, as Isabel's ideals had been.

The most revealing images are introduced in connection with Goodwood's final attack at Gardencourt. He touches exactly on the very points of her unhappiness, so that she gives "a long murmur, like a creature in pain": "The world ... seemed ... to take the form of a mighty sea, where she floated in fathomless waters. She had wanted help, and here was help; it had come in a rushing torrent ... she believed that to let him take her in his arms would be the next best thing to dying. This belief, for a moment, was a kind of rapture, in which she felt herself sinking and sinking. In the movement she seemed to beat with her feet, in order to catch herself, to feel something to rest on[74]." The image stresses above all Isabel's feeling of helplessness before Goodwood's strong presence. But although she sees in his propositions a kind of help for her "tormented soul" she is extremely frightened by the thought of his taking possession of her. The importance of the passage from the point of view of the whole novel is that here Isabel declines the offered help of the man of whom she had thought at one time that he could be a "blessing in disguise—a clear and quiet harbor inclosed by a fine granite breakwater[75]".

The Old Things, as *Roderick Hudson* and *The Portrait,* is primarily a novel of action. It is, therefore, obvious that there is not much room to render the emotions of the characters[76]. In *The Ambassadors,* on the other hand, images are used to render feelings to an extent which is unparalleled in any other of James's novels. Strether's impression of Madame de Vionnet is not that of a vicious, dreadful woman, as she had been pictured by Mrs. Newsome, but "The air of supreme respectability—that was the strange blank wall for his adventure to have brought him to break his nose against. It had in fact, as he was now aware, filled all the approaches, hovered in the court as he passed, hung on the staircase as he mounted, sounded in the grave rumble of the old bell ... it formed, in short, the clearest medium of its particular kind that he had ever breathed[77]." The feeling of "a strange blank wall" makes Strether doubt whether his mission is justified, makes him wonder whether Madame de Vionnet's influence on Chad is not more of a benefit than a means to his corruption. This impression of Madame de Vionnet is essential to Strether's own development. His feeling about Gloriani is the realization of the great difference between them. But he does not trust the artist: "He was conscious now of the final reality, which was that there was not so much a doubt as a difference altogether; all the more that over the difference the famous sculptor seemed to signal almost condolingly, yet oh how vacantly! as across some great flat sheet of water. He threw out the bridge of a charming hollow civility on which Strether wouldn't have trusted his own full weight a moment[78]." We may divine the reason for Strether's hesitancy from a metaphor which shows how the atmosphere of Gloriani's garden affects him: "The open air ... was all a chamber of state. Strether had presently the sense of a great convent, a convent of missions ... a nursery of young priests ... he had the sense of names in the air, of ghosts at the windows, of signs and tokens, a whole range of expression, all about him, too thick for prompt discrimination[79]." The old established institution of a convent, representing a long and uninterrupted tradition, stands for European culture. Almost helpless, Strether stands in the middle of these surroundings. The next important revelation of his feelings takes place at a *déjeuner* when, alone opposite Madame de Vionnet "for an hour, in the matter of letting himself go, of diving deep, Strether was to feel that he had touched bottom. He was to feel ... that he had travelled far since that evening, in London ... it was at present as if he had either soared above or sunk below them—he couldn't tell which ... the sense that the situation was running away with him, had never been so sharp as now; and all the more that he could perfectly put his finger on the moment it had taken the bit in its teeth[80]." In this passage we are told not only that Strether is a different being from the one he had been when he landed in Europe, that he had parted far from his mission of "saving" Chad, but also that he has lost command over himself to a great extent. The situation "is running away with him". There are other, stronger forces which draw him along, without his being able to resist, and the fact that these feelings reveal themselves when he is in the company of Marie de Vionnet makes it evident that she is one of the major influences on him.

After the arrival of the Pococks, James stresses Strether's transformation by contrasting Sarah's and his views about Chad's development. "Everything Mrs. Pocock had failed to give a sign of recognizing in Chad as a particular part of a transformation—everything that had lent intention to this particular failure affected him as gathered into a large loose bundle and thrown, in her words, into his face[81]." And a little later, when Sarah has remarked that Madame de Vionnet's influence on Chad has been hideous, he has the feeling that "she had let fly at him as from a stretched cord, and it took him a minute to recover from the sense of being pierced. It was not the penetration of surprise; it was that, much more, of certainty[82]." On the whole, the images concerning Strether's feelings are not very powerful, but they elucidate some aspects which had been missing among the metaphors reflecting his thoughts.

In James's last two novels there are not many metaphors of significance concerning the feelings. In *The Golden Bowl* especially we have the impression that every action that is taken by each character is the result of careful thought and calculation. It is a novel which deals with strategic and tactical moves. In *The Wings* the same is true of Mrs. Lowder and Kate Croy, for none of their feelings is emphasized by means of metaphors. But there is one important passage in the course of the scenes in Venice which reveals to us Merton's feelings about his relationship with Milly. "He felt her as diffusing, in wide warm waves, the spell of a general, a kind of beatific mildness ... he seemed to stand in it up to his neck. He moved about in it, and it made no plash; he floated, he noiselessly swam in it; and they were all together, for that matter, like fishes in a crystal pool ... but he couldn't be invidious, even to profit by so high a tide; he felt himself too much 'in' it, as he might have said: a moment's reflection put him more in than any one[83]." It is a secret and mutual affection which is pictured here, and, still more important, no one of the many people present is aware of it. The mute understanding between Milly and Merton is a proof of the depth and sincerity of their love and affection for each other. His attitude here and after her death is strangely discrepant with the fact of his intercourse with Kate and his high feelings about it afterwards. He cherishes the memory as "an inestimable value", as "the part of a treasure kept, at home, in safety and sanctity, something he was sure of finding in its place when, with each return, he worked his heavy old key in the lock. The door had but to open for him to be with it again and for it to be all there; ... Wherever he looked or sat or stood ... it was in view as nothing of the moment, nothing begotten of time or of chance could be, or ever would[84]." If this discrepancy in Merton's character was intentional, Densher is endowed with a strong element of perversity.

One significant image is introduced in the course of Milly's reflections, which makes it evident that she is very much guided by others and is not acting for herself. "It pressed upon her then and there that she was still in the current determined ... by others; that not she but the current acted, and that somebody else, always, was the keeper of the lock or the dam. Kate for example had but to open the floodgate: the current moved in its mass—the current, as it had been, of her doing as Kate wanted[85]." That the most active and decisive forces in Mrs. Stringham's life are the views of Mrs. Lowder is most strikingly brought home to the reader by the following metaphorical passage: "She felt that she believed in her bones what Milly believed, and what would now make working for Milly such a dreadful upward tug. All this, within her, was confusedly present—a cloud of questions out of which Maud Manningham's large seated self loomed, however, as a mass more and more definite, taking in fact for the consultative relation something of the form of an oracle[86]."

In *The Golden Bowl* the few images that are introduced in connection with feelings are more decorative than significant, and are, at any rate, of no importance for the understanding of the characters, as an image that occurs in Fanny's reflections after a talk with Charlotte and Amerigo may exemplify: "For what she was most immediately feeling was that she *had*, in the past, been active, for these people, to ends that were now bearing fruit and that might yet bear a larger crop. She but brooded at first, in her corner of the carriage; it was like burying her exposed face, a face too helplessly exposed, in the cool lap of the common indifference[87]." We can compare such a metaphorical passage to an aria in an opera which, as often happens, may be a beautiful piece in itself, but does not tell us anything about the character concerned that we do not already know. This is exactly true of the passage just quoted. We are told in the first chapter that Fanny has done a great deal for Charlotte and Amerigo, while we are also made aware that her activities are "bearing fruit" in the scene of Charlotte's and Amerigo's attempted purchase of the golden bowl. This image seems to be one of those which James has introduced "purely because his eye fell on a dull patch of canvas, and he set out to brighten it up[88]". The significance of such an image is, however, almost nil.

Within this chapter images expressing states of dependence are functionally the most significant. The metaphors dealt with in the present section elucidate the attitude of certain characters to one another and, above all, give us important hints about the factors which govern some of these major relationships. What renders these metaphors so important is that they do not concern the externally apparent relations, but rather the inward reasons for them which reveal themselves only in the thoughts of the characters. To mention only one example: we know from the external action that Adam Verver has accepted Amerigo as a son-in-law and that he has later made Charlotte Stant his wife so as to be less lonely. But what were the deeper motives which made this mercenary man accept these two persons, neither of whom had any means at all? The images in this section are concerned with these deeper motives[89].

The Portrait both contains many significant metaphors for the expression of states of dependence and already makes use of its central symbol: the *objet d'art*. James has introduced it in this novel quite obviously in order to contrast Americans with Europeans, and to show the dependence of the former on the latter. The relationship to which it is successfully applied is that between Gilbert Osmond and Isabel Archer: "His egotism, if egotism it was, had never taken the crude form of wishing for a dull wife; this lady's intelligence was to be a silver plate, not an earthen one,—a plate that he might heap up with ripe fruits, to which it would give a decorative value, so that conversation might become a sort of perpetual dessert. He found the silvery quality in perfection in Isabel; he could tap her imagination with his knuckle and make it ring[90]." The way in which Osmond looks upon human beings merely as *objets d'art* foreshadows the similar, but even more pronounced, attitude of Adam Verver. Osmond's meditations about his daughter run along the same lines: "He wished to do something sudden and arbitrary, something unexpected and refined; to mark the difference between his sympathies and her [Isabel's] own, and to show that if he regarded his daughter as a precious work of art, it was natural he should be more and more careful about the finishing touches[91]." Another *objet d'art* image, introduced when the friendship between Madame Merle and Isabel is still in its early stages, prefigures the dependence of the heroine upon the other woman: "Sometimes she took alarm at her candor: it was as if she had given to a comparative stranger the key to her cabinet of jewels. These spiritual gems were the only ones of any magnitude that Isabel possessed, but there was all the greater reason why they should be carefully guarded[92]." From these three examples, which are the only representatives of their kind in *The Portrait,* we conclude that James is not yet introducing *objet d'art* images consistently as a central symbol for the dependence of certain characters upon others. But he is equally successful when he pictures Isabel's subordination to her husband in the following way: "Her mind was to be his,—attached to his own like a small garden-plot to a deer-park. He would rake the soil gently, and water the flowers; he would weed the beds and gather an occasional nosegay. It would be a pretty piece of property for a proprietor already far-reaching[93]." Osmond has acquired Isabel almost as one purchases a piece of land rather as Mr. Verver buys human beings as valuable pieces for his art collection. In the end both men's attitude is the same.

The relationship which remains most in the dark until very deep into the second part of the novel is that between Madame Merle and Osmond. Before James reveals the truth about it there are two extremely significant passages, the first as early as the nineteenth chapter. It is a self-characterization of Madame Merle, but neither Isabel, to whom it is made, nor the reader at this point can possibly know in every detail to what Madame Merle is referring: "There are more iron pots ... than porcelain ones. But ... every one has something; even the hardest iron pots have a little bruise, a little hole somewhere ... I am rather stout porcelain, but ... I have been chipped and cracked! I do very well for service yet, because I have been cleverly mended; and I try to remain in the cupboard—the quiet, dusky cupboard, where there is an odor of stale spices—as much as I can. But when I have to come out, and into a strong light, then, my dear, I am a horror[94]." From the context it is obvious what Madame Merle means by "iron pots" and "porcelain ones". The former are people with no feelings at all, people whom nothing can injure. The latter are delicate and sensitive characters. The second part of her metaphor gives us a hint that she has had experiences in the past which have left deep marks upon her character, marks which she managed, however, ingeniously to hide. It is important to note that she says "I have been chipped and cracked" and "I have been cleverly mended". Both these expressions make it evident that at least one other person must have been intimately concerned in the dreadful experience she has had. Thirty chapters later we read a passage which immediately relates it to the one just quoted because the same kind of imagery is used. James reveals another piece of truth: the person intimately concerned in Madame Merle's past is Gilbert Osmond. Another point to be noticed is that the earlier passage is purely metaphorical, whereas the following contains a strong connection between image and reality, so that we are made to feel that what had once been mere pictorial language can now become real at any moment. In the course of a discussion with Madame Merle Osmond gets up and looks at some "delicate specimens of rare porcelain". "He took up a small cup and held it in his hand; ... Madame Merle kept her eye upon her cup ... 'Please be very careful of that precious object.' 'It already has a small crack,' said Osmond dryly, as he put it down." When she was alone again "Madame Merle went and lifted from the mantel-shelf the attenuated coffee-cup in which he had mentioned the existence of a crack; but she looked at it rather abstractedly. 'Have I been so vile all for nothing?' she murmured to herself[95]." It might be argued that what is described here is reality and not an image. But the passage is certainly meant as a sequel to the earlier one. Madame Merle, whom we can identify with the "small cup", has now come out of her hiding-place, the "dusky cupboard" of the earlier passage. She is on the mantel-shelf to be seen by everybody with her "crack". Osmond's behaviour has dragged her out, and she realizes that it will probably not take long for Isabel and others to become aware of the true relationship between her and Osmond. His seizing the small cup and holding it in his hand is also an expression of Madame Merle's dependence on him. She is completely at his mercy. Therefore she is so anxious that he should be careful with the small cup. She is afraid that he might drop it and that it would break to pieces; in other words that he might ruin her life, that he might unmask her and show her wicked, corrupt self to the world. And her last words are an indication that Osmond *is* going to denounce her.

In *The Old Things* the true centre is not a human being but the works of art themselves. Therefore it is not so much the relationship between certain characters of the novel which forms the main source of interest, but rather their relation to the *objets d'art,* the spoils of Poynton. Everything that happens is ultimately caused by the struggle for possession of the treasures. But only two persons have a direct interest in their acquisition: Mrs. Gereth in the first place and Mona Brigstock in the second. Mrs. Gereth's dependence on her *objets d'art* is emphasized in a series of significant images. "In the sense of having passed the threshold of Poynton for the last time, the amputation, as she called it, had been performed. Her leg had come off,—she had now begun to stump along with the lovely wooden substitute; she would stump for life, and what her young friend was to come and admire was the beauty of her movement and the noise she made about the house[96]." By "the amputation" James refers to the removal of a part of her treasures from Poynton, which, to her, means as much as the loss of a limb. Fleda receives a similar impression when the parts of the treasures at Ricks seemed to her "to suffer like chopped limbs[97]". Mrs. Gereth's passion for her *objets d'art* is again stressed after she has sent everything back to Poynton, supposing that the break between Owen and Mona has taken place. "The chill struck deep as Fleda thought of the mistress of Ricks reduced, in vulgar parlance, to what she had on her back: there was nothing to which she could compare such an image but her idea of Marie Antoinette in the Conciergerie, or perhaps the vision of some tropical bird, the creature of hot, dense forests, dropped on a frozen moor to pick up a living[98]." All these images have the effect of almost identifying Mrs. Gereth with her works of art. They are her life. If they are taken away from her she is brought into the immediate vicinity of death, as is amply stressed by the two pictures of "Marie Antoinette in the Conciergerie" and "the tropical bird ... on a frozen moor".

Mona's dependence upon the spoils of Poynton is not elucidated by such powerful images. This is justified, because her relation to these treasures can never be so intensely immediate as Mrs. Gereth's. With Mona the possession of the *objets d'art* is simply the goal of her stubbornness, and a suspicion which every attentive reader must have from the early stages of the novel is proved to be correct by a significant image: "To have loved Owen apparently, and yet to have loved him only so much, only to the extent of a few tables and chairs, was not a thing she [Fleda] could so much as try to grasp[99]." Mona loves Owen only for the sake of the works of art at Poynton which will go over into her possession after her marriage. Owen, on the other hand, is too stupid to realize this in time. He is too dependent upon her. "He was hollow, perfunctory, pathetic; he had been girded by another hand. That hand had naturally been Mona's, and it was heavy even now on his strong, broad back[100]." After their marriage another image speaks in even plainer language: "There was a person to whom it was clear that she led her wretched husband by the nose[101]." Owen is, from the very beginning, completely in Mona's hand. She does with him whatever she wants and, as the last image emphasizes, he seems to obey her entirely.

The most interesting image in view of the development of *objet d'art* metaphors in the later novels is one applied to the relationship between Mrs. Gereth and Fleda. After she has lost all her treasures she says to Fleda: "Moreover, with nothing else but my four walls, you'll at any rate be a bit of furniture. For that, you know, a little, I've always taken you,—quite one of my best finds[102]." Osmond's similar attitude towards Isabel was not yet so explicitly expressed as this.

It is in *The Ambassadors* that the greatest number of relationships are elucidated by means of metaphors. At the beginning of the novel Strether is almost entirely dependent upon Maria Gostrey's opinions and views. "It was always the case for him in these counsels that each of her remarks, as it came, seemed to drop into a deeper well. He had at all events to wait a moment to hear the slight splash of this one[103]." But by the end of the novel he has completely freed himself of this dependence. "The time seemed already far-off when he had held out his small thirsty cup to the spout of her pail. Her pail was scarce touched now, and other fountains had flowed for him; she fell into her place as but one of his tributaries; and there was a strange sweetness—a melancholy mildness that touched him—in her acceptance of the altered order[104]." By the "other fountains" that had begun to flow for Strether, James clearly alludes to Chad and Madame de Vionnet and their circle. Strether, in fact, shifts gradually over from Maria's influence into a stronger dependence upon Marie de Vionnet. This change alone is evidence of his enormous transformation during his short stay in Paris[105]. There he remains subject to yet another influence, the indirect dependence upon Mrs. Newsome. It has never been his intention to break with her, and when she has ceased to trust him he rightly wonders whether he can win back her confidence. "It was quite his present theory that he would leave no stone unturned to do so[106]." During the days of her complete silence he is made to feel her omnipresence with great intensity: "he had never so lived with her ... He walked about with her, sat with her, and dined face-to-face with her ... Her vividness ... became for him, in the special conditions, almost an obsession ... He knew it for the queerest of adventures ... that in Paris itself, of all places, he should find this ghost of the lady of Woollett more importunate than any other presence[107]." As long as he received letters from her he felt secure. It needed her complete silence to make him realize anew how dependent on her he still was. And if we recall that she is in the last analysis a symbol of his "old self", the above passage becomes even more significant. In spite of his immense transformation Strether cannot deny, and does not want to give up, his "old self". He is too old to do that. The most he can achieve is to establish a communication with the lost spirit of his youth.

The dependence of Kate Croy and Merton Densher upon Mrs. Lowder has already been exemplified in some of the animal images. But there are also other kinds of images which emphasize her supreme command over the two lovers. They cannot do without her. She is always there in control of them: "It was impossible to keep Mrs. Lowder out of their scheme. She stood there too close to it and too solidly; it had to open a gate, at a given point, do what they would, to take her in. And she came in always, while they sat together rather helplessly watching her, as in a coach-and-four; she drove round their prospect as the principal lady at the circus drives round the ring, and she stopped the coach in the middle to alight with majesty[108]." But whereas Merton seems only occasionally to be the subject of Mrs. Lowder's influence Kate is perpetually governed by her. "That was the story—that she was always, for her beneficent dragon, under arms; living up, every hour, but especially at festal hours, to the 'value' Mrs. Lowder had attached to her[109]." The power of her personality is not only felt by Kate and Merton. Her strength appears even more impressive by the command she seems to have over a character like Lord Mark. "They were all swimming together in the blue ... he was personally the note of the blue—like a suspended skein of silk within reach of the broiderer's hand. Aunt Maud's free-moving shuttle took a length of him at rhythmic intervals; and one of the intermixed truths that flickered across to Milly was that he ever so consentingly knew he was being worked in[110]." We may interpret Mrs. Lowder's taking "a length" of Lord Mark "at rhythmic intervals" and his knowing that he "was being worked in" as meaning that Mrs. Lowder is trying to marry Kate to him, as he happens to possess some money. The image, therefore, throws light on the background of the relationship between Mrs. Lowder, Lord Mark and Kate. This is the more important because Lord Mark remains a rather shallow figure throughout the whole novel. When he appears in Venice Milly's rejection of him is quite clearly emphasized by a series of images. The first evokes the atmosphere in which their whole discussion takes place: "The charm turned on them a face that was cold in its beauty, that was full of poetry never to be theirs, that spoke, with an ironic smile, of a possible but forbidden life[111]." This already serves as a preparation for Milly's subsequent rejection of Lord Mark. The second passage stresses the impossibility of a life together. It also contains his realization of the rejection.

> The way she let him see that she looked at him was a thing to shut him out, of itself, from services of danger, a thing that made a discrimination against him never yet made... The gathering dusk of *her* personal world presented itself to him, in her eyes, as an element in which it was vain for him to pretend he could find himself at home, since it was charged with depressions and with dooms, with the chill of the losing game ... What somehow happened, however, ... — the sadness, to her vivid sense, of his being so painfully astray, wandering in a desert in which there was nothing to nourish him — was that his error amounted to positive wrongdoing[112].

The whole long episode describing the encounter between Milly and Lord Mark conveys a note of ambiguity, an uncertainty as to James's meaning, but images like "a thing to shut him out", "the chill of the losing game" or the picture of his "wandering in a desert in which there was nothing to nourish him" put a strong emphasis on Milly's rejection.

In *The Golden Bowl* James takes up the *objet d'art* image again. The immediate reason for its application is Mr. Verver's being the most thoroughgoing collector of works of art whom James ever created; life and *objets d'art* have become inseparable. For Adam Verver the primary consideration in everything he acquires is its value as a "museum-piece". And he does not restrict this question merely to dead matters, actual works of art, but extends it to human beings. At the very beginning of the novel Maggie tells Amerigo that for her father he is "a part of his collection", "one of the things that can only be got over here. You're a rarity, an object of beauty, an object of price. You're not perhaps absolutely unique, but you're so curious and eminent that there are very few others like you—you belong to a class about which everything is known. You're what they call a *morceau de musée*." But Maggie has no idea how much the prince has cost her father. She tells

Amerigo furthermore that Adam "stores" the bigger things everywhere. "We've been like a pair of pirates—positively stage pirates, the sort who wink at each other and say 'Ha-ha!' when they come to where their treasure is buried." The smaller pieces they take with them on their travels "to make the hotels we stay at and the houses we hire a little less ugly". The prince draws the only possible conclusion, namely that he is to be "one of the little pieces that you unpack at the hotels, or at the worst in the hired houses, like this wonderful one, and put out with the family photographs and the new magazines. But it's something not to be so big that I have to be buried[113]." A few pages later an image is introduced in Amerigo's reflections which shows an immediate connection with the passage just quoted: "It was as if he had been some old embossed coin, of a purity of gold no longer used, stamped with glorious arms, mediaeval, wonderful, of which the 'worth' in mere modern change, sovereigns and half-crowns, would be great enough, but as to which, since there were finer ways of using it, such taking to pieces was superfluous ... he was to constitute a possession, yet was to escape being reduced to his component parts[114]." It is interesting to note the change in the application of *objet d'art* images when compared with *The Portrait*. There Osmond, the poor European, treated the wealthy American, Isabel, as if she were a valuable piece of art; her money is her value in his eyes. In *The Golden Bowl* the positions are reversed. It is now the wealthy Americans in whose eyes the poor Europeans have only a value in so far as they represent history and tradition. They have no ethical value, as individuals, but only as representatives of their race. In *The Portrait* Osmond had been the strong force, in spite of his poverty; in the present novel, Amerigo, Osmond's counterpart from this point of view, is completely dependent on the Ververs and their money. His marriage with Maggie does not lead to a strengthening of his weak position. Amerigo's dependence is, in the first place, upon Mr. Verver. The prince was for him a "representative precious object" like "great ancient pictures and other works of art, fine eminent 'pieces' in gold, in silver, in enamel, majolica, ivory, bronze", which "had for a number of years multiplied themselves round him and, as a general challenge to acquisition and appreciation, so engaged all the faculties of his mind, that the instinct, the particular sharpened appetite of the collector, had fairly served as a basis for his acceptance of the Prince's suit[115]". This passage gains particular weight because it shows us Adam Verver's own view of the matter; it points to the very reason for his acceptance of the prince as a possible husband for Maggie: because he satisfied the "appetite of the collector" within him. Another metaphor emphasizes Amerigo's dependence upon Adam most clearly: "He was living, he had been living these four or five years, on Mr. Verver's services: a truth scarcely less plain if he dealt with them, for appreciation, one by one, than if he poured them all together into the general pot of his gratitude and let the thing simmer to a nourishing broth[116]." We are made aware of another important point: Amerigo does not mind in the least being dependent on Adam; it is compensated for by his being able to live in greater freedom because he is allowed to share Maggie's fortune. Mr. Verver relieved him "of all anxiety about his married life in the same manner in which he relieved him on the score of his bank account[117]". To secure the prince and to keep up his "value", Adam was obliged to sacrifice some of his money, which gives the prince not only a feeling of security, but also one of satisfaction. "From time to time, the amount of the Prince was made sure. He was being thus, in renewed instalments, perpetually paid in; he already reposed in the bank as a value, but subject, in this comfortable way, to repeated, to infinite endorsement. The net result of all of which, moreover, was that the young man had no wish to see his value diminish[118]." Adam Verver's dreadful habit of putting works of art and human beings in the same class is even more strikingly brought out in his relation to Charlotte Stant, for it is as an "acquisition" that he looks upon his marriage with her. In his thinking there is practically no difference between persons and objects. Charlotte is for him one of "his great 'finds'". He applied the "same measure of value to such different pieces of property as old Persian carpets, say, and new human acquisitions". But James is even more explicit when he says that Adam had a little glass into which he put everything in order to judge it as one does with wine. As this glass "had served him to satisfy himself, so to speak, both about Amerigo and about the Bernadino Luini he had happened to come to knowledge of at the time he was consenting to the announcement of his daughter's betrothal, so it served him at present to satisfy himself about Charlotte Stant and an extraordinary set of oriental tiles of which he had lately got wind[119]." *Objets d'art* and human beings are interchangeable in Adam's thoughts. His identifying human beings with works of art is indication enough that he has perfect control over both Amerigo, and, later on, Charlotte. There is in fact a strong resemblance between Amerigo's dependence on Maggie on the one hand and that of Charlotte upon Adam on the other. Both Amerigo and Charlotte are in a stronger position in the first part of the novel. They profit by Adam's and Maggie's complete absorption in each other. But, with Maggie's knowledge, the dependence of the mercenary prince grows rapidly again, causing a similar, even stronger dependence of Charlotte upon Adam in her ignorance. Maggie and Adam, towards the end of the novel, are in fact completely superior to the others, particularly in regard to Charlotte. This point is impressively emphasized in the following passage which describes Maggie's reflections on the "daily round" which Adam and Charlotte take together at Fawns: "the likeness of their connection would not have been wrongly figured if he had been thought of as holding in one of his pocketed hands the end of a long silken halter looped round her beautiful neck. He didn't twitch it, yet it was there; he didn't drag her, but she came." On the other hand there exists a mute understanding between father and daughter, facial intimations which "amounted perhaps only to a wordless smile, but the smile was the soft shake of the twisted silken rope". But such small hints are full of meaning for Maggie, as if her father had said something like: "I lead her now by the neck, I lead her to her doom, and she doesn't so much as know what it is, though she has a fear in her heart which, if you had the chances to apply your ear there ... you would hear thump and thump and thump. She thinks it *may* be, her doom, the awful place over there ... but she's afraid to ask, ... just as she's afraid of so many other things that she sees multiplied round her now as portents and betrayals[120]." The "long silken halter" around Charlotte's neck is a clear enough intimation that she is here pictured as a domesticated animal. Thus she has been gradually degraded from a "huntress" enjoying complete freedom, first into one of Adam's museum-pieces, and then into a domesticated animal; the growth of her dependence is quite apparent.

The father-daughter relationship in *The Golden Bowl* is one of the most curious. Until the very end of the novel Adam and Maggie appear almost as an indivisible unity, and she sacrifices her father in the end only because she must for the sake of her own happiness with Amerigo. The bond between the two seems to have a stronger force in Adam: Maggie appears to him like "some slight, slim draped 'antique' of Vatican or Capitoline halls, late and refined, rare as a note and immortal as a link, set in motion by the miraculous infusion of a modern impulse and yet ... keeping still the quality, the perfect felicity, of the statue; the blurred, absent eyes, the smoothed, elegant, nameless head, the impersonal flit of a creature lost in an alien age and passing as an image in worn relief round and round a precious vase[121]". Maggie also, then, is associated above all, in Adam's mind, with *objets d'art*. She is more than anything else his own, his most beloved possession.

One other important relationship remains to be considered, that between Amerigo and Charlotte. It is characteristic that this particular relationship is not emphasized by many significant images. The reason is that the nature of the relation between them is made obvious enough by the events of the novel. The most significant image occurs at the beginning of the third chapter, where it fulfils the function of making the attentive reader aware of the intimacy between them in the past. Looking at Charlotte's face, her eyes and her mouth in particular, it was "as a cluster of possessions of his own that these things, in Charlotte Stant, now affected him; items in a full list, items recognised, each of them, as if, for the long interval, they had been 'stored'—wrapped up, numbered, put away in a cabinet. While she faced Mrs. Assingham the door of the cabinet had opened of itself; he took the relics out one by one, and it was more and more, each instant, as if she were giving him time[122]." The circumstance that Amerigo could feel these things as a "cluster of possessions of his own" is evidence enough that he must have been on very intimate terms with her in the past. Introduced at this early point, the function of this image is mainly to prepare for their resumption of the old intimacy. But it is made quite clear in a further image that they have not consciously worked in that direction. It has been brought about rather by a series of fortunate circumstances: both their marriages into the same family, and above all the particularly strong bond between Maggie and her father. "What had happened, in short, was that Charlotte and he had, by a single turn of the wrist of fate—'led up' to indeed, no doubt, by steps and stages that conscious computation had missed—been placed face to face in a freedom that partook, extraordinarily, of ideal perfection, since the magic web had spun itself without their toil, almost without their touch." But the continuation of the metaphor stresses the point that a renewal of the intimacy with Charlotte has been at the back of Amerigo's mind ever since his marriage; "there sounded through their safety, as an undertone, the very voice he had listened to on the eve of his marriage ... Dimly, again and again, ... he had seemed to hear it tell him why it kept recurring; but it phrased the large music now in a way that filled the room. The reason was ... that just this truth of their safety offered it now a kind of unexampled receptacle, letting it spread and spread, but at the same time elastically enclosing it, banking it in, for softness, as with billows of eider-down[123]." Although the main significance of this image is that it shows the prominence of Charlotte in Amerigo's thoughts, it also establishes an immediate connection with the prince's meditations at the opening of the novel. The theme of the "freedom" on the other hand connects this passage with a later image. "It had all been just in order that his—well, what on earth should he call it but his freedom?—should at present be as perfect and rounded and lustrous as some huge precious pearl. He hadn't struggled nor snatched; he was taking but what had been given him; the pearl dropped itself, with its exquisite quality and rarity, straight into his hand. Here, precisely, it was, incarnate; its size and its value grew as Mrs. Verver appeared, afar off, in one of the smaller doorways[124]." It is not easy to interpret the word "freedom" in this context. But it seems that James here clearly alludes to the adultery committed by the former lovers. The image, moreover, is another example which shows the smooth transition from picture to reality with Charlotte's appearance. Another image applied to the relationship between Amerigo and Charlotte is very significant, because it emphasizes that their understanding has come to an end. A gulf of the unknown has opened between them which Charlotte cannot bridge because of Amerigo's absolute silence as to Maggie's knowledge. "It was as if he were singing to himself, *sotto voce,* as he went—and it was also, on occasion, quite ineffably as if Charlotte, hovering, watching, listening, on her side too, kept sufficiently within earshot to make it out as a song, and yet, for some reason connected with the very manner of it, stood off and didn't dare[125]." The harmony between the two has gone, and she tries in vain to find "her part" again, for Amerigo's strange behaviour makes it impossible.

We have seen that, especially in *The Golden Bowl,* the interpretation of *objet d'art* images is essential for a correct appreciation of some relationships, particularly those between Adam Verver and the other major characters. The metaphors expressing states of dependence show a steady increase in functional significance from novel to novel. And some of the examples from James's last works make us realize that the metaphors in their highest form of achievement are no longer elements foreign to the novel, but form an organic part of its structure. This aspect of James's imagery will be our main concern in the following chapter.

CHAPTER 6

The Constructive Image

The most important metaphors from the point of view of their function are those which contribute to the structure of a novel. The images introduced by most of the Victorian novelists were only floral decorations. James lifted many of them to a level where they form an essential part of the structure of the house of fiction.

He developed two devices in order to strengthen the structure of his novels by means of imagery. As they are, first and foremost, dramatic devices, they are more frequently and powerfully applied in James's later novels. The use of iterative imagery was in many instances adopted because most of the novels were written in serial form. The second device may be called the preparatory metaphor, because it foreshadows events that will happen at later points in the novel. These images help particularly to develop the plot as an organic growth.

A. ITERATIVE IMAGERY

Being a dramatist himself, James must have realized the dangers and difficulties to be faced in the application of iterative imagery in a long piece of prose like the novel. In a drama the single images in a series can follow each other after comparatively short intervals. In a novel this is not possible if the iterative image is to fulfil its essential function, which is to emphasize important stages in the development of either a person or an action; many chapters, therefore, separate one image from the next in the series with the result that the intended effect is occasionally lost on the reader. The application of iterative imagery in a novel requires therefore the careful choice of metaphors which shall be effective and yet not too complicated and obscure in their meaning[1].

1. Water Images

Certainty or uncertainty, safety or danger, are among the states which water images are called upon to express, while their specifically constructive function consists in the oscillation between two of these extremes. In the case of boat images stress is laid on the side in a conflict taken by a particular person.

With the exception of one image the iterative water metaphors in *Roderick Hudson* are not original enough to be really effective. There are four images in all, but the connection between them is not too obvious. They have in common that they all are Rowland's comments upon Roderick's development as an artist in Rome. From them alone we can draw the conclusion that the sculptor does not develop as Rowland had thought he would. When the first image is introduced all is still well, but there is already a slight allusion to the possible danger which Roderick's genius could hold for his development. Rowland remarks to Sam Singleton: "You sail nearer the shore, but you sail in smoother waters[2]." It is Roderick whom Rowland pictures as sailing far out at sea, although he does not say this explicitly. The image evokes a contrast between the little artist represented by Sam Singleton, who never creates great works of art, but who is also more balanced and safe, and Roderick, the genius, who, sailing far out on the treacherous sea, is at any moment likely to be surprised by a storm, and is always surrounded by an element which might destroy him. The next three images are introduced in comparatively quick succession and their interrelation is therefore more apparent. The first image stresses that Roderick's development is at a point of stagnation: "It is not such smooth sailing as it might be, and I am inclined to put up prayers for fair winds[3]." In the next image Roderick is seen involved in a current (Christina Light and her world), which, in Rowland's opinion, is utterly detrimental to his development as an artist: "There are doubtless many good things you [Christina] might do, if you had proper opportunity ... But you seem to be sailing with a current which leaves you little leisure for quiet benevolence. You live in the whirl and hurry of a world into which a poor artist can hardly find it to his advantage to follow you[4]." The last image is the most elaborate and significant. It sums up the major stages of Roderick's evolution and describes the desperate situation in which Rowland then sees himself with Roderick: "We had passed at a bound into the open sea, and left danger behind." This refers to Roderick's first big successes as a sculptor, his Adam and Eve. "But in the summer I began to be puzzled, though I succeeded in not being alarmed." Here Rowland alludes to Roderick's keen interest in Christina Light. "When we came back to Rome, however, I saw that the tide had turned and that we were close upon the rocks." This indicates his unproductivity. "It is, in fact, another case of Ulysses alongside of the Sirens; only Roderick refuses to be tied to the mast[5]." The relation between Roderick and Christina Light is further elucidated in this last part of the metaphor.

In *The Ambassadors* we find the most significant series of water images. Taken together they are also a comment upon Strether's transformation. The first two images emphasize the contrast between Strether and Waymarsh. The latter refuses to accept Europe: "But this very proof of the full life, ... would have made, to Strether's imagination, an element in which Waymarsh could have floated easily had he only consented to float[6]." Strether surrenders at once: "Was what was happening to himself then, was what already *had* happened, really that a woman of fashion was floating him into society, and that an old friend deserted, on the brink, was watching the force of the current?[7]" The two persons alluded to are Maria Gostrey and Waymarsh. In both images Woollett appears as the place of safety, the shore, the secure ground, whereas Europe is pictured as the mighty stream with dangerous currents. With this symbolism in mind we must study all the subsequent water images. Waymarsh, by his keen interest in Miss Barrace, momentarily reaches a point where he also is seen "floating". But the main point is that Strether is continuing to drift away from Woollett. "Waymarsh himself, for the occasion, was drawn into the eddy; it absolutely, though but temporarily, swallowed him down, and there were days when Strether seemed to bump against him as a sinking swimmer might brush a submarine object. The fathomless medium held them—Chad's manner was the fathomless medium; and our friend felt as if they passed each other, in their deep immersion, with the round, impersonal eye of silent fish[8]." The general note struck by all three passages is that of passivity. Something clearly happens to both Strether and Waymarsh, without their being able to do much about it. How strong the forces at work are is made obvious when even Waymarsh, though only temporarily, surrenders. Another point to which attention must be drawn is that in both instances the active force is a woman. The same is true for the subsequent water images, in which the central symbol is no longer the water itself but the boat on the water; this enables James to contrast Woollett and Europe much more sharply. The first boat image is significant only in relation to those following. "She had settled in Paris, brought up her daughter, steered her boat. It was no very pleasant boat—especially there—to be in; but Marie de Vionnet would have headed straight.[9]" The word "life" could be easily substituted for "boat" to make the meaning quite apparent. But the image is too conventional to be really effective. The elements in the following one are not much different, but the formulation makes it more significant: "that hangs together with the conviction we [Strether and Chad] now feel—this certitude that Mrs. Pocock will take him [Waymarsh] into her boat. For it's your mother's own boat that she's pulling[10]." Both these boat images are in a way preparatory to the two in which Strether is described as being drawn into Madame de Vionnet's boat. The first of these significant metaphors occurs when Sarah Pocock, in Strether's company, meets her for the first time. She "greeted him more familiarly than Mrs. Pocock; she put out her hand to him without moving from her place; and it came to him, in the course of a minute", that "she was giving him over to ruin ... She wanted to show as simple and humble ... but it was just this that seemed to put him on her side ... the consciousness of all this, in her charming eyes, was so clear and fine that as she thus publicly drew him into her boat she produced in him such a silent agitation as he was not to fail afterwards to denounce as pusillanimous." Strether is fully aware that

Sarah would draw wrong conclusions from Madame de Vionnet's behaviour. We can understand his feeling that the French lady is giving him over to ruin. His retreat back to Woollett and Mrs. Newsome will be completely cut off by the impression made on Sarah and Waymarsh. "They were at this very moment ... attributing to him the full license of it, and all by the operation of her own tone with him; whereas his sole license had been to cling, with intensity, to the brink, not to dip so much as a toe into the flood." Only now does James elaborate the original boat metaphor and thereby give it significance. "To meet his fellow visitor's invocation and, with Sarah's brilliant eyes on him, answer, *was* quite sufficiently to step into her boat. During the rest of the time her visit lasted he felt himself proceed to each of the proper offices, successively, for helping to keep the adventurous skiff afloat. It rocked beneath him, but he settled himself in his place. He took up an oar, and since he was to have the credit of pulling, he pulled[11]." At the beginning of the following chapter, James takes up the metaphor again. "If Mme de Vionnet, under Sarah's eyes, had pulled him into her boat, there was by this time no doubt whatever that he had remained in it and that what he had really most been conscious of for many hours together was the movement of the vessel itself. They were in it together this moment as they had not yet been[12]." The first metaphor makes it obvious that Madame de Vionnet is the active force, and that Strether stands completely under her influence; the second that he feels completely on her side. Thus we have two contrasting movements: that of Waymarsh into Sarah's and Mrs. Newsome's boat—in other words the movement back to Woollett and activity. On the other hand there is Strether being drawn into Madame de Vionnet's boat, which signifies a change from action to that passivity represented by Europe. But with both men their movements are guided. The last boat image, although short, is extremely significant; it gains weight because it grows immediately out of the two metaphors which elucidate Strether's relation to Madame de Vionnet. When she announces that her daughter is to be married to some one other than Chad, Strether's reaction is: "He had struck himself at the hotel, before Sarah and Waymarsh, as being in her boat; but where on earth was he now?[13]" After this news, which destroys his belief that Chad is in love with Jeanne de Vionnet, he is neither in her mother's boat any more, nor has he a chance left of moving back into Mrs. Newsome's. When we have followed the water images as a guide to Strether's movements up to this point, we realize that they describe an oscillating line which leads from safety (Woollett) to danger (Europe), then to comparative safety (Madame de Vionnet) and again back to danger. But the cycle is not yet complete. Strether is yet able to reach safety again. At the end of the novel he "was well in port, the outer sea behind him, and it was only a matter of going ashore; there was a question that came and went for him, however, as he rested against the side of his ship, and it was a little to get rid of the obsession that he prolonged his hours with Miss Gostrey[14]". The last image leads us back to those at the beginning where Strether had been pictured as leaving the shore of safety and involving himself in the dangerous currents of Europe. He has, in his own opinion, completed his mission successfully, because, in the course of his stay in Europe, its purpose had undergone a transformation similar to his own.

The water images in *The Wings* show no real consistency. In the early stages, we encounter three such metaphors which are undoubtedly connected with one another. After the ninth chapter a few other water images are introduced, but they are neither related to the three earlier examples, nor are they of any significance[15]. The three water images at the beginning give us very important hints about the relationship between Milly and Mrs. Stringham. She is more helpless than Milly and, moreover, quite stupid. Throughout the novel the heroine makes all her vital decisions without the counsel of her confidante, and this lady's uselessness is exclusively emphasized by the three iterative water images in the first chapters. Mrs. Stringham "had seen little of the girl ... before accepting her proposal; and had accordingly placed herself, by her act, in a boat that she more and more estimated as, humanly speaking, of the biggest, though likewise, no doubt, in many ways, by reason of its size, of the safest[16]". Quite clearly a new meaning is presented in this boat image. The "size" of Milly's "boat" refers to her enormous wealth which gives Mrs. Stringham a feeling of safety as she gradually realizes its extent. It is just this safety which Mrs. Stringham enjoys; she is passively drawn along by Milly, whose nature reminds her "of the term always used in the newspapers about the great new steamers, the inordinate number of 'feet of water' they drew; so that if, in your little boat, you had chosen to hover and approach, you had but yourself to thank, when once motion was started, for the way the draught pulled you. Milly drew the feet of water, and ... her companion floated off with the sense of rocking violently at her side[17]." Mrs. Stringham "fondly embarked" because she thought that she was "supremely for leading Milly's" life, as she had none of her own to lead. But the image above emphasizes clearly enough that she, in her "little boat", is in no position to assume such leadership. Her inability to help Milly becomes most apparent in the third water image, which is introduced at a point when the girl is already in close contact with Mrs. Lowder, Kate and Merton. After Milly has said that she does not know what it is she wants to run away from, Mrs. Stringham's thoughts are rendered in the following way: "The sense was constant for her that their relation was as if afloat, like some island of the south, in a great warm sea that made, for every conceivable chance, a margin, an outer sphere of general emotion; and the effect of the occurrence of anything in particular was to make the sea submerge the island, the margin flood the text. The great wave now for a moment swept over. 'I'll go anywhere else in the world you like.'[18]" This is certainly not leading Milly, but rather leaving it entirely to her to decide.

The use of iterative water images in *The Golden Bowl* shows some similarity to that in *The Ambassadors*. The centre of gravity is occupied by Amerigo. He starts, at the beginning of the novel, "on the great voyage—across the unknown sea". His "ship"—that of his marriage to Maggie—is "all rigged and appointed; the cargo's stowed away and the company complete". But the prince is afraid that he might lose his way "in the waste of the waters", and he entreats Fanny to be his "lead"; "I don't ask you to stay on board with me, but I must keep your sail in sight for orientation." The continuation of the metaphor leaves no doubt that it was Fanny who brought Amerigo and Maggie together, and that he now depends completely upon her further help and guidance. "You've provided the ship itself, and, if you've not quite seen me aboard, you've attended me, ever so kindly, to the dock. Your own vessel is ... in the next berth, and you can't desert me now." Fanny is of a different opinion when she concludes this first image sequel with a reference to the wealth of the Ververs: "You talk about ships, but they're not the comparison. Your tossings are over—you're practically *in* port ... of the Golden Isles[19]." This passage already points forward to the prince's helplessness after Maggie's discovery. Fanny has then ceased to help him, and it is his wife who, in the end, leads him into the port of safety and happiness.

The following images are mostly boat metaphors, elucidating the positions of one or more characters in relation to the two sides of America and Europe. Even though the single images of the series are not very original in themselves, they gain much weight in their cumulative effect and their clarifying analysis of the true relationships between the major characters. Indeed they hold the whole conversation between Fanny and Amerigo together. He initiates the series when he says: "We're in the same boat", referring to Charlotte and himself. Fanny contradicts him: "I don't know what you mean by the 'same' boat. Charlotte is naturally in Mr. Verver's boat." This at once allows the prince to bring up the question of money: "And, pray, am *I* not in Mr. Verver's boat too? Why, but for Mr. Verver's boat, I should have been by this time ... away down, down, down." Fanny knows exactly what he is alluding to, "how it had taken his father-in-law's great fortune, and taken no small slice, to surround him with an element in which ... he could pecuniarily float". Amerigo now touches upon the question of his intimacy with Charlotte. "The 'boat' ... is a good deal tied up at the dock, or anchored ... out in the stream. I have to jump out from time to time to stretch my legs, and ... Charlotte really can't help occasionally doing the same ... one has to take a header and splash about in the water. Call our having remained here together tonight ... one of the harmless little plunges, off the deck, inevitable for each of us ... We shan't drown, we shan't sink—at least I can answer for myself. Mrs. Verver too, moreover ... visibly knows how to swim[20]." From the very conventional beginning this passage works gradually up to an extremely elaborate and significant picture. It renders the situation very clearly. Charlotte and Amerigo form one side; but at the same time they are dependent upon Mr. Verver as far as the vital question of money is concerned. They are not in a "boat" of their own but rather in his. They can leave it from time to time to stretch their legs, to take one of their "harmless little plunges", but they cannot go off completely without sacrificing the advantages of Mr. Verver's money.

The next image occurs when Bob Assingham, at Matcham, has "a consciousness of deep waters" and the notion that his wife "had been out on these waters". With this image James refers to one of Fanny's dangerous adventures, during which her husband "had not quitted for an hour ... the shore of the mystic lake".

He had on the contrary stationed himself where she could signal him at need. Her need would have arisen if the planks of her bark had parted—*then* some sort of plunge would have become his immediate duty. His present position, clearly, was that of seeing her in the centre of her sheet of dark water, and of wondering if her actual mute gaze at him didn't perhaps mean that her planks *were* now parting. He held himself so ready that it was quite as if the inward man had pulled off coat and waistcoat. Before he had plunged, however ... he perceived, not without relief, that she was making for land. He watched her steadily paddle, always a little nearer, and at last he felt her boat bump. The bump was distinct, and in fact she stepped ashore. "We were all wrong. There's nothing." "Nothing—?" It was like giving her his hand up the bank[21].

Fanny has been trying to find out the true relationship between Charlotte and Amerigo, and she sums up the result of her inquiry by saying to her husband: "I *see* the boat they're in, but I'm not, thank God, in it myself[22]." This places a renewed emphasis on the facts stated in the second of the discussions quoted between Amerigo and Fanny. Maggie's position and her attitude towards the adulterous relationship is elucidated when Mrs. Assingham says to her husband that the princess "irresistibly *knows* that there's something between them. But she hasn't 'arrived' at it ... at all; that's exactly what she hasn't done, what she so steadily and intensely refuses to do. She stands off and off, so as not to arrive; she keeps out to sea and away from the rocks, and what she most wants of me is to keep at safe distance with her—as I, for my own skin, only ask not to come nearer[23]." Here we are given the clue to Maggie's behaviour until the breaking of the bowl. Although she knows that there is something between her husband and her stepmother, she pretends not to know, as it serves her plans better. But Maggie has to choose between sacrificing her father or her marriage. When she has made up her mind we realize how much of a sacrifice it is for her to leave Adam. This becomes evident when she is alone together with him for the last time, which "was wonderfully like their having got together into some boat and paddled off from the shore where husbands and wives, luxuriant complications, made the air too tropical. In the boat they were father and daughter." And in this felicity Maggie asks the silent question: "Why, into the bargain ... couldn't they always live, so far as they lived together, in a boat?[24]"

The cycle of these images is again completed by a direct reference to the very first image, that of Amerigo's setting out on the "unknown sea". The concluding one makes it evident that all the unnatural relations which have developed in the course of the novel have been destroyed. Maggie and Amerigo are together as they should have been from the very outset. But much has been lost over the course of the years. They have to start from the beginning again, but are full of hopes for attaining safety and happiness: "'Wait!' It was the word of his own distress and entreaty, the word for both of them, all they had left, their plank now on the great sea[25]." They are no longer in Mr. Verver's big, safe "boat", which has been wrecked and has left them with only a "plank" as a hope for survival. Only through patience and mutual understanding can they be saved and reach their goal.

2. Architectural Images

Architectural images serve a purpose directly contrary to that fulfilled by water metaphors, for they indicate firmness and security, and, sometimes, intimacy and confidence between two persons. They occur iteratively only in two novels[26].

Isabel Archer is the keystone in the structure of *The Portrait*. She is the centre about which everything and everybody circles. In order to enhance this impression, James has endowed her with metaphors that picture her as a beautiful edifice which is the object of every one's interest. All the persons in contact with her walk around it, most of them trying to find an entrance—that is to get into her confidence. Ralph is one of those who tries incessantly, but never with success. "He surveyed the edifice from the outside, and admired it greatly; he looked in at the windows, and received an impression of proportions equally fair. But he felt that he saw it only by glimpses, and that he had not yet stood under the roof; the door was fastened[27]." Isabel, screened by reserve, is a mystery to him. He tries in vain to open that locked door. The relationship between Isabel and Madame Merle is different. Here the door is no longer fastened: "The gates of the girl's confidence were opened wider than they had ever been; she said things to Madame Merle that she had not yet said to any one. Sometimes she took alarm at her candor[28]." There is a clear distinction between Madame Merle, who is allowed to take possession of Isabel's "interior", and Ralph, who is only allowed to look in "at the windows". His only comfort is the thought that all her suitors so far are doomed in the same way, and he hopes that the same fate will befall Osmond: "He found much entertainment in the idea that ... he should see a third suitor at her gate ... Ralph looked forward to a fourth and fifth *soupirant;* he had no conviction that she would stop at a third. She would keep the gate ajar and open a parley; she would certainly not allow number three to come in[29]." There is a very subtle difference between Ralph's relationship to Isabel and that of Warburton, Goodwood and Osmond. Because of his illness he cannot be one of her suitors. To him she will open herself up completely or not at all. With the other men she has to open a "parley" with the result that each of them is left with some hope before she decides definitely in favour of one of them.

A significant architectural metaphor attributed to Pansy emphasizes the affinity between her and her stepmother; at the same time it contrasts the simplicity of her character to the secrecy of Isabel's. Warburton has taken an interest in Pansy but, as a result of Isabel's interference, has not persisted in his attentions. Osmond, angered at the loss of such an enormously rich suitor, says that he "comes and looks at one's daughter as if she were a suite of apartments; he tries the door-handles and looks out of the windows, raps on the walls, and almost thinks he will take the place ... Then, on the whole, he decides that the rooms are too small; he doesn't think he could live on a third floor; he must look out for a *piano nobile*. And he goes away, after having got a month's lodging in the poor little apartment for nothing[30]." The culmination of the architectural images is reached, when Isabel's edifice, after she has been married a short while, has become identical with the "house of suffocation" in which she is living. And it is after she has heard about the real relationship between Osmond and Madame Merle that "the truth of things, their mutual relations, their meaning, and for the most part, their horror rose before her with a kind of architectural vastness[31]". It overshadows the beauty of her own edifice completely. She may be horrified, but she is condemned to live with it.

The two most complicated and elaborate architectural metaphors are introduced into *The Golden Bowl*. They are over-ingenious and therefore difficult to understand. Although there is no direct relationship between them they may still be regarded as iterative because they develop very similar conceptions. Adam, in retrospect, sees Amerigo's interference in his relationship with his daughter, "as if his son-in-law's presence ... had somehow filled the scene and blocked the future ... though the Prince ... was still pretty much the same 'big fact,' the sky had lifted, the horizon receded, the very foreground itself expanded, quite to match him, quite to keep everything in comfortable scale". This is an indication that Maggie's marriage had incurred certain changes on the part of the Ververs, an adjustment to the prince's "size", because the "little old-time union" between them had "resembled a good deal some pleasant public square, in the heart of an old city". What had happened with Amerigo's advent was that into this "square" "a great Palladian church ... had suddenly been dropped; so that the rest of the place, the space in front, the way round, outside, to the east end, the margin of street and passage, the quantity of overarching heaven, had been temporarily compromised". The phenomenon which had occurred since then was that "no visibility of transition showed, no violence of adjustment, in retrospect, emerged. The Palladian church was always there, but the *piazza* took care of itself ... the limit stood off, the way round was easy, the east end was as fine, in its fashion, as the west, and there were also side doors for entrance, between the two ... as for all proper great churches. By some such process ... had the Prince, for his father-in-law, ... ceased to be ... a block." At this point the metaphorical rendering of the facts is at an end. The prince, in Mr. Verver's eyes, had clearly threatened to destroy the harmony between him and his daughter. The continuation of the metaphor now brings Adam's explanation why he was willing to accept Amerigo all the same as a son-in-law and why he was able to adjust himself to his "size". "It all came then, the great clearance, from the one prime fact that the Prince ... hadn't proved angular ... Oh, if he *had* been angular!—who could say what might *then* have happened? He spoke ... as if he grasped the facts ... for which angularity stood ... He might have been signifying by it the sharp corners and hard edges, all the stony pointedness, the grand right geometry of his spreading Palladian church." The prince is "variously and inexhaustibly round", when he might have been "abominably square". Mr. Verver is most explicit towards Amerigo himself. "Say you had been formed ... in a lot of pyramidal lozenges like that wonderful side of the Ducal Palace in Venice—so lovely in a building, but so damnable, for rubbing against, in a man, and especially in a near relation. I can see ... all the architectural cut diamonds that would have scratched one's softer sides. One would have been scratched by diamonds ... but one would have been more or less reduced to a hash. As it is, for living with, you're a pure and perfect crystal[32]." Adam was, in other words, able to discard his gnawing fears that the prince would prove unaccommodating, cantankerous and eccentric. Once he has come to this conclusion he never suspects Amerigo of doing something indecent and unlawful, and he trusts him entirely. The above extracts from a metaphorical passage about twice as long raise the question why James uses so many words to express these thoughts, why he erects such a huge construction. In the first place a short objective statement of the circumstances would fail to emphasize the importance of these facts for the whole development and understanding of the novel. In the second place the symbolical impact of the passage would be completely lost. The picture of the mutual relation of Maggie and Adam shows how closed in their whole life is, being solely directed to a centre which is their own relationship, without a true connection with the outward world—until the arrival of Amerigo and his marriage to Maggie. Only then do the Ververs realize how limited their past life has been, how much they have been lacking the larger experience. The sudden drop of the "great Palladian church" makes them aware of all these shortcomings and they hasten to adjust themselves, to expand their horizon, to enlarge the quantity of "overarching heaven". But they are prepared to make this adjustment only if it will not involve sacrificing their "*piazza*"; and Adam makes sure of this before accepting the prince. The fact that Amerigo was not "angular" guaranteed the fulfilment of this condition. Adam is concerned with Amerigo only in so far as he has a bearing on the father–daughter relationship. Apart from that he is, for Mr. Verver, only a "pure and perfect crystal", the most valuable piece in his collection of works of art. The central problem which James tackled in Mr. Verver is the destructive effect of money on human relationships. As exemplified in his case money threatens to destroy all natural attachments in life. It tears Maggie from her husband and deprives Charlotte of a true married life with Adam. Therefore his way of living is much more immoral than that of Charlotte and Amerigo. Although theirs is adulterous it is, basically, natural. Maggie gradually becomes aware of the abnormal relationship with her father and the impossibility of its leading to real happiness. This realization is formulated in the second architectural metaphor which opens Book II of the novel. She had made, "by the mere touch of her hand", a difference in the situation which "had been occupying, for months and months, the very centre of the garden of her life, but it had reared itself there like some strange, tall tower of ivory, or perhaps rather some wonderful, beautiful but outlandish pagoda, a structure plated with hard, bright porcelain, coloured and figured and adorned, at the over-hanging eaves, with silver-bells that tinkled, ever so charmingly, when stirred by chance airs". The meaning of the "pagoda" is left rather ambiguous at this point[33]. But a few pages later James makes it clear what it stands for. "The pagoda in her blooming garden figured the arrangement ... by which, so strikingly, she had been able to marry without breaking, as she liked to put it, with her past. She had surrendered herself to her husband without the shadow of a reserve or a condition, and yet she had not, all the while, given up her father by the least little inch[34]." Bearing this in mind, the continuation of the pagoda metaphor is clearer. Maggie had "walked round and round it ... looking up, all the while, at the fair structure that spread itself so amply and rose so high, but never quite making out, as yet, where she might have entered had she wished ... though her raised eyes seemed to distinguish places that must serve, from within, and especially far aloft, as apertures and outlooks, no door appeared to give access from her convenient garden level. The great decorated surface had remained consistently impenetrable and inscrutable." It is the arrangement between the four of them, at which she marvelled again and again, as if it were a mystery, just to be wondered at, but not to be really understood. The exotic elements in the metaphor express this mystery, which is enhanced by the picture of the "Mahometan mosque, with which no base heretic could take a liberty; there so hung about it the vision of one's putting off one's shoes to enter, and even, verily, of one's paying with one's life if found there as an interloper". In the past Maggie had simply enjoyed the beauty of these almost sacred arrangements. The meaning of her walking around the pagoda is given at a later point when we read that she "had compassed the high felicity of seeing the two men beautifully take to each other[35]". This allusion establishes an immediate connection with the earlier image of the "Palladian church". All the possible relationships between the four major characters, except those of the two marriages, are alluded to when we read that "so it was that their felicity had fructified; so it was that the ivory tower ... had risen stage by stage[36]". Thus the first part of the metaphor is a kind of summary of the situation during the first half of the novel. The second part refers to the situation as it appears to Maggie on that particular evening which "had made the abrupt bend in her life", when she had resolved to take a decisive action and had so "ceased merely to circle and to scan the elevation, ceased ... to stare and wonder". Her courage had even been surprising to herself, but there was no doubt that she had "caught herself distinctly in the act ... of stepping unprecedentedly near". She even went further in that she "had sounded with a tap or two one of the rare porcelain plates. She had knocked, in short—though she could scarce have said whether for admission or for what; she had applied her hand to a cool smooth spot and had waited to see what would happen. Something *had* happened; it was as if a sound, at her touch, after a little, had come back to her from within; a sound sufficiently suggesting that her approach had been noted[37]." Maggie's sudden knock refers to one particular step she has taken, whereas the "sound" from within indicates the prince's reaction to her step. "For it had been a step, distinctly, on Maggie's part, her deciding to do something, just then and there, which would strike Amerigo as unusual[38]." This was to await his return from Matcham, not, as was her custom, with her father at Eaton Square, but in her own home at Portland Place. The silent question which she puts to herself on that particular evening—"What if I've abandoned *them,* you know? What if I've accepted too passively the funny form of our life?[39]" — refers clearly to the meaning of the "pagoda" and her realization that if an intimacy has developed between Charlotte and Amerigo, it was a good deal her own fault. By her unusual step she "wanted him to understand from that very moment that she was going to be *with* him again, quite with *them,* together, as she doubtless hadn't been since the 'funny' changes—that was really all one could call them—into which they had each, as for the sake of the others, too easily and too obligingly slipped[40]". The second part of the image, then, foreshadows Maggie's efforts to re-establish a happy married life between herself and Amerigo as well as between her father and Charlotte, yet without destroying the equilibrium that had existed in the past.

3. Flying Images

The primary functions of flying images are the expression of freedom (which contains at the same time an element of danger), superiority, high moral behaviour and—with wing images—the suggestion of protection or safety. There are only two novels in which James clearly made an iterative use of such images: *The Portrait* and *The Old Things*[41].

In the first of these novels they are applied to Isabel Archer as a comment upon her descent from her high flight of freedom and unlimited will-power to her imprisoned and earthbound state after her marriage. In the first chapter Warburton says to Ralph: "You know you told me the other day that I ought to 'take hold' of something. One hesitates to take hold of a thing that may the next moment be knocked sky-high." Ralph then suggests that he should "take hold of a pretty woman". "'The pretty women themselves may be sent flying!' Lord Warburton exclaimed[42]." These images prefigure two subsequent events: firstly Warburton's trying to take hold of Isabel, secondly her being "knocked sky-high" by the large sum of money which she inherits. At this very early stage of the novel these two images appear to have no connection. But in this way James very subtly prepares the ground for Isabel's appearance and some important coming events. The next image is introduced in Goodwood's thoughts, after Isabel has stressed her fondness for personal freedom and the wish to retain her liberty. "To his mind she had always had wings, and this was but the flutter of those stainless pinions[43]." Isabel, in Goodwood's eyes, is capable of very great flights, or, in other words, of doing great things. When she, after entering into her inheritance, frankly confesses to Ralph that she is troubled, he gives her the advice: "Spread your wings; rise above the ground. It's never wrong to do that[44]." He wants her to be rich so that she can make the utmost of her freedom, in his particular sense of remaining unmarried. The most significant of these flying images is introduced after Isabel's marriage to Osmond, when Ralph says: "You seemed to me to be soaring far up in the blue,—to be sailing in the bright light, over the heads of men. Suddenly some one tosses up a stone,—a missile that should never have reached you,—and down you drop to the ground[45]." In "some one tosses up a stone" he is unmistakably referring to Osmond. It stresses his worthlessness; in Ralph's eyes he is a character to whom Isabel should never have responded; one does not give up one's freedom for the sake of a "stone". Now that she is down on the earth again her freedom is at an end. Her innocence, weakness, and compassion had delivered her into the hands of evil and corruption. Her reaction to Ralph's image is a further proof of her innocence: "What do you mean by my soaring and sailing? ... You talk about one's soaring and sailing, but if one marries at all one touches the earth[46]." This is exactly what Ralph had tried to prevent; for his own selfish reasons he did not want her to marry. On the other hand it is just the large fortune that allows Isabel to do something she could not have done without it, namely a charitable deed; that is what marrying Osmond amounts to. She believes in his goodness because she has not known evil in her past life. The extent of the loss of her freedom is emphasized in a final wing image, introduced after Warburton has told her that he thinks Ralph is dying. Isabel's immediate wish is to see him without delay, but she cannot: "she looked, as she sat there, like a winged creature held back[47]." Her wings of freedom had been horribly clipped; she could fly no longer. The inter-relation of these flying images cannot be doubted, but they are only partly effective because, with one exception, they are too near the conventional to be significant enough; their organic relation and structural function will, therefore, be lost on the majority of readers.

In *The Old Things* the flying images show the beauty of Fleda's intentions, her high moral and heroic behaviour, and the most important stages in the failure of her high-minded purposes. After her talk with Owen at Ricks she recognizes that it is her moral duty to act in Mona's and Owen's interest, which gives her a feeling of superiority and greatness. "To know that she had become to him an object of desire gave her wings that she felt herself flutter in the air: it was like the rush of a flood into her own accumulations. These stored depths had been fathomless and still, but now, for half an hour, in the empty house, they spread till they overflowed[48]." This image helps to emphasize that she is a "free spirit", capable of great flights. "The rush of a flood" on the other hand indicates the danger involved in her knowledge of Owen's feelings towards her, for in her presumption she might do something wrong. The next significant flying image occurs when Owen meets Fleda in London and tells her that he reported their conversation at Ricks to Mona who, of course, thinks Fleda dishonest, interested in Owen herself. Fleda "had coloured up to her eyes, where, as with the effect of a blow in the face, she quickly felt the tears gathering. It was a sudden drop in her great flight, a shock to her attempt to watch over what Mona was entitled to. While she had been straining her very soul in this attempt the object of her magnanimity had been pronouncing her 'not honest'[49]." This image marks a very important point in her inner development. If she had secretly hoped for a possible union between her and Owen, it was her conviction at the same time that they could only be entirely happy if the break between Mona and Owen were not caused by her. But his telling Mona of his encounter with Fleda puts her in an impossible position. Her whole heroism and magnanimity have become questionable. The third flying image occurs after Fleda's breakdown, when her heroic plans have become a complete failure: "The stillness all round had been exactly what Fleda desired, but it gave her for the time a deep sense of failure, the sense of a sudden drop from a height at which she had all things beneath her. She had nothing beneath her now; she herself was at the bottom of the heap[50]." The course of her flight is now quite evident. The images mark three important points in her inner development, and there is no doubt that they are intentionally related to one another. They help to stress the tragic fate of her intentions. Her heroism has all been for nothing. It has helped neither herself, Owen, Mrs. Gereth nor Mona. She has given away all her secrets, her moral greatness has come to grief, and now she feels low, base and miserable.

So far the curves of Isabel's and Fleda's flights have been similar. But in *The Old Things* James has extended the series of flying images, and though the following metaphor has nothing to do with flying, it is obviously an extension of the preceding images. James has ended the last flying image by saying that Fleda "herself was now at the bottom of the heap". It is exactly at this point that he begins his next image, which is introduced when Mrs. Gereth tells Fleda what has happened during Mrs. Brigstock's visit at Ricks. "Fleda had listened in unbearable pain and growing terror, as if her interlocutress, stone by stone, were piling some fatal mass upon her breast. She had the sense of being buried alive, smothered in the mere expansion of another will; and now there was but one gap left to the air. A single word, she felt, might close it, and with the question that came to her lips as Mrs. Gereth paused she seemed to herself to ask, in cold dread, for her doom[51]." The image is inserted when Mrs. Gereth tells Fleda that Mrs. Brigstock had asked her whether she wanted Owen to marry Fleda. It not only heightens the tension, but also permits us to have another look into her much troubled mind. If she should now hear that Mrs. Gereth had informed her visitor of her being in favour of a marriage between her son and Fleda, then all her hopes would definitely be at an end. Her whole behaviour would then appear, in the eyes of the Brigstocks at any rate, horrid and disgusting. They could then only see her interference as part of a hideous plan between Mrs. Gereth and herself in order to get Owen away from Mona.

The iterative use of flying images in *The Old Things* is more successful than that in the earlier novel. The relationship between the four metaphors is much more apparent, and most of the images show more originality in their formulation. They are, moreover, a continuation of the structural principle which, for the greater part of the first half of the novel, has been fulfilled by the war images.

4. Princess and Dove Images in "The Wings of the Dove"

The two predominant groups of images in *The Wings* are the princess images with their many variations and above all the dove images, which constitute the central symbol of the novel. Their iterative use demonstrates more effectively than any other group of images in James's work the transition from mere metaphors to characteristic symbols. The single example taken by itself appears still as an image, but through the recurrent introduction its symbolic significance becomes apparent.

The princess images create the impression of a fairy tale, lifting the particular story of Milly on to a universal plane. The novel is James's ultimate expression of what he had to say of mankind and humanity. "He wanted to raise his international theme to its ultimate potentiality[52]." Like a princess in a fairy tale, Milly appears as the ideal of human kind, in her combination of wealth, beauty, generosity, suffering and death. It is mainly Susan Stringham who likens her to a princess. "After but two or three meetings, the girl with the background, the girl with the crown of old gold and the mourning ... had told her she had never seen anyone like her[53]." Although not explicitly a princess image the "crown of old gold" points forward to the first true image of this kind a few pages later, when certain qualities about Milly affect Mrs. Stringham at moments "as the princess in a conventional tragedy might have affected the confidant if a personal emotion had ever been permitted to the latter ... Mrs. Stringham was a woman of the world, but Milly Theale was a princess, the only one she had yet had to deal with, and this in its way, too, made all the difference ... Service was in other words so easy to render that the whole thing was like court life without the hardships[54]." This image leads directly to another, which is introduced when Mrs. Stringham watches Milly looking down from a dangerous position in the Swiss Alps upon the world stretching below her; "If the girl was deeply and recklessly meditating there, she was not meditating a jump; she was on the contrary, as she sat, much more in a state of uplifted and unlimited possession that had nothing to gain from violence. She was looking down on the kingdoms of the earth, and though indeed that of itself might well go to the brain, it wouldn't be with a view of renouncing them. Was she choosing among them, or did she want them all?[55]" This is a stronger and more obvious repetition of the theme already stated in the first image. The dangerous point from which Milly looked down "on the kingdoms of the earth" emphasizes on the one hand her unlimited freedom of action; on the other we are also made aware of the persistent nearness of danger and death. Susan's conviction that Milly is "not meditating a jump" allows us to look ahead to her struggle for the possession of the "kingdoms", her struggle for life in the face of death.

James discriminates very carefully between the various relations in which other characters stand to Milly. Mrs. Stringham's is that of a confidante to a princess, Kate's that of the "worthiest maiden, the chosen daughter of the burgesses", who waited upon the "wandering princess" at the "city gate[56]". "It was the real thing again, evidently, the amusement of the meeting for the princess too; princesses living for the most part, in such an appeased way, on the plane of mere elegant representation. That was why they pounced, at city gates, on deputed flower-strewing damsels; that was why, after effigies, processions and other stately games, frank human company was pleasant to them[57]." In this significant metaphor another motive is touched upon: as a "princess" Milly is condemned to "mere elegant representation", as a result of her wealth and the legend that surrounds and accompanies her wherever she goes. Nevertheless she longs for true and intimate relationships with human beings; Kate offers herself at once as a satisfaction to this yearning, and Milly seizes the opportunity without any hesitation or further consideration. Kate becomes, for a certain time, Milly's confidante, whereas with Mrs. Stringham her feeling of "representation" is strongest. This lady "dropped at times into inscrutable, impenetrable deferences—attitudes that, though without at all intending it, made a difference for familiarity, for the ease of intimacy. It was as if she recalled herself to manners, to the law of court-etiquette ... It was definite for her ... that to treat her as a princess was a positive need of her companion's mind; wherefore she couldn't help it if this lady had her transcendent view of the way the class in question were treated[58]." The novel reaches a point at which Kate is also reduced to Mrs. Stringham's status, becoming mere "lady of her [Milly's] court[59]", although she once enjoyed the privilege of a royal favourite. This moment is reached in Venice when the picture of Milly as "the angular, pale princess, ostrich-plumed, black robed, hung about with amulets, reminders, relics, mainly seated, mainly still", is contrasted to that of Kate as "the upright, restless, slow-circling lady of her court, who exchanges with her, across the black water streaked with evening gleams, fitful questions and answers. The upright lady, with thick, dark braids down her back, drawing over the grass a more embroidered train, makes the whole circuit, and makes it again, and the broken talk, brief and sparingly allusive, seems more to cover than to free their sense[60]." The next princess image, unpretentious though it first appears, derives great significance from the context in which it occurs, which is the moment when Milly begins to conceive the idea of using the whole of her wealth for something or some one "as a counter-move to fate": "She was more prepared than ever to pay enough, and quite as much as ever to pay too much. What else—if such were points at which your most trusted servant failed—was the use of being, as the dear Susies of earth called you, a princess in a palace?[61]"

For Merton Milly is no princess but remains throughout the novel the "little American girl" whom he had met in New York. "Mrs. Lowder, Susan Shepherd, his own Kate, might, each in proportion, see her as a princess, as an angel, as a star, but for himself, luckily, she hadn't as yet complications to any point of discomfort: the princess, the angel, the star were muffled over, ever so lightly and brightly, with the little American girl who had been kind to him in New York and to whom, certainly ... he was perfectly willing to be kind in return[62]." Only towards the end of the novel does the true significance of the princess image become apparent. Milly is raised from the level of the earth to that of heaven. Her picture is glorified like that of some saint, and she is transfigured into a symbol of purity and sublimity. Merton admits that to live around Milly is "quite court life". But Mrs. Stringham elucidates the meaning when she adds: "If you understand it of such a court as never was: one of the courts of heaven, the court of an angel ... That's just the beauty here; its why she's the great and only princess. With her, at her court, ... it does pay ... You'll see for yourself[63]." Merton does so only after Milly's death. Before that event he honestly wonders in what way it would "pay" to be at Milly's "court", and he receives the answer when Kate suggests to him that he should marry Milly in order to be in possession of the fortune after her death.

> When Densher at last spoke it was under cover. 'I might stay, you know, without trying.'
> 'Oh, to stay *is* to try.'
> 'To have for herself, you mean, the appearance of it?'
> 'I don't see how you can have the appearance more.'
> Densher waited. 'You think it then possible she may *offer* marriage?'
> 'I can't think—if you really want to know—what she may *not* offer!'
> 'In the manner of princesses, who do such things?'
> 'In any manner you like. So be prepared.'[64]

With this the series of princess images is completed. We see from them that although each image has in itself a particular significance and throws light on certain relationships, the function of the whole group is nevertheless different from that of the other iterative images we have studied in preceding paragraphs. The structural principle of those was mainly to illustrate the course of one particular development. The function of the princess images, however, is to keep constantly before us one particular aspect which remains basically the same throughout the novel. Milly Theale appears as a princess from beginning to end. Such changes as take place are in the relationships between herself and the persons surrounding her, such as Mrs. Stringham and Kate Croy.

The dove image appears first of all in the utmost contrast to the many animal images connected with Mrs. Lowder, Kate and, indirectly, Merton. From that point of view we are confronted with a symbolic contrast of innocence, peacefulness and weakness on the one hand, and corruption, aggression and strength on the other. But from another point of view the dove image also shows a connection with the meaning of the flying images in *The Portrait*. Milly, by means of her fabulous wealth, is also capable of great and wondrous flights, of unpredictable actions which have a lasting effect on others. Those who come into contact with Milly in all her innocence and gentleness cannot help comparing her to a dove. Kate is the first to make this comparison. After she has said to Milly: "Oh, you may very well loathe me yet!", her friend asks: "Why do you say such things to me?" And the answer comes in the form of: "Because you're a dove." After this Milly "felt herself ever so delicately, so considerately, embraced; not with familiarity or as a liberty taken, but almost ceremonially and in the manner of an *accolade;* partly as if, though a dove who could perch on a finger, one were also a princess with whom forms were to be observed. It even came to her, through the touch of her companion's lips, that this form, this cool pressure, fairly sealed the sense of what Kate had just said." And now follows the most significant part in connection with this first dove image. Kate's name for her is "like an inspiration" to Milly: "she found herself accepting as the right one ... the name so given her. She met it on the instant as she would have met the revealed truth; it lighted up the strange dusk in which she lately had walked. *That* was what was the matter with her. She was a dove. Oh, *wasn't* she?" Kate's name gives Milly a valuable clue to the way she and Mrs. Lowder regard her. She decides at once to assume the part, to act as a dove should, and so make use of the impression she leaves on others for her own ends. This gives her an immense advantage over them, the first time when she faces Mrs. Lowder afterwards, whose words affect her as those "of dove cooing to dove". And Milly's answer to that lady's vital question "had prepared itself while aunt Maud was on the stair; she had felt in a rush all the reasons that would make it the most dovelike; and she gave it, while she was about it, as earnest, as candid. 'I don't *think,* dear lady, he's [Merton] here.' It gave her straightway the measure of the success she could have as a dove: that was recorded in the long look of deep criticism, a look without a word, that Mrs. Lowder poured forth." Although Milly is convinced from her talk with Kate that Merton has returned to England, she lies to Mrs. Lowder. This answer, of course, strengthens aunt Maud's conviction that Milly is very innocent and can easily be exploited. And when the girl is left alone with Mrs. Stringham, "she studied again the dovelike and so set her companion to mere rich reporting that she averted all inquiry into her own case. That, with the new day, was once more her law ... She should have to be clear as to how a dove *would* act[65]." Now that we know that Milly is shrewd enough to "act" like a dove quite consciously, we may be sure that, in Venice, she soon sees through Mrs. Lowder's and Kate's plans for Merton and herself. These intentions are emphasized when Kate says to Merton: "Everything suits her so—especially her pearls ... She's a dove ... and one somehow doesn't think of doves as bejewelled. Yet they suit her down to the ground." Densher's subsequent reflections on Kate's remarks are most revealing. "Milly was indeed a dove; this was the figure, though it most applied to her spirit. But he knew in a moment that Kate was just now ... exceptionally under the impression of that element of wealth in her which ... was a great power, and which was dovelike only so far as one remembered that doves have wings and wondrous flights, have them as well as tender tints and soft sounds ... such wings could in a given case—*had*, in fact, in the case in which he was concerned—spread themselves for protection. Hadn't they, for that matter, lately taken an inordinate reach, and weren't Kate and Mrs. Lowder, weren't Susan Shepherd and he, wasn't *he* in particular, nestling under them to a great increase of immediate ease?[66]" In this passage are contained all the elements expressed through the dove image. For Kate, Milly's dove-like character becomes a means to an end; she thinks it possible to gain possession of her "pearls", which stand for Milly's fortune, by animating Merton to make up to the doomed "dove". To him, however, another important aspect becomes apparent, as he reflects on the power which this wealth represents. Milly has "wings and wondrous flights", and may do things not in the least expected by others. Yet another point touched upon here is that the wings can be used for protection, and it is Merton himself who feels that he, more than any one else, is "nestling under them". Shortly after Milly's death Mrs. Lowder says to Merton: "Our dear dove then, as Kate calls her, has folded her wonderful wings." And she adds: "Unless it's more true ... that she has spread them the wider." With this remark she shows that she still thinks to have secured Milly's money for Merton and Kate. When he takes up Mrs. Lowder's thought with "Rather, yes—spread them the wider[67]", he certainly attaches a different meaning to Milly's spreading of her wings, which is also referred to when Kate says, at the very end of the novel: "I used to call her, in my stupidity—for want of anything better—a dove. Well, she stretched out her wings, and it was to *that* they reached. They cover us[68]." From one point of view Milly's wings cover Merton and Kate, for has she not left the best part of her fortune to him? But they also cover him in a special way, for through her death he comes to understand her: he has realized the greatness and beauty of her mind and spirit. If he was not in love with Milly during her lifetime, he is now in love with her memory. And this as well as his awareness of his detestable behaviour towards Milly prevents him from accepting her money. He is willing to marry Kate without it, but Milly's magnanimity prevents him from making use of it in a marriage with Kate. Thus her wings cover the two lovers in a different sense from that which Mrs. Lowder and Kate had anticipated, turning into a heavy oppression Merton's feeling of guilt on account of their despicable behaviour during Milly's lifetime.

Thus the first dove images reveal to us, as we have seen, that Milly has already realized how much she stands to gain by entering whole-heartedly into the part assigned to her; and from that moment onwards all her actions seem to be a preparation for her death and her last supreme deed of generosity. In the end it is not the weakness and helplessness of the dove which triumphs, but her purity and power as shown in her "wondrous flight" which indeed Merton's reflections had anticipated.

5. Minor Forms of Iterative Imagery

In *The Ambassadors* a golden nail image, which is used recurrently, is of particular interest. It emphasizes Strether's growing dependence upon Madame de Vionnet and is, therefore, supplementary to the iterative boat metaphors. When the image first appears he has just thought to be in "the very act of arranging with her for his independence". He had asked a small favour of her, and she had obliged him, adding "Thank you" with "peculiar gentleness". "The sound of it lingered with him, making him fairly feel as if he had been tripped up and had a fall ... he had, ... quite stupidly, committed himself, and, with the subtlety sensitive on the spot, to an advantage, she had driven in, by a single word, a little golden nail, the sharp intention of which he signally felt. He had not detached, he had more closely connected himself[69]." He had come out from Woollett in order to act, but now his was merely a passive rôle of observation and discrimination. Other people, Madame de Vionnet for instance, act. He is not in a position to meet her "subtlety"; he has become a mere tool in the hands of the magnificent French lady, a situation which, to a great extent, has been made possible by his admiration for her. He appears as the most valuable and precious weapon that she has, for she uses a "golden nail" to fasten him to her. By doing him a favour she obliges him to do her one in return. When she, therefore, sees a certain danger that she might lose Chad, she makes Strether promise that he will "see him" and, by implication, also herself "through". The first of the golden nail images occurs at the end of the sixth instalment which was published in June, while the second is introduced at the beginning of the July issue. After Strether has given his promise "she pushed back her chair and was the next moment on her feet. 'Thank you!' she said with her hand held out to him across the table and with no less a meaning in the words than her lips had so particularly given them after Chad's dinner. The golden nail she had then driven in pierced a good inch deeper[70]." Although James recalls the occasion by his reference to "Chad's dinner" and by having Madame de Vionnet say "Thank you" again, it is primarily by the golden nail image that the reader's mind is carried back to the particular scene. The slight change in the image itself signifies that Strether has now committed himself even more deeply.

A recurrent image which occurs in *The Golden Bowl* is less impressive because the two sequels to the initial elaborate image are rather weak, though the reference to the introductory metaphor is still obvious. The images convey Amerigo's reflections about the obscurity of the motives of people like Fanny Assingham.

> He remembered to have read ... the story of the shipwrecked Gordon Pym, who, drifting in a small boat further toward the North Pole—or was it the South?—than any one had ever done, found at a given moment before him a thickness of white air that was like a dazzling curtain of light, concealing as darkness conceals, yet of the colour of milk or of snow ... The state of mind of his new friends had resemblances to a great white curtain. He had never known curtains but as purple even to blackness—but as producing where they hung a darkness intended and ominous. When they were disposed as to shelter surprises the surprises were apt to be shocks[71].

The comparison with Poe's short story emphasizes Amerigo's inability to make out the intentions and motives of the people he is in contact with. He cannot understand them properly, least of all perhaps Fanny Assingham. At best the prince can discern the facts of the situations in which he finds himself, but hardly ever does he perceive the reasons which lie behind them—a condition which may be seen when the image is taken up again two pages later. "Lost there in the white mist was the seriousness in *them* that made them so take him. It was even in Mrs. Assingham, in spite of her having ... a more mocking spirit. All he could say as yet was that he had done nothing, so far as to break any charm. What should he do if he were to ask her frankly this afternoon what *was,* morally speaking, behind their veil? It would come to asking what they expected him to do[72]." The prince wishes just to enjoy being taken seriously without attempting to find out why, for he knows he might be burdened with a responsibility. At the opening of the second chapter he confesses to Fanny that he has fears as to his recent marriage. Here a second reference to the Poe image is introduced: "'Terribly afraid. I've now but to wait to see the monster come. They're not good days; they're neither one thing nor the other. I've really *got* nothing, yet I've everything to lose. One doesn't know what still may happen.' The way she laughed at him was for an instant almost irritating; it came out, for his fancy, from behind the white curtain. It was a sign, that is, of her deep serenity, which worried instead of soothing him[73]." These three images are significant only in so far as they powerfully prepare for the first elaborate water metaphor, used soon afterwards by Amerigo in a further discussion with Fanny. But as they form a separate group in themselves, they cannot be regarded as belonging to the iterative water images[74].

B. PREPARATORY IMAGES

James developed two forms of the preparatory image. It may either serve as a preparation of an event happening immediately afterwards, or for something occurring only much later. The constructive function is particularly evident in the second form of the preparatory metaphor. Frequently, it is only when one remembers an image introduced, it may be, many pages previously, that later happenings seem plausible or sufficiently motivated. Both forms of the preparatory image are used to a great extent in the last three novels, but in the early works only occasional use is made of them.

Cecilia points forward to Roderick's failure as an artist by doubting whether he will really develop in the way Rowland and he himself anticipate. "Circumstances, with our young man, have a great influence, as is proved by the fact that although he has been fuming and fretting here for the last five years, he has nevertheless ... found it easy ... to vegetate. Transplanted to Rome, ... he'll put forth a denser leafage ... I hope with all my heart that the fruit will be proportionate to the foliage. Don't think me a bird of ill omen; only remember that you will be held to a strict account[75]." A remark made by Gloriani, who is an artist himself carries more weight as a prophecy and preparation for Roderick's failure. When he sees a photograph of Roderick's statuette of the water-drinker, he admires the earlier masterpiece greatly, but at the same time utters the following warning: "This sort of thing is like a man trying to lift himself up by the seat of his trousers. He may stand on tip-toe, but he can't do more. Here you stand on tip-toe, very gracefully, I admit; but you can't fly; there's no use trying[76]." Gloriani sees in the water-drinker the highest achievement possible, but he foresees too that Roderick will never mount any higher. These two examples show clearly that the preparatory metaphors are not yet very powerful. Nor are they used systematically; they do not, therefore, fulfil a structural purpose.

It is only in *The Portrait* that the first few examples of any significance occur. In the preface James says that the main question is what Isabel would *do*. In order to heighten suspense about this question he inserted some suggestions as to what she *might* do. Among these are some of the images which may be called prophetic as well as preparatory. Henrietta Stackpole is one of the characters who, now and then, utters her fears about Isabel's development. She says to Ralph for instance: "Isabel is changing every day; she is drifting away,—right out to sea. I have watched her, and I can see it[77]." She is here referring to the dangers of Europe with which her innocent and inexperienced compatriot is confronted, and to which, she fears, the girl will sooner or later fall a victim. The water image may here be interpreted in the same way as those at the beginning of *The Ambassadors,* where America represents the shore of safety, and Europe the treacherous and dangerous sea. Ralph uses a similar image for Isabel's attitude towards her suitors. But he is much more confident about Isabel's journey upon the sea of Europe: "She has started on an exploring expedition, and I don't think she will change her course, at the outset, at a signal from Gilbert Osmond. She may have slackened speed for an hour, but before we know it she will be steaming away again[78]." Henrietta's and Ralph's views again stress the opposing attitudes they take to Isabel; Henrietta's is pessimistic, Ralph's is optimistic.

When Isabel's impression of her meeting with Goodwood in Florence is given in retrospect, the thought of this encounter inspires an image in her mind, which serves as a preparation for his final attack at Gardencourt, described nine chapters later. Isabel recalls that their meeting "had had quite the character of a complete rupture", but his extreme aggressiveness has made a lasting impression upon her: "He left her, that morning, with the sense of an unnecessary shock; it was like a collision between vessels in broad daylight. There had been no mist, no hidden current, to excuse it, and she herself had only wished to steer skilfully. He had bumped against her prow, however, while her hand was on the tiller, and ... had given the lighter vessel a strain, which still occasionally betrayed itself in a faint creaking[79]." If we turn back to the chapter in which this particular encounter is described, we find that there he at first affected her as "straight, strong and fresh". Then she is afraid of her visitor, who looks at her "with his stiff persistency,—a persistency in which there was almost a want of tact; especially as there was a dull, dark beam in his eye, which rested on her almost like a physical weight[80]". Her memory of Caspar's visit was that of his foremost wish for physical possession, an impression that is fortified by his behaviour after Ralph's death.

Isabel's unhappiness and its extent is foreshadowed when Madame Merle, even before the marriage, says to Osmond: "You're unfathomable ... I am frightened at the abyss I shall have dropped her into[81]." This image prepares for the scene in which Isabel becomes aware of the gulf that has opened up between her husband and herself, and sees herself as in a dungeon with Osmond's mind peeping down from a high window. Another scene which is prepared much earlier is the Countess Gemini's revelation. Isabel does not like her very much; nevertheless it appears to the Countess "that, different as they were in appearance and general style, Isabel and she had a patch of common ground somewhere, which they would set their feet upon at last. It was not very large, but it was firm, and they should both know it when once they touched it[82]." This "patch of common ground" is the Countess's knowledge about the true relationship between Madame Merle and Osmond, which primarily concerns Isabel.

Mrs. Gereth's sudden removal of the works of art might have been as surprising to the reader as it is to Fleda had not James prepared us for this move through an image, in which Poynton is pictured as a ship of which Mrs. Gereth is the captain. "Pale but radiant, her back to the wall, she planted herself there as a heroine guarding a treasure. To give up the ship was to flinch from her duty; there was something in her eyes that declared she would die at her post[83]." She has to save her collection of *objets d'art* at any cost. Should she have to leave Poynton without the treasures, it would mean certain shipwreck. She has, therefore, to guard them as a whole, although Fleda had thought that the mistress of Poynton had made a concession and "had finally accepted the problem of knocking together a shelter with the small salvage of the wreck[84]". The image quoted above can also be regarded as foreshadowing the battle images.

Fleda's final breakdown and the disclosure of her last secret is also partly inferred by an image which is introduced after she has left Mrs. Gereth at Ricks. But without her she feels lonely. She seems to be bereft of friends and the easy comradeship they bring. "The lady of Ricks had made a desert round her, possessing and absorbing her so utterly that the others had fallen away ... Her only plan was to be as quiet as a mouse, and when she failed in the attempt to lose herself in the flat suburb she resembled a lonely fly crawling over a dusty chart[85]." She has nobody to take into her confidence, and deliberately avoids meeting or seeing any one; meanwhile her inner burden grows and grows. We can already foresee a moment when she will no longer be able to bear alone the burden which has steadily been accumulating on her spirit. The breaking point arrives during her second meeting with Owen in town.

We also find in *The Old Things* the first application of the device of preparing a remark by a preceding image. Thus its impact is made much greater; it gains weight and stands out in its true significance in relation to the totality of the plot. The example occurs during the great scene of climax when

Mrs. Gereth discloses, to Fleda's unspeakable horror, that as a result of her wrong calculations she has sent all the *objets d'art* back to Poynton. "Mrs. Gereth stood there in all the glory of a great stroke. 'I've settled you.' She filled the room, to Fleda's scared vision, with the glare of her magnificence. 'I've sent everything back.'[86]" The image of her filling the whole room with her "magnificence" anticipates the importance of the following remark, and it makes us pause and think over everything that her sudden action implies. As the image occurs in Fleda's consciousness we have to judge Mrs. Gereth's remark from her point of view. Fleda, of course, knows at once that Poynton with its beautiful works of art is now irretrievably lost to Mona, which also means that she now must bury all her hopes relating to Owen. It is not surprising that James should have made use of this kind of imagery for the first time in this novel, for it is essentially a dramatic device which heightens the tension of the passage.

In *The Ambassadors* we find several images which prepare for the complications and obstructions which Strether encounters in his efforts to fulfil his mission. After his first meeting with Chad he is at a complete loss as to what he should do, how he should judge his "almost monstrous" change. But he resolves to find out first every element that has contributed to Chad's transformation. His "note" is that of "discrimination". How much there is still to be found out and Strether's realization of how difficult it will be to do so is expressed in one of his remarks to Maria Gostrey: "It's a plot ... there's more in it than meets the eye ... It's a plant![87]" The significance and preparatory part of this remark is that he likens the plot to a "plant", thus implying that it will grow from day to day, that new elements will always show up, and that it will be a very long time before he has found out everything that concerns his mission. Shortly afterwards we find two other important images. Both Strether and Maria are convinced that a woman is playing a decisive part in Chad's life. "Consider and judge her only in *him*", she says to Strether. But it is exactly in the logic of such a statement that his great danger lies. "He had the courage at least of his companion's logic. 'Because then I shall like her?' He almost looked, with his quick imagination, as if he already did, though seeing at once also the full extent of how little it would suit his book[88]." This image anticipates his later dependence upon Madame de Vionnet and the effect it has upon his mission. When it is introduced, she has not yet made her appearance. But he is quite aware that, should he like her, it would mean taking a positive attitude towards Chad's development and moving away from the duty he had come to fulfil. In the same connection Maria, "the priestess of the oracle", makes a prophecy which foreshadows the outcome of the relationship between Chad and Marie de Vionnet. "His disavowal of her isn't, all the same, pure consideration. There's a hitch ... It's the effort to sink her[89]." The truth of this remark only becomes apparent at the very end of the novel, when Chad drops Madame de Vionnet. Maria's picture also establishes a direct relation to the much later scene when they appear together in a boat.

Strether's failure, from the point of view of Woollett, is prepared for by another significant metaphor: "He failed quite to see how his situation could clear up at all logically except by some turn of events that would give him the pretext of disgust. He was building from day to day on the possibility of disgust, but each day brought forth meanwhile a new and more engaging bend of the road. That possibility was now ever so much further from sight than on the eve of his arrival[90]." He gets more and more involved in Chad's affairs, moves further and further away from home. He has now reached a point where he sees but one remote chance of his taking Mrs. Newsome's side again: the "possibility of disgust", which she had thought he should find from the very beginning. But he had got quite a different impression, and now the likelihood of his being disgusted is much remoter than on the day of his arrival in Europe. His failure is almost certain, and he is convinced that should disgust come his way it would be "at best inconsequent and violent".

One of the most important preparatory images is Maria's hint as to what Strether's future will be after his return to Woollett. As it occurs at the very end of the novel it is to be considered rather as a prophecy. Referring to Mrs. Newsome and Chad she says to Strether: "What I mean is ... that with such a spirit—the spirit of curses!—your breach is past mending. She has only to know what you've done to him never again to raise a finger[91]." Strether's future life will have to be lived entirely away from Mrs. Newsome. In other words he will have to start a completely new one.

Among the images immediately preparing an important statement the most striking is that which precedes Sarah's ultimatum to Strether. It is given indirectly as occurring in his thoughts, thus welding the metaphor and Sarah's ultimatum together:

> when Strether had spoken of Waymarsh's leaving him, and that had necessarily brought on a reference to Mrs. Pocock's similar intention, the jump was but short to supreme lucidity. Light became indeed after that so intense that Strether would doubtless have but half made out, in the prodigious glare, by which of the two the issue had been in fact precipitated. It was, in their contracted quarters, as much there between them as if it had been something suddenly spilled, with a crash and a splash, on the floor. The form of his submission was to be an engagement to acquit himself within the twenty-four hours[92].

The ultimatum formulated in the last sentence gains a tremendous emphasis from the preceding pictorial passage, particularly from the "crash and splash, on the floor". Again we have a form of "drama through metaphor".

James has slightly extended this device in *The Wings*. Here the images not only point to the importance of a subsequent remark, but sometimes also its nature or the effect it has on another character. When Milly and Mrs. Stringham are together in the Swiss Alps the following incident takes place: "It was now as if, before this repast, Milly had designed to 'lie down'; but at the end of three minutes more she was not lying down, she was saying instead, abruptly, with a transition that was like a jump of four thousand miles: 'What was it that, in New York, on the ninth, when you saw him alone, Dr. Finch said to you?'[93]" This question initiates the theme of Milly's illness which hovers in the background throughout the novel. She has a suspicion that she is incurably ill, and she is preoccupied with this idea. By her abrupt outbreak into this question, and by means of the image that leads up to it, the significance of this problem is duly stressed. It prepares us for the importance which Milly herself attributes to the state of her health.

It is essential to the understanding of the development of the plot that the reader should be well aware of the fact that in the early stages of her friendship with Kate Milly does not suspect that she cares for Merton. To keep this secret from her is one of the major conditions for the success of Kate's plans. This is elucidated when she says to Merton: "'She regards me as already ... her dearest friend ... We're in, she and I, ever so deep.' And it was to confirm this that, as if it had flashed upon her that he was somewhere at sea, she threw out at last her own real light. 'She doesn't, of course, know I care for *you*. She thinks I care so little that it's not worth speaking of.' That he *had* been somewhere at sea these remarks made quickly clear, and Kate hailed the effect with surprise. 'Have you been supposing that she does know—?'[94]" Apart from giving Kate's central remark the required weight, the image of Merton's being "at sea" again stresses the fact that he is not the most intelligent of men. He is very slow in grasping certain obvious matters, and is even more clumsy in certain things he *does*. In the description of one of his meetings with Milly in Venice a metaphor makes it apparent that his subsequent remark is bound to have just the opposite effect upon her to what he had desired. "It pleased him to think of 'tact' as his present prop in doubt ... It had to serve now, accordingly, to help him not to sweeten Milly's hopes. He didn't want to be rude to them, but he still less wanted them to flower again in the particular connection; so that, casting about him, in his anxiety, for a middle way to meet her, he put his foot, with unhappy effect, just in the wrong place. 'Will it be safe for you to break into your custom of not leaving the house?'[95]" Only through the image do we know that he realizes at once that he has said the wrong thing, because his question is the expression of his belief that she is extremely ill. "He had done what ... she had asked him in London not to do; he had touched, all alone with her here, the supersensitive nerve of which she had warned him[96]."

Apart from these immediately preceding images there is a large group of metaphors which anticipate events that take place only much later. Mrs. Lowder's efforts to marry Kate to Lord Mark are carefully prepared by a very early image in which it is said of Kate that "she was to set forth in pursuit of Lord Mark on some preposterous theory of the premium to success. Mrs. Lowder's hand had attached it, and it figured at the end of the course as a bell that would ring, break out into public clamour, as soon as touched[97]." The "premium to success" is an unmistakable allusion to Lord Mark's money. Another image prepares us for Milly's illness and also for the final break between her and Kate. In the very early stages of the friendship between the two it is said of Kate—though in a "dead" metaphor—that she "had, at such a point as this, no suspicion of a rift within the lute—by which we mean not only none of anything's coming between them, but none of any definite flaw in so much clearness of quality[98]". The "lute" signifies Milly; the "rift" within this precious and delicate instrument has a double meaning, which is hinted at in the subsequent explanatory remarks. What will finally come between Kate and Milly is simply the latter's fortune, while the "flaw" alludes to Milly's state of health. By the choice of the image James is also able to convey the impression that her illness is not an obvious defect, and cannot easily be detected.

Her early death and the manner of it is foreshadowed at a comparatively early point. Susan has said to Milly that she is not "as sound and strong" as she insists on having her, to which Milly's rejoinder is: "The day I *look* as sound and strong as that, ... on that day I shall be just sound and strong enough to take leave of you sweetly for ever. That's where one is ... when even one's *most* 'beaux moments' aren't such as to qualify, so far as appearance goes, for anything gayer than a handsome cemetery. Since I've lived all these years as if I were dead, I shall die, no doubt, as if I were alive— which will happen to be as you want me[99]." It is as if Milly has, at this moment, a presentiment of her early death. And its effect on Merton and Kate strengthens the truth of her remark that she is more "alive" after her death than in her life[100].

We are prepared for her final act of magnanimity, overwhelming in its surprise, during Merton's last discussion with Mrs. Stringham in Venice. The tension and suspense occasioned by Milly's unfathomable behaviour makes this a most dramatic scene. Mrs. Stringham's first words are in the form of an image, which conveys the whole atmosphere of her encounter with Densher: "She has turned her face to the wall[101]." The meaning of this image is that she refuses to communicate with any one; she just silently clings to life. A little later during that talk the initial image is taken up again in Densher's thoughts, but this time with more power and intensity: "He recognised in her personal ravage that the words she had just uttered to him were the one flower she had to throw. They were all her consolation for him, and the consolation, even, still depended on the event. She sat with him, at any rate, in the grey clearance—as sad as a winter dawn—made by their meeting. The image she again evoked for him loomed in it but the larger. 'She has turned her face to the wall.'[102]" In this passage we see a combination of the two forms of the preparatory image. The significance of "she has turned her face to the wall" is emphasized by the picture of the atmosphere in which Merton's and Mrs. Stringham's discussion takes place, while it also makes us anticipate some unexpected events of great consequence still to come. The sadness of the "winter dawn" is also an indirect characterization of their spiritual condition at that particular moment.

The consummate artistry displayed by James in some of his preparatory images can perhaps be best shown by an example from *The Golden Bowl*. In the first chapter he gives us a very significant metaphor from which we can draw valuable conclusions about Maggie's reaction to her decisive discovery. She says to Amerigo: "I believe things enough about you, my dear, to have a few left if most of them, even, go to smash. I've taken care of *that*. I've divided my faith into water-tight compartments. We must manage not to sink." The prince wants to know more explicitly what she means by her metaphor. "You do believe I'm not a hypocrite? You recognise that I don't lie or dissemble or deceive? Is *that* water-tight?" And Maggie's answer must come as a relief to him and give him confidence: "Water-tight—the best compartment of all? Why, it's the best cabin and the main deck and the engine-room and the steward's pantry! It's the ship itself—it's the whole line. It's the captain's table and all one's luggage—one's reading for the trip[103]." This passage, with the word "smash" as a clear allusion, points forward to the scene of the breaking of the bowl. What is more important is that this early passage emphasizes the fact that Maggie sees so many virtues in her prince that even this future trying incident will not completely shake her confidence in him; she is, on the contrary, determined to make every effort possible to ensure their happiness.

In *The Golden Bowl* the device of the immediately preparing image is developed to serve a wider purpose. Not only does it prepare us for the importance of a subsequent remark, but also for a whole passage essential for the understanding of the novel. One such consists of Adam's reflections about his marriage. He is, at the beginning, unable to find a satisfactory solution to the problem of forming a new and intimate tie for himself without abandoning his daughter. But then, all of a sudden, he is in possession of a key: "Light broke for him at last, indeed, quite as a consequence of the fear of breathing a chill upon this luxuriance of her spiritual garden. As at a turn of his labyrinth he saw his issue, which opened out so wide, for the minute, that he held his breath with wonder[104]." Through this metaphorical passage we are made aware that his justification of his marriage is about to follow. The image acts like a signal, giving us a kind of warning, and marking the importance of the subsequent sentences.

Yet another newly-developed variation of the immediately preceding image is that in some cases it does give us the clue to the attitude which a particular character will take during the following discussion. An image which occurs just before the first conversation between Amerigo and Maggie after the breaking of the bowl shows us the line she will take in her dispute with her husband: "Mrs. Verver rose between them there, for the time, in august and prohibitive form; to protect her, defend her, explain about her, was, at the least, to bring her into the question—which would be by the same stroke to bring her husband. But this was exactly the door Maggie wouldn't open to him[105]." Thus all her efforts are directed towards avoiding the subject of Charlotte and consequently that of her father. Neither of them is mentioned once during their discussion. There are, of course, allusions to her, but she always appears as part of the "we" which comprises Amerigo and Charlotte. But such examples are comparatively rare; it is the usual form of the immediately preparing image which is still predominant. This may be seen in one example where an important remark of Charlotte's to Amerigo is prepared for as follows: "As soon as they were alone together, however, she mounted, as with the whizz and the red light of a rocket, from the form to the fact, saying straight out, as she stood and looked at him: 'What else, my dear, what in the world else can we do?'[106]" Here her exclamation refers to their intimacy, and the lies and subterfuges they are forced to take refuge in so that they may be able to continue their secret meetings.

All James's preparatory images have one thing in common: They are always comparatively short and concise, especially the immediately preceding images, a fact which is explained by their function. They must not carry too much weight themselves, but rather add it to that for which they prepare us. Only in those images which foreshadow later happenings does James sometimes allow himself to extend the metaphor to greater epic length. In these cases they have to produce a stronger effect, because it must be a lasting one, as for instance in the metaphors relating to Goodwood's aggressiveness, Milly's death or Maggie's faith in her husband. They have to form the basis of later events, and in them the constructive function of the preparatory image is most apparent.

CHAPTER 7

The Transition from Metaphor to Symbol

A careful study of the symbolism in James's work yields material enough for an extensive work. Therefore a comprehensive treatment of his symbols will not be attempted in this chapter. They are considered only in so far as the study of the imagery in the preceding chapters leads up to certain conclusions concerning the use of symbols.

A first important hint of the difference in treatment between the early and the late works is the titles of the novels themselves. *Roderick Hudson* or *The Portrait of a Lady* suggest a literal and predominantly obvious approach, whereas the titles of the last novels—for example *The Wings of the Dove*—point to central symbols that govern each of these works[1]. The treatment of the plots confirms the impression conveyed by the titles. We witness a gradual change of emphasis, from the literal and specific to the symbolic and general. This evolution can be most directly studied in the development of the imagery, the function of which in the early works is to characterize and to emphasize the particular, thus adding colour to the narrative. In the later works the metaphors still have a special meaning, but as well as this they often become symbols of important fundamental matters, conveying James's own views about the relation of life, art and money, as exemplified, in most cases, in the meeting of Europeans and Americans.

Consistent or pronounced symbolism in any form is still quite remote from the style of *Roderick Hudson*. Seen in relation to the later novels, Christina Light may be conceived as the first character who symbolizes the destructive powers of beauty and corruption. The power of money to mar and destroy is also revealed in her. She is a "beauty of beauties", and "her face is her fortune[2]". But this symbolism is not supported by any significant images, as for instance in the case of Madame Merle or Kate Croy. The most obvious symbolism is that which brings out the contrast between light and darkness, life and death. Christina Light represents the dangerous, delusive light which is the chief agent leading Roderick to destruction. The "white light of a splendid pearl", which is the way her appearance is described, and the previous image quoted above belong—although they are very conventional—to the earliest, and still weak sketches of the theme of the relation between money, beauty and corruption, which James made central in *The Wings*. Symbolism of light and darkness becomes most apparent at the end of *Roderick Hudson,* where the happenings seem to be a proof of the correctness of Rowland's feelings about Roderick at an earlier point. We read there of the "sunshine of genius" which has also its "storms[3]". And it is in a heavy storm in the Swiss Alps that Roderick's genius is extinguished. But his death appears as a redemption for him, as the beginning of a new life in a better world, in pure and continual light, for such is the effect of the image introduced, when Rowland and Sam Singleton have reached the place from which he has fallen to his death: "They looked up through their horror at the cliff from which he had apparently fallen, and which lifted its blank and stony face above him, with no care now but to drink the sunshine on which his eyes were closed[4]." A religious aspect is introduced by this thought of life after death.

One of the most interesting features of the novel is the symbolism inherent in the relationship between Rowland and Roderick. They leave a strange impression of unity, composed of complementary qualities, so that they appear as the projections of two opposing forces in one and the same human being. Roderick's nature is "strong in impulse, in talk, in responsive emotion", qualities lacking in Rowland, who is possessed instead by a strength "in will, in action, in power to feel and to do singly[5]". More evidence to strengthen the supposition that they symbolize two divergent forces in one and the same human being is the fact that *Roderick Hudson* belongs, together with *The Ambassadors,* to James's most autobiographical novels. Rowland's and Roderick's experiences in Europe have much in common with James's own, particularly in the year 1874, most of which he spent in Italy[6]. In Roderick, James portrayed the kind of artist he himself did not want to become. And as he identifies himself very much with Rowland, the governing unity becomes apparent in James himself. The fact that Roderick is really a projection, as it were, of Rowland's mind, is also stressed in James's preface[7]. In the novel itself we find only one image which expresses the symbolic unity. It occurs at the beginning of the first chapter, when Rowland says to Cecilia: "Do you know I sometimes think that I'm a man of genius, half-finished? The genius has been left out, the faculty of expression is wanting; but the need of expression remains, and I spend my days groping for the latch of a closed door[8]." Soon afterwards Rowland finds the "genius" that has been left out, in the person of Roderick Hudson.

The theme of the corruption of European civilization is symbolized much more strongly in *The Portrait*. And it is very powerfully strengthened by significant images. The two metaphors in which Madame Merle is characterized as a "porcelain cup" that has been "chipped and cracked" has a similar symbolic value to that of the golden bowl, which has a fault. Madame Merle's crack is the fault in her relationship with Osmond. Both in *The Portrait* and *The Golden Bowl* the flaws are discovered by the persons from whom they should have been hidden. The difference is that Maggie is able to mend the golden bowl of her married life again, whereas Isabel has been too completely deceived by the evil force incarnate in Madame Merle. New England innocence, as symbolized by Isabel Archer, thus becomes a victim of corrupt, decadent Europe, represented by Madame Merle and Osmond.

Nature plays a more significant part in *The Portrait* than in any other of James's novels. Most of the important scenes occur either in a garden, or at least in the open air, especially the proposals of Isabel's many suitors, and Goodwood's final attempt to win her. The garden image gives the happenings in real gardens a strong connection with Isabel's soul. It is as if Goodwood and Warburton were walking across Isabel's soul when they cross the lawn at Gardencourt in order to propose to her. Each of these proposals appears, therefore, as a temptation offered to her innocence. But the garden image symbolizes more than that. It is also an expression of her freedom, the restriction of which after her marriage is brought out by the picture in which Isabel's mind is described as a "small garden-plot" attached to Osmond's. In these garden scenes we have, then, an indirect characterization of Isabel's spiritual condition.

In *Roderick Hudson* the acquisition of wealth is only a minor theme accompanying Mrs. Light's efforts to marry her daughter to the wealthy prince Casamassima; the passion for the possession of works of art is not even raised as a subject. Both themes are prominent in James's mature novels, together with that of the familiar conflict between good and evil, innocence and corruption. Art, in James's first novel, is clearly a symbol for a positive value, the best that Europe represents. In *The Portrait* we already perceive a different conception of the relation between life and art, and significantly enough we encounter, in connection with Gilbert Osmond, the first *objet d'art* images. But their symbolism is not yet fully worked out, although Osmond's passion is certainly already a destructive force in his life, and therefore also in those lives which are closely bound up with his. *Objet d'art* images become the symbol for the inhuman, the overridingly selfish. As a result of the worship of his own ego he feels the urge to "acquire" Isabel as a visible idol standing for his selfishness. Osmond is the first in the series of such characters in James's novels. And this line is continued in Lord Mark and reaches its culmination in Adam Verver.

In *The Old Things* art and an overmastering desire for the possession of *objets d'art* have become the central subject. Art no longer represents a positive value, for it is too dominant in the lives of those concerned. It is a curse, which in the end destroys Mrs. Gereth's life and Fleda's hopes, and it is only in the complete destruction of the treasures that a positive value becomes apparent. The spoils, then, have the same symbolic importance as the golden bowl in the later novel; each is central to the whole work, and indeed composes the structure of the entire novel. Every step taken by either Mrs. Gereth or Mona Brigstock is governed by the *objets d'art*. The moral of *The Old Things* can perhaps best be summarized by saying that if art is to be a positive value in life, it must not be allowed to become dominant and exclusive, but should be restricted to its due place in one's life. From this point of view Fleda appears as the symbol of the truly human attitude towards life which, in her case, is governed by a sense of moral duty. Fleda, therefore, becomes a second structural centre of the novel, a pivot about which revolves everything that is positive and good. The iterative flying images symbolize the inevitable fate of the good woman in a world of corruption (as shown in Mrs. Gereth and Mona) and obtuseness (as represented by Owen). The fire which, in the end, consumes Poynton with all its treasures symbolizes, therefore, the destruction of the principal object of Mona's philistinism, and opens the way to a possible happiness between Owen and herself.

The Ambassadors is, in many ways, a more mature and complicated version of the theme which James treated in Roderick Hudson. There are, of course, many differences of emphasis. The whole novel describes the struggle within Strether of two opposing views, that with which he arrives in England, in which he sees Europe as the dwelling-place of evil, vice and corruption, and that which gradually begins to predominate in him, viz. that with its art, tradition and history, it offers more positive than negative values. The principal symbolic projections of these views are the characters of Mrs. Newsome on the one hand, and Madame de Vionnet on the other. If the former represents Strether's "old self", then, by analogy, Madame de Vionnet symbolizes his "new self". Gradually he moves away from Mrs. Newsome and Woollett to Madame de Vionnet and Paris. It becomes apparent, in this novel, that the various places on both sides of the Atlantic which figure in James's works symbolize different ways of living. In the preface to The Ambassadors he states clearly what he was aiming at when he chose Paris as the main scene for Strether's drama: "Which friendly test indeed was to bring him out, through winding passages, through alternations of darkness and light, very much in Paris, but with the surrounding scene itself a minor matter, a mere symbol for more things than had been dreamt of in the philosophy of Woollett. Another surrounding scene would have done as well for our show could it have represented a place in which Strether's errand was likely to lie and his crisis to await him[9]." And when James chose Woollett, he did not mean that town in particular, but just "an American city of the second order ... an old and enlightened Eastern community, in short, which is yet not the seat of one of the bigger colleges[10]". What matters, then, in James's choice of his places is the background which they represent. The provincial character of Woollett makes the scene of climax in Gloriani's garden possible and plausible. That scene, which is full of significant images, symbolically marks the turning point in Strether's life.

James emphasized the significance of Strether's transformation by three different groups of images. First there are those which show Paris as a symbol of everything that is best—a complete contrast to Woollett. It is a "jewel brilliant and hard", where Strether has the feeling of being in possession of a "bag of gold". Gold and jewels are here not symbols for damnation, destructive and inhuman forces but, on the contrary, the most desirable and edifying values that Europe can offer. The most outstanding human representative of these values is Madame de Vionnet, and Strether's realization and acceptance of them, his growing sense for all that human history, tradition and culture represents, is symbolically worked out in his increasing passion and dependence upon Madame de Vionnet, again emphasized most significantly by the golden nail images and elaborate water metaphors.

The iterative use of architectural metaphors in *The Ambassadors* presents a case on the border-line between imagery and symbolism; the transition from the former to the latter can here best be studied. The passages in question do not contain what might be called true images; they rather create three different pictures of symbolical meaning in regard to Strether's transformation. In these passages we have in fact the most effective stress on his evolution, and moreover a proof of his positive attitude to it. The three phases could best be compared to the piers of a bridge; they carry the weight of the whole structure. The first passage shows Strether on the way to Chad's apartment for the first time. It is "a third floor on the Boulevard Malesherbes" with "windows of a continuous balcony". Looking at it from the opposite side of the street Strether has the feeling that "the balcony in question didn't somehow show as a convenience easy to surrender ... What call had he ... to like Chad's very house? High, broad, clear ... it fairly embarrassed our friend by the quality that ... it 'sprang' on him." Before he crosses the road in order to enter the house a significant incident occurs. On the balcony "a young man had come out ... and ... resting on the rail, had given himself up, while he smoked, to watching the life below". The most significant part of the passage is Strether's passionate wish about the young man on the balcony. "There was youth in the surrender to the balcony, there was youth, for Strether, at this moment, in everything but his own business; and Chad's thus pronounced association with youth had given the next instant, an extraordinary quick lift to the issue. The balcony ... testified suddenly ... to something that was up and up; they placed the whole case materially ... on a level that he found himself at the end of another moment rejoicing to think he might reach[11]." It is certainly not mere chance that James placed Chad's apartment on a third floor. It is an intentional contrast of levels: Strether down in the street and little Bilham standing high up on the balcony. The word "youth" is the one most frequently used in the above passage. Strether's hope to reach that level is therefore a symbolic expression of his wish to re-establish a contact with his own lost youth and the happiness of those early days of his life. The first stage towards the fulfilment of his wish is reached very quickly, by his contact with Chad's friend, and by his dining with him, Waymarsh and Miss Barrace in Chad's apartment. At this point the next important passage is introduced, the second pier of the bridge: "There was no great pulse of haste yet in this process of saving Chad ... as he sat, ... with his legs under Chad's mahogany, ... and with the great hum of Paris coming up in softness, vagueness—for Strether himself indeed already positive sweetness—through the sunny windows towards which, the day before, from below, his curiosity had raised its wings. The feeling that had been with him at that moment had borne fruit almost faster than he could taste it, and Strether literally felt, at the present moment, that there was a precipitation in his fate[12]." Several parts of this passage emphasize the fact that Strether is rapidly changing in his outlook, is moving away from Woollett and his mission. He sees no reason for "haste" in "saving Chad"; the "hum of Paris" already affects him as "positive sweetness", and he has reached the level on which he wished to be the day before. But he has not yet established communication with the lost spirit of his youth. Nor is he able to do it on the several occasions we meet him in Chad's apartment in the course of the novel. It happens only towards the end when he is pictured in the same position in which he, at the beginning, had seen little Bilham: he is alone on Chad's balcony looking down on the life of Paris. It is as if he had become identical with the little Bilham of the first passage quoted: "He spent a long time on the balcony; he hung over it as he had seen little Bilham hang the day of his first approach ... he passed back into the rooms, ... and, while he circulated and rested, tried to recover the impression that they had made on him three months before, to catch again the voice in which they had seemed then to speak to him. That voice ... failed audibly to sound; which he took as the proof of all the change in himself." Although only three months have elapsed since his arrival in Paris, this time appears much longer to him, so that the events during the early stages of his stay seem "a point in the far past". What brought about the change in him was that he felt free again and so could establish a relationship with "the youth of his own that he had long ago missed". During the time he waits for Chad, he realizes that he has gone as far as he can and as he wants to. It is for him "an hour full of strange suggestions, persuasions, recognitions; one of those that he was to recall, at the end of his adventure, as the particular handful that most had counted". But he is also made to realize that many things are irretrievably lost, that everything in Chad's apartment "represented the substance of his loss, put it within reach, within touch, made it, to a degree it had never been, an affair of the senses. That was what it became for him at this singular time, the

153

youth he had long ago missed—a queer concrete presence, full of mystery, yet full of reality, which he could handle, taste, smell, the deep breathing of which he could positively hear. It was in the outside air as well as within." This passage, in its richness and variety of metaphorical expression and poetic pictures is like a summary of the essential points in the novel. For Strether, this hour is the culmination of his stay in Paris, when he best recognizes his achievements and failures. Just before the meditations quoted above we see him looking at the objects lying on a table in Chad's apartment. Among them is, typically enough, one of those "lemon-coloured" novels of which he had once taken a few back to America, when he was still young and the world open to him. The whole atmosphere surrounding him in Chad's apartment is characterized by the "mellowest lamplight", which creates, in Strether's mind, a "soft circle" within which the novel has been pushed by Chad's servant[13]. The "soft circle" symbolically represents all that Strether has missed. He can now walk around it, but is no longer able to enter. After Chad's arrival the symbolic meaning of Strether's being on a higher level than he had been a few months before is strengthened: "It was as if their high place really represented some moral elevation from which they could look down on their recent past[14]." He is now completely on Chad's side. His contact with him and his friends has made him younger. But he finally goes back to Woollett because his reawakening has also shown him that he is too old to "live".

In *The Wings* James has found the most poignant symbols for his contrast between good and evil, innocence and corruption, American and European, in the image of the dove for Milly and that of the beast for Mrs. Lowder. We can consider the princess images on the one hand and the war images on the other as secondary symbols for this same contrast, but only the first group is consistently worked out. Whereas the beast images clearly denote brute force and treachery, the inhuman and vicious, the meaning of the dove symbol is much more intricate. It helps to lift James's international theme on to a level of great human tragedy. The dove is the symbol of peace and purity, but also of unlimited freedom. It is capable of great wondrous flights, but can also stretch out its wings to afford protection. Milly's freedom is her wealth of which she can, however, make only a limited use, as she is doomed to an early death. But her wealth is also her curse, because it is the prime cause of her tragedy, as well as of the downfall of Merton and Kate. It induces those pure creatures who strive for its possession to become vicious, treacherous and unscrupulous. It makes them inhuman, as it does Kate. All she comes to see in Milly is her fortune, and she shrinks from no means that might bring her into possession of it. In the scene of climax in Venice when Kate suggests to Merton that he should marry the dying Milly, her wealth comes to symbolize the whole difference between the two women: "Milly's royal ornament had—under pressure now not wholly occult—taken on the character of a symbol of differences, differences of which the vision was actually in Kate's face. It might have been in her face too that, well as she would certainly look in pearls, pearls were exactly what Merton Densher would never be able to give her. Wasn't *that* the great difference that Milly to-night symbolised?[15]" Milly's pearls represent not only the difference between her and Kate but between two worlds, that of America with its growing monetary potentiality and that of our Western civilization with its history, traditions, titles and ceremonies, but also its state of poverty. Kate is not wicked in herself, but represents the evil of the world into which she has been born. Her efforts to overcome this state lead ultimately to the frustration of her and Merton's hopes, and to the ruin of their possible happiness. Money thus becomes a symbol of the damned, who comprise both those born with it and those who try to acquire it. And from this we can understand the real symbolic meaning of Milly's stretching out her wings to cover Merton and Kate in protection. This picture creates a kind of unity between these three characters, making them foreigners in the world in which they are living. At the end of the novel James does not condemn Kate or Merton for their behaviour; he rather criticizes the civilization into which they were born, which has lost the ability to recognize true moral values. Mrs. Lowder, Lord Mark and Kate's father are immoral and selfish. Kate and Merton are moral in so far as they never intend to do Milly any harm. They want to enable her to enjoy as much happiness as her short life will allow. If they do it with selfish, personal ends in mind, it is, James suggests, the civilization they live in that forces them to do it.

This brings us to the symbolism of the Bronzino portrait which so resembles Milly. "She was the image of the wonderful Bronzino[16]." The most obvious symbolism in that scene which shows Milly and Lord Mark admiring the beautiful portrait is that it foreshadows Milly's short-lived happiness, her early death. She herself has a notion of it, when standing in front of the picture: "The lady in question, at all events, with her slightly Michaelangelesque squareness, her eyes of other days, her full lips, her long neck, her recorded jewels, her brocaded and wasted reds, was a very great personage—only unaccompanied by joy. And she was dead, dead, dead. Milly recognised her exactly in words that had nothing to do with her. 'I shall never be better than this.'[17]" This remark, the tears in her eyes, and Lord Mark's not understanding her, are indications that she is thinking of death, and that she will never be able to live her life to the full. The bringing together of Milly and the Bronzino points forward to her own future. But this symbolism, which relates the picture to Milly's illness and death, is the result of her own perceptiveness, the reflection of her own mind. We must also interpret this scene from James's point of view. He likens her to a beautiful Renaissance lady with whom Milly becomes identified through her death. Only in the past can her moral magnitude find a true equivalent. Such values are completely lost in the world in which she moves during her lifetime, a world that pays no heed to moral judgments. "It's another life[18]", Milly says later about the painting. Death appears as the beginning of a better life, just as in *Roderick Hudson*. In both novels death is but a symbol; with Roderick it stands for the dangers which may threaten a young American artist in Europe; for Milly it represents the dangers facing a valuable human being in surroundings where moral and ethical values are no longer respected.

In James's last novel, it is obvious why the golden bowl has a central symbolic value. It is the most comprehensive symbol that he ever found. It refers to every major theme treated in the novel, that of the contrast between good and evil, that of the collector's attitude towards *objets d'art,* and that of the influence of money on human relationships. Moreover, as a symbol, it is full of potentialities which are continually exploited. When it is first introduced, it stands for the relationship between Amerigo and Charlotte, which in the past had been a perfect gilded crystal bowl, but now shows a crack on the eve of his marriage. It is characteristic that only the prince is aware of it, when he, together with Charlotte, is shown the bowl in the little Bloomsbury shop. He is superstitious and anticipates that his relations to Charlotte may become a serious impediment to his happiness with Maggie, and later on to Charlotte's with Adam. From the Ververs' point of view the symbolism of the bowl at the beginning seems to be a different one. For them it is the prince, for whom Mr. Verver has paid with the sacrifice of his own "marriage" with his daughter. Neither he nor Maggie are aware of the flaw, and the question which looms in the background is always whether Mr. Verver has not paid too high a price. "But shall you at least get your money back?[19]" is what Amerigo asks his wife after her discovery, and this is the crucial question for the rest of the novel. Will she be able to restore her happiness? When Maggie gets hold of the bowl and becomes aware of the crack in it, it means not only that she knows of the intimacy between Charlotte and Amerigo, but also that she becomes aware of the flaw in the relationship between them all, in the order of their lives, and she knows that she and her father are as guilty as Amerigo and Charlotte. From the point of view of Maggie's discovery, the golden bowl becomes a symbol for both her and her father's marriages. The three pieces into which it splits, when Fanny smashes it on the floor, symbolize the triangle in which Maggie sees herself involved: Charlotte-Amerigo-herself. Adam is left out, because it is he above every one else whom she wants to spare. He must be kept innocent. All her subsequent efforts are to achieve a "happiness", as she says to Fanny Assingham, "without a hole in it big enough for you to poke in your finger". She wants "the golden bowl—as it *was* to have been ... The bowl with all our happiness in it. The bowl without the crack[20]." Without the "crack" in Maggie's faith. It really comes to the question of Blake's verses, to which Matthiesson rightly refers, although there is nowhere any indication that James had thought of them: "Can wisdom be kept in a silver rod,/ Or love in a golden bowl?[21]" Maggie, in the end, gives a triumphant "yes" to this question, but she can only do it after the complete sacrifice of her little platonic union with her father after she and her husband have left Adam's safe "boat". It is the triumph of love and humanity over morbidity and a life that is entirely governed by abstract laws of the god of money. Money has been the curse and destruction of Roderick, Isabel and Milly, and, in the form of works of art, of Mrs. Gereth. It threatens, in the same form again, the lives of the four major characters of *The Golden Bowl,* as is duly emphasized by the many *objet d'art* images which characterize the relationship of Adam Verver with the three others. And Maggie's desperate, but in the end victorious, struggle is best reflected in the many pictures of death and suffocation that predominate in her imagination. Horror, pain and evil are constantly before her eyes. She has visions of "bare blades", of her stuffing her handkerchief in her mouth, night and day, so as not to be heard moaning, or she feels assaulted, "as a beast might have leaped at her throat[22]". It is such images of suffering and death that take the lead in Maggie's visions. But it is just because she is so sensitive to evil that she does not become a victim. She restores the golden bowl in the end without the crack, and when she has finally reached her goal it is symbolized by an image that shows a clear allusion to the central symbol of the golden bowl: "Here it was, then, the moment, the golden fruit that had shone from afar[23]." The bowl becomes in the end the symbol for the victory of humanity and love, for the will to live in a world of growing terror, where money threatens to become a destructive power.

All James's symbols are derived from his own experience, from his acute observation of the world as it really is. In his later novels he gradually comes to use these symbols as a means of unfolding the thoughts, feelings and imaginations of his characters, thus providing the background to their actions with realistic images which analyse the essential differences between them. This deep and skilful exploration of the hidden springs of his characters' hopes and fears, desires and imaginations, is made possible by imagery which in its highest form has passed into a symbolism of profound and universal significance.

NOTES

The following abbreviations are used in these notes:

NYE   *The Novels and Tales of Henry James*, New York Edition, 24 volumes, London 1908–9.

N   *The Notebooks of Henry James*, edited by F. O. Matthiessen and K. B. Murdock, New York 1947.

AM   *The Atlantic Monthly.*

NAR   *The North American Review.*

C   Henry James, *The Wings of the Dove*, London (Constable) 1902.

M   Henry James, *The Golden Bowl*, London (Methuen) 1904, 2 volumes.

    In the notes the large roman after the symbol refers to the volume (the small roman in quotations from the NYE to the page in the preface), and the arabic to the page. An * after the page number refers to the appendix where the images to which the note refers are quoted in their context.

Chapter 1: The Significance of Imagery in the Work of Henry James

1 See Bibliography C.
2 *Neuenglische Stilistik*, p. 102 f.
3 NYE.
4 NYE, XVII, xxvii.
5 *Henry James: Les années dramatiques.*
6 James used to destroy these scenarios afterwards, and only in the cases of *The Ambassadors, The Ivory Tower* and *The Sense of the Past* have they been preserved.
7 *Henry James at Work.*
8 Ibid., p. 9
9 S. J. Brown, *The World of Imagery*, p. 33.
10 NYE, II, xxi.
11 NYE, V, xii.
12 NYE, VII, xii.
13 Ibid.
14 NYE, VII, xi.
15 *The Old Things* was the original title of *The Spoils of Poynton*. The nature of this study makes it necessary to analyse the imagery in the first versions of the novels.
16 *Henry James: The Major Phase.*
17 See Bibliography B.

Chapter 2: The Rhetorical Image

A. Comparison and Simile

1 See chapter 4, A.
2 Examples of "dead" images in James's novels: "as pretty as an angel"; "as pure as a pearl"; "as thin as air"; "as firm as a rock"; "as thick as thieves"; "as light as air"; "as free as air"; "behaving like an angel".
3 Examples: "as bright as the morning"; "as clear as noon"; "as soft as dusk"; "as fresh as morning light" (Thackeray uses the more common comparison to the rose); "the response was as prompt as if he had pressed a spring"; "as white as a corpse" (Thackeray always makes the common comparison between whiteness and snow).

4 AM, Dec. 1875, 661.

5 AM, June 1875, 650.

6 AM, Nov. 1875, 565.

7 AM, Dec. 1881, 759.

8 Ibid.

9 AM, May 1896, 631.

10 Owen Gereth "had his delicacies, but he hid them away like presents before Christmas" (AM, June 1896, 731); or: "It affected her like the crack of a whip." (AM, July 1896, 60); or: "the atmosphere of West Kensington, purified by the wind, was like a dirty coat that had been bettered by a dirty brush." (AM, Oct. 1896, 521.) The irony and sarcasm in this last example are obvious. Nevertheless, these images are merely decorative.

11 NAR, Jan. 1903, 141.

12 NAR, July 1903, 139. A further example of this kind comes from *The Wings:* "for many days other questions and other possibilities sounded with as little effect as a trio of penny whistles might sound in a Wagner overture." (C, 96.)

13 Under these fall those comparisons which seem to contain a forced relationship, as for instance: "the young girl's face remained serious, like the eastern sky when the opposite sunset is too feeble to make it glow." (AM, Feb. 1875, 153.) Or: "Florence in midsummer was perfectly void of travelers, and the dense little city gave forth its aesthetic aroma with a larger frankness, as the nightingale sings when the listeners have departed." (AM, Nov. 1875, 567.) In the first of these examples the linking of phenomena between which there is no similarity, is unconvincing, in the second the comparison of a passive state with an active doing.

14 M, I, 237.

15 M, II, 270.

B. Metaphor

16 As for instance: "The conversation ... furnished Rowland with food for reflection"—"he felt a profound disinclination to tie the knot again"—"It had the stamp of genius"—"he thought it would break the ice"—"the fatal hour ... had struck"—"leaning on the pure bosom of nature". Certain common metaphorical expressions occur in all James's fiction. Among these are: "to care a straw"; "to care a fig"; "to wash one's hand of something"; "to put one's finger on something"; "to hang fire", and so on.

17 James says that Roderick was "up to his knees in debt", and in *Castle Rackrent* we read "when a man's over head and shoulders in debt". Phrases with the expression "to care a straw" are frequently used both by James and Edgeworth and, for that matter, many other Victorian novelists. And compare the following examples from Edgeworth with the metaphors from *Roderick Hudson* quoted in the previous footnote: "to see through the thin veil with which politeness covers domestic misery"; "Sir Philip Baddely had the field to himself"; "I embraced the first opportunity ... of retaliation"; "Her Ladyship was running on to a fresh train of ideas"; "she shall find my doors shut."

18 M, I, 180.

19 M, I, 365.

20 A similar effect is achieved in a short addition to another quite ordinary metaphor. When James gives Maggie's impression of Charlotte and Amerigo, he writes: "the particular sense of them that she had taken home tonight had done her the service of seeming to break the ice where that formation was thickest." (M, II, 55.)

21 AM, June 1875, 647.

22 AM, Dec. 1880, 761.

A. Revised and Added Images

1 NYE, I, xviii.

2 NYE, I, 324.*

3 Of Roderick's face and glance we read in the first version: "with his head high and his brilliant glance unclouded." (AM, Oct. 1875, 385.) The one metaphorical adjective "unclouded" is too weak to create a vivid picture in the mind of the reader. Therefore James revised it into "with his head high and his face as clear as a beach at the ebb". (NYE, I, 355.) This simile certainly leaves a more lasting impression, and, at this point of the novel, James particularly wants to stress the fact that Roderick was yet without sorrows and doubts about his success as an artist. A similar improvement is brought about through the alteration of a description of the Cavaliere's smile. In the first edition the image is extremely vague and hardly pictorial. "This time, unmistakably, the Cavaliere smiled, but still in that very out-of-the-way place." (AM, Oct. 1875, 397.) It is impossible to imagine what James means by "out-of-the-way place". Only the final version brings clarity: "The Cavaliere's smile was like the red tip of a cigar seen for a few seconds in the dark." (NYE, I, 389.) This comparison conveys especially the uncertainty of the onlookers whether the Cavaliere has really smiled or whether it was only their imagination.

4 AM, March 1875, 310.

5 NYE, I, 119.

6 AM, Dec. 1881, 770.

7 NYE, IV, 436. Two other examples concern Ralph Touchett.

B. Added Images

8 AM, Sept. 1875, 276.

9 NYE, I, 342.

10 AM, Oct. 1875, 391.

11 NYE, I, 371.

12 "The truth was that he had simply accepted the situation" (AM, Nov. 1880, 606) is replaced by "His serenity was but the array of wild flowers niched in his ruin." (NYE, III, 54.) The situation which Ralph had accepted was his illness and unhappiness. The final version, however, expresses much more. It tells us that he tries to hide his unhappiness by pretending to be happy, gay, and serene, and that a sensitive person could very well discover his real state behind the mask he is wearing.

13 "If he had English blood in his veins it had probably received some French or Italian commixture; but he suggested, fine gold coin as he was, no stamp nor emblem of the common mintage that provides for general circulation; he was the elegant complicated medal struck off for a special occasion." (NYE, III, 329.) As a collector of *objets d'art* and because of the importance they have in his life Osmond foreshadows Adam Verver. He also shows a tendency to judge people from the art-collector's point of view.

14 NYE, III, 218.

15 NYE, III, 165.

16 NYE, III, 232.

17 NYE, IV, 433f.

18 When James, for instance, adds that Mrs. Gereth "felt a return of the tide of last night's irritation, a renewal of everything she could secretly suffer from ugliness and stupidity". (NYE, X, 3.) With this personification of ugliness and stupidity we identify Mona Brigstock. But the pictorial character of the image is so remote that it fails to impress the reader. The same is true when James adds that "Fleda Vetch was dressed

with an idea, though perhaps with not much else". (NYE, X, 5.) This is hardly more than a rhetorical image with little suggestive quality.

19 NYE, X, 149.

20 NYE, X, 193.

21 NYE, X, 253.

22 Mr. Leon Edel has shown that James "did not, in reality, 'interpolate' passages in his text, but rather restored such portions as he had been forced to remove for purpose of abridging the serial instalments". Mr. Edel points out further that James revised *The Ambassadors* extensively from serial to first edition, but that there were few changes from the latter to the NYE. (See "Henry James's Revisions for *The Ambassadors*", in *N & Q*, vol. CC, January 1955, pp. 37–38.)

23 NYE, XXI, 89.

24 The second important restored part is a whole chapter at the beginning of the eleventh book, which, in the NYE, opens with a chapter between Strether and Maria Gostrey, followed by one between the former and Chad, which the serial edition does not contain. Because of a publishing error which James himself seems never to have noticed, the order of these two chapters in the NYE is wrong. The new chapter between Strether and Chad should precede the one between Maria Gostrey and Strether, and should form the conclusion of Book X. The only correct edition of *The Ambassadors* in book-form is the English one, published by Methuen in 1903. (See also Edel, L., *Selected Letters of Henry James*, London 1956, p. 130.) Because of its highly symbolic meaning this restored passage will be dealt with in chapter 7.

C. Obscuring Images

25 NYE, III, 48.

26 AM, Nov. 1880, 604.

27 M, II, 350.

28 A confrontation of the same passage in first and final versions may show that the revision does not clarify but complicates the already intricate construction even more. The passage gives Isabel Archer's thoughts about Goodwood's character.

first version	final version
Isabel knew that his was not a soft nature, from which pin-pricks would draw blood; and from the first of her acquaintance with him, and of her having to defend herself against a certain air that he had of knowing better what was good for her than she knew herself, she had recognized the fact that perfect frankness was her best weapon. To attempt to spare his sensibility or make her opposition oblique, as one might do with men smaller and superficially more irritable,— this, in dealing with Caspar Goodwood, who would take everything of every sort that one might give him, was superfluous diplomacy. It was not that he had not susceptibilities, but his passive surface,	It wasn't certainly as if his nature had been soft, so that pin-pricks would draw blood from it; and from the first of her acquaintance with him, and of her having to defend herself against a certain air that he had of knowing better what was good for her than she knew herself, she had recognised the fact that perfect frankness was her best weapon. To attempt to spare his sensibility or to escape from him edgewise, as one might do from a man who had barred the way less sturdily— this, in dealing with Caspar Goodwood, who would grasp at everything of every sort that one might give him, was wasted agility. It was not that he had not susceptibilities, but his passive surface, as well

as well as his active, was large and firm,   as his active, was large and hard, and he
and he might always be trusted to dress   might always be trusted to dress his
his wounds himself. (AM, Feb. 1881,   wounds, so far as they required it, him-
187.)   self. (NYE, III, 219.)

The revisions and additions in this passage show a clear tendency to render it more ambiguous. Other examples of obscure or artificial imagery: a) Concerning Mary Garland's smile: "Rowland indeed had not yet seen this accident produced; but something assured him that when, on [sic] due course shown, she should cease to be serious, it would be like the final rising of the plain green curtain of the old theatre on some — not very modern—comedy." (NYE, I, 54.) b) Ralph's reflections on Henrietta Stackpole: "Her presence proved somehow less irreducible to soft particles than Ralph had expected in the natural perturbation of his sense of the perfect solubility of that of his cousin; for the correspondent of the *Interviewer* prompted mirth in him, and he had long since decided that the *crescendo* of mirth should be the flower of his declining days." (NYE, III, 122.) c) Concerning Madame Merle: "After their union Isabel discovered that her husband took a less convenient view of the matter; he seldom consented to finger, in talk, this roundest and smoothest bead of their social rosary." (NYE, IV, 158.) d) of Strether: "He presently recovered his inward tone and ... many a fresh flower of fancy was to bloom in the same air." (NAR, Sept. 1903, 476f.) e) of Kate Croy: "She lived under her mother's roof, as she considered, obscurely, and was acquainted with few persons who entertained on that scale; but she had had her dealings with two or three connected, as appeared, with such—two or three through whom the stream of hospitality, filtered or diffused, could thus now and then spread to outlying receptacles." (C, 45.) f) of Bob Assingham: "But it was a question that he had promptly dropped at the returning brush of another, of which she had shortly before sown the seed." (M, I, 386.) g) of Maggie Verver: "She might have been wishing, under this renewed, this still more suggestive visitation, to keep him with her for remounting the stream of time and dipping again, for the softness of the water, into the contracted basin of the past." (M, II, 266.) h) of Charlotte Stant: "Maggie had seen her, unmistakably, desire to rise to the occasion and be magnificent—seen her decide that the right way for this would be to prove that the reassurance she had extorted there, under the high, cool lustre of the saloon, a twinkle of crystal and silver, had not only poured oil on the troubled waters of their question, but had fairly drenched their whole intercourse with that lubricant." (M, II, 287.)

29 NAR, Jan. 1903, 156.
30 Ibid.
31 See for instance T. S. Eliot's notes at the end of "The Waste Land". In the final version of *The Portrait* an image occurs which is most certainly based on a literary allusion, but which, for most readers, remains ineffective because the work to which it refers is hardly ever read nowadays. The image, concerning Osmond, reads: "When not in the right mood he could fall as low as any one, saved only by his looking at such hours rather like a demoralized prince in exile." (NYE, III, 351f.) There can be hardly any doubt that James was thinking of Alphonse Daudet's *Les Rois en Exil* when he created this image. (He refers to Daudet in "Partial Portraits", p. 195ff.)

D. Comic Effects through Images

32 AM, Feb. 1875, 153.*
33 AM, May 1875, 522.

34 AM, Oct. 1875, 391. After Christina and Roderick have gone away together it is said of Casamassima that he "continued to pass to and fro, stiffly and solemnly, like a pendulum marking the time allowed for the young lady to come to her senses". (AM, June 1875, 655.) The Cavaliere Giacosa has "a little black eye which glittered like a diamond and rolled about like a ball of quicksilver, and a white mustache, cut short and stiff, like a worn-out brush". (AM, March 1875, 3 of.)

35 Henrietta: "I'm drifting to a big position — to being the queen of American Journalism. If my next letter isn't copied all over the west, I'll swallow my pen-wiper!" (AM, Feb. 1881, 194.) Isabel of Rosier: "he has about the extent of one's pocket-handker-chief — the small ones, with lace." (AM, Aug. 1881, 218.) Mrs. Gereth of Mrs. Brig-stock: "If a cow should try to calculate, that's the kind of happy thought she'd have." (AM, Sept. 1896, 379.)

36 Miss Barrace: "She seemed, with little cries and protests and quick recognitions, movements like the darts of some fine high-feathered, free-pecking bird, to stand before life as before some full shop-window. You could fairly hear, as she selected and pointed, the tap of her tortoise-shell against the glass." (NAR, May 1903, 798.) Of Waymarsh: "He *is* a success. Moses, on the ceiling, brought down to the floor; over-whelming, colossal, but somehow portable." (NAR, May 1903, 799.) In the case of the Pococks it is always clear irony or sarcasm, achieved either very simply by an adjective: "Poor Jim ... drank in the sparkling Paris noon" (NAR, Aug. 1903, 308), or by the nature of the comparison, as in the case of Sarah: "Her marked, thin-lipped smile, intense without brightness and as prompt to act as the scrape of a safety-match." (NAR, Aug. 1903, 302.)

37 "She wrote short stories, and she fondly believed she had her 'note', the art of showing New England without showing it wholly in the kitchen. She had not herself been brought up in the kitchen; she knew others who had not; and to speak for them had thus become with her a literary mission." (C, 90.) She "flitted in and out of the Public Library with the air of conscientiously returning or bravely carrying off in her pocket the key of knowledge itself". (C, 91.)

38 M, I, 66.

39 M, I, 250.

40 Ibid.

41 M, I, 33.

E. Illustrative Images

1. General

42 AM, June 1875, 646f.

43 AM, June 1875, 647.

44 AM, March 1875, 297. Other examples from *Roderick Hudson*. Of Roderick: "He rode his two horses at once with extraordinary good fortune; he established the happiest *modus vivendi* betwixt work and play." (AM, March 1875, 304.) "For forty-eight hours there swam before Rowland's eyes a vision of Roderick, graceful and beautiful as he passed, plunging, like a diver, from an eminence into a misty gulf. The gulf was destruc-tion, annihilation, death." (AM, Aug. 1875, 137.)

45 AM, March 1881, 349.

46 AM, Aug. 1881, 228.

47 AM, July 1881, 82.

48 AM, July 1881, 84.

49 "Fleda was slow to take in Mrs. Gereth's announcement [that she had sent all the spoils back to Poynton], but when she had done so she felt it to be more than her cup

of bitterness would hold. Her bitterness was her anxiety, the taste of which suddenly sickened her." (AM, Sept. 1896, 381.) Of Kate Croy's confirmation of her love for Merton: "She said it out so splendidly that it was like a new profession of faith, the fulness of a tide breaking through." (C, 83.) Of Milly's freedom: "on top of all to enjoy boundless freedom, the freedom of the wind in the desert—it was unspeakably touching to be so equipped." (C, 93.) The new element in this simple example is that the illustrative picture is reduced to a subordinate clause, a kind of apposition, and has thus become an organic part of the whole rhythmic structure of the sentence.

50 After Fleda's meeting with Owen at her sister's: "She felt as if for ten days she had sat in darkness, looking to the east for a dawn that had not yet glimmered." (AM, Sept. 1896, 376.) Fleda has given away one of her secrets, and Mrs. Gereth is going to make full use of her newly gained knowledge. "One of the straightest of these strokes, Fleda saw, would be the dance of delight over the mystery Mrs. Gereth had laid bare,—the loud, lawful, tactless joy of the explorer leaping upon the strand. Like any other lucky discoverer, she would take possession of the fortunate island." (AM, July 1896, 66.) This rather unpretentious image contains an explanation of all Mrs. Gereth's subsequent moves.

51 NAR, March 1903, 471.
52 C, 368.
53 M, I, 334.*

2. Path Images

54 As for instance: If "Roderick chose to follow a crooked path, it was no fault of his". (AM, May 1875, 516.) Or: "there was a very straight path" (AM, Dec. 1881, 770) that lay before Isabel Archer. Of Fleda Vetch: "The girl's heart gave a tremendous bound; the right way dawned upon her in a flash. Obscurity, indeed, the next moment engulfed this course, but for a few thrilled seconds she had understood." (AM, July 1896, 60.) To Strether it seemed "at present as if the backward picture had hung there, the long crooked course, gray in the shadow of his solitude". (NAR, Feb. 1903, 315.)

55 AM, Feb. 1881, 193.
56 NAR, Oct. 1903, 616.*
57 M, II, 170.

3. Light Images

58 "this qualification of it as a policy or a remedy was straightway ... a light that her own light could answer" (C, 469), "her interest came out for at least the minimum of light." (C, 512.) "The light of admiration was in Rowland's eyes, and it speedily kindled a wonderful illumination on Hudson's handsome brow." (AM, Jan. 1875, 14.) "Fleda had gathered fuller confidence as he continued; so plain was it that she had succeeded in not dropping into his mind the spark that might produce the glimmer invoked by his mother." (AM, Aug. 1896, 201.) "Strether, in contact with that element [glory] as he had never yet so intimately been, had a consciousness ... of letting this rather gray interior [his mind] drink in, for once, the sun of a clime not marked in his old geography." (NAR, May 1903, 794.) Charlotte Stant is about to make her point: "To make it now with force for Fanny Assingham's benefit would see her further, in the direction in which the light had dawned, than any other spring she should, yet awhile, doubtless, be able to press. The direction was that of her greater freedom— which was all in the world she had in mind." (M, I, 256.)

59 AM, May 1875, 525.
60 AM, Sept. 1881, 361.
61 AM, Sept. 1881, 353.

62 AM, Aug. 1881, 232.

63 AM, Dec. 1881, 752.

64 NAR, Aug. 1903, 297f.*

65 Referring to what Kate and Mrs. Lowder had told him, Merton Densher feels that "so far as his late lights had opened the door to any want of the natural in their meetings, he might trust her to take care of it for him as well as for herself". (C, 310.) In regard to Milly we read: "With that there came to her a light: wouldn't her value, for the man who should marry her, be precisely in the ravage of her disease?" (C, 373.) "But that was an old story, and Kate's multiplied lights led him on and on." (C, 432.) "it was fairly as if light broke, though not quite all at once." (C, 433.) The expression of uncertainty and doubt is the main function of light images like: "on the case thus postulated our young American had as yet had no light: she only felt that when the light should come it would greatly deepen the colour." (C, 143f.) Or: "The clear shadow, from whatever source projected, hung, at any rate, over Milly's companion the whole week, and Kate Croy's handsome face smiled out of it, under bland skylights." (C, 144.) Or: Milly "became conscious of being here on the edge of a great darkness." (C, 158.)

66 M, II, 188.

67 M, II, 215f.

68 M, II, 257.

4. Theatre Images

69 Of Mrs. Hudson we read that she "had an illness which for many months was liable at any moment to terminate fatally, and during her long-arrested convalescence she removed the mask she had worn for years by her husband's order". (AM, Jan. 1875, 6.) After Christina's marriage to Casamassima "the dark little drama ... had played itself out". (AM, Nov. 1875, 555.) Isabel's "mask had dropped for an instant, but she had put it on again, to Ralph's infinite disappointment. He had caught a glimpse of her natural face, and he wished immensely to look into it." (AM, Sept. 1881, 349.) "Mrs. Gereth turned up a dead gray mask." (AM, Oct. 1896, 519.) A curtain image shows, in its formulation and conception, a noticeable originality: "With a formal rupture he [Owen] would be at large; and she [Fleda] had only to tighten her fingers round the string that would raise the curtain on that scene." (AM, Aug. 1896, 206.)

70 AM, Oct. 1875, 405.

71 AM, Sept. 1896, 389.

72 NAR, Oct. 1903, 623.

73 NAR, Oct. 1903, 626.

74 NAR, Nov. 1903, 793.

75 NAR, Nov. 1903, 793f.*

76 C, 277ff.*

77 "it [the intimacy] was in view as, when the curtain had risen, the play on the stage is in view, night after night, for the fiddlers. He remained thus, in his own theatre, in his single person, perpetual orchestra to the ordered drama, the confirmed 'run'; playing low and slow, moreover, in the regular way, for the situations of most importance. No other visitor was to come to him ... he couldn't, for his life, he felt, have opened his door to a third person. Such a person would have interrupted him, would have profaned his secret or perhaps have guessed it; would at any rate have broken the spell of what he conceived himself—in the absence of anything 'to show'—to be inwardly doing." (C, 442f.)

78 C, 363.*

79 M, II, 34.

80 M, II, 213.
81 M, II, 242.*
82 M, I, 172f.

F. *Emphasizing Images*

1. General

83 AM, Aug. 1881, 228.
84 Ibid.
85 Ibid.
86 AM, Nov. 1881, 630. The final version of this image is even more powerful: "She had expected to kindle some responsive blaze, but had barely extracted a spark. Isabel showed as scarce more impressed [sic] than she might have been, as a young woman of approved imagination, with some fine sinister passage of public history." (NYE, IV, 366.)
87 AM, Dec. 1880, 747.
88 As for instance when Madame Merle stresses the fact that there are already marked points of difference between Isabel and Osmond, saying to Edward Rosier: "But don't for the present try to make her take up the cudgels for you. Her husband may have other views, and, as a person who wishes her well, I advise you not to multiply points of difference between them." (AM, July 1881, 62.) Isabel's lost freedom of action makes her give "an envious thought to the happier lot of men, who are always free to plunge into the healing waters of action". (AM, July 1881, 76.)
89 AM, April 1896, 442.
90 AM, July 1896, 66.
91 AM, Sept. 1896, 377.
92 Strether's overwhelming impression of Jeanne: "What was in the girl was indeed too soft, too unknown for direct dealing; so that one could only gaze at it as at a picture, quite staying one's own hand." (NAR, May 1903, 807.) Strether's conviction of the affection between Jeanne and Chad: "'It's the child!' ... and though her [Maria's] direct response was for some time delayed he could feel in her meanwhile the working of this truth. It might have been simply as she waited, that they were now in presence, altogether, of truth spreading like a flood and not, for the moment, to be offered her in the mere cupful." (NAR, May 1903, 808.) During a talk between Maria Gostrey and Strether the influence which Marie de Vionnet has gained over Strether is emphasized: "They had, in the matter that so much interested them, come so far as this without sounding another name—to which, however, their present momentary silence was full of a conscious reference. Strether's question was a sufficient implication of the weight it had gained during the absence of his hostess; and just for that reason a single gesture from her could pass for him as a vivid answer." (NAR, July 1903, 160.) Waymarsh, on the other hand, has lost his influence on Strether completely: "Quit!" he says to Strether, meaning the whole circle of people in which his friend is involved in Paris. His exhortation is followed by: "But it lacked its old intensity; nothing of it remained; it went out of the room with him." (NAR, Oct. 1903, 634.)
93 NAR, March 1903, 478.
94 NAR, April 1903, 635.
95 Ibid. It is most likely that James has, consciously or unconsciously, derived this image from John Greenleaf Whittier's poem "Barbara Frietchie". The image clearly shows a resemblance to the following lines from Whittier's poem:

Up rose old Barbara Frietchie then,
Bowed with her fourscore years and ten;

Bravest of all in Fredrick town,
She took up the flag the men hauled down;

In her attic window the staff she set,
To show that one heart was loyal yet.

Up the street came the level tread,
Stonewall Jackson riding ahead

Under his slouched hat left and right
He glanced: the old flag met his sight.

"Halt!"—the dust-brown ranks stood fast.
"Fire!"—out blazed the rifle blast.

It shivered the window, pane and sash;
It rent the banner with seam and gash.

Quick, as it fell, from the broken staff
Dame Barbara snatched the silken scarf.

She leaned far out on the window-sill,
And shook it forth with a royal will.

"Shoot, if you must, this old grey head,
But spare your country's flag", she said.

96 NAR, May 1903, 804.
97 NAR, May 1903, 804f.*
98 C, 162.
99 C, 132.
100 C, 155.
101 C, 156.
102 Ibid. Another important fact which James stresses repeatedly, though not with related images, is Mrs. Stringham's incapacity to understand Milly's character fully. "Mrs. Stringham found herself from that hour, in other words, in presence of an explanation that remained a muffled and intangible form, but that, assuredly, should it take on sharpness, would explain everything and more than everything, would become instantly the light in which Milly was to be read" (C, 98); and: "She had almost the sense of tracking her young friend as if at a given moment to pounce. She knew she shouldn't pounce, she hadn't come out to pounce; yet she felt her attention secretive, all the same, and her observation scientific." (C, 98.)
103 C, 167.
104 M, I, 187f.
105 M, I, 411f.
106 M, II, 114.
107 At the beginning of the second part of the novel we are told that Maggie knows the true relationship between her husband and Charlotte.
108 M, II, 212. This image occurs at the opening of the chapter which describes Maggie's development from a mere "actress" to an "author", from an acting to a directing person (see chapter 3, E, 4.).
109 Examples from other novels: In The Ambassadors the immediate effect on Strether of one of Sarah's remarks: "She had let fly at him as from a stretched cord, and it took him a minute to recover from the sense of being pierced." (NAR, Oct. 1903, 640.) In The Wings Merton's reaction to one of his own remarks towards Milly is given with: "And he couldn't have said when he had uttered it if it were loyal to Kate or

disloyal. It gave her, in a manner, away; it showed the tip of the ear of her plan."
(C, 452.)
110 M, II, 275.

2. *Key Images*

111 "the letter needed, to Rowland's mind a key: the key arrived a week later." (AM,
April 1875, 424.) "Daniel Touchett had been neither at Harvard nor at Oxford, and
it was his own fault if he had put into his son's hands the key to modern criticism."
(AM, Nov. 1880, 605.) Waymarsh's "look had recurred to Strether as the key of
much that he had since observed". (NAR, Jan. 1903, 149.) Two related images (not
in the serial version): After Chad "had expressed a hope that he would let him put
him up for the night Strether was in full possession of the key, as it might have been
called, to what had lately happened" (NYE, XXII, 307) and: "It placed his present
call immediately on solid ground, and the effect of it was to enable him quite to play
with what we have called the key." (NYE, XXII, 308.)
112 AM, June 1875, 649.
113 AM, Aug. 1875, 130.
114 AM, Nov. 1880, 605.
115 AM, Dec. 1880, 748.
116 There are two reasons for this fact. Firstly it is a very short and dramatically concise
novel in which James had to concentrate on essentials. Secondly, and more important,
all relations between the few characters seem clear to themselves. And as the function
of key images is mainly to point out uncertainties and doubts in such relationships,
their introduction in this novel was superfluous.
117 The reason in this novel seems to be different. Strether is the absolute centre of the
novel, and therefore the whole of the imagery depends largely on his character and
his mind. As James himself pointed out in his preface, this novel is mainly a drama
of discrimination. Strether is deciphering everything piece by piece, and in these
efforts he shows a remarkable patience. This quality of his character means that he
always seems to get the answers to his own questions in time. If he is confronted
with a riddle he is determined to solve it, and in these efforts Maria Gostrey plays
an essential part as a "ficelle". In many instances it is she who provides the keys for
Strether or gives valuable information for finding them.
118 C, 92.
119 Ibid.
120 C, 97.
121 C, 235.
122 C, 263 f.*
123 M, I, 5.
124 M, II, 242.

3. *Images Based on Games*

125 Madame Grandoni stresses Christina's advantages in being beautiful: "She has been
told twenty times a day by her mother, since she was five years old, that she is a beauty
of beauties, that her face is her fortune, and that if she plays her cards, she may marry
a duke." (AM, April 1875, 434.) Roderick: "When I have played my last card, I shall
cease to care for the game." (AM, June 1875, 649.) Speaking of Casamassima, Rowland says to Mrs. Light: "I certainly hope you'll keep him ... You have played a
dangerous game with your daughter; it would be a pity not to win!" (AM, June
1875, 657 f.)
126 AM, Oct. 1875, 405.

127 As when Ralph says to Lord Warburton: "I suspect we have each been playing our little game" (AM, July 1881, 83), or when Osmond says to Isabel: "You've played a very deep game; you've managed it beautifully." (AM, Sept. 1881, 359.)

128 AM, Dec. 1881, 751.

129 AM, July 1896, 62.

130 AM, July 1896, 64.

131 AM, Sept. 1896, 382.

132 NAR, March 1903, 475.

133 NAR, April 1903, 649.

134 NAR, April 1903, 655.

135 NAR, Sept. 1903, 465.

136 NAR, July 1903, 159.

137 NAR, Aug. 1903, 302.

138 NYE, XXII, 234 (not in the serial version).

139 They are first described as "being able to play a waiting game with success". (C, 75.) After Merton's return from America: "'respect', in their game, seemed somehow ... a fifth wheel to the coach." (C, 255.) At the same point Merton is made to think "that waiting was the game of dupes". (C, 257.) He was uneasy because they had not announced their engagement nor taken the further step of marriage. "He had really at this to make out a little what he thought, and the first thing that put itself in evidence was of course the oddity, after all, of their game, to which he could but frankly allude." (C, 267.) During a discussion with Kate, he mentions Mrs. Lowder's strength: "Remember, after all, that supremely clever as we are, and as strong a team, I admit, as there is going—remember that she can play with us quite as much as we play with her." To which Kate answers: "She doesn't want to play with *me*, my dear ... she doesn't want to make me suffer a bit more than she need. She cares for me too much, and everything she does, or doesn't do, has a value." (C, 267f.) The exploitation of Milly's innocence marks a new stage of their game, at the beginning of which Kate says to Merton: "Only be nice to her. Please her; make her see how clever you are—only without letting her see that you're trying. If you're charming to her you've nothing else to do." Merton has his doubts: "I can be 'charming' to her, so far as I see, only by letting her suppose I give you up—which I'll be hanged if I do! It *is* ... a game." Kate replies: "Of course it's a game. But she'll never suppose you give me up—or I give *you*—if you keep reminding her how you enjoy our interviews." (C, 269.) With the certainty of Milly's approaching death Densher says to his fiancée: "We've played our dreadful game, and we've lost." (C, 531.)

140 M, II, 35f.*

141 M, II, 110f.*

142 It is not justified to say, as Joseph J. Firebaugh has done, that "Maggie is a heartless Machiavellian absolutist, willing to compromise with her absolutes to gain her selfish ends, willing to build a false world of appearances to conceal the truth about her life, interested primarily in maintenance of ownership" (in his article "The Ververs", in *Essays in Criticism*, vol. IV, Oct. 1954, p. 406).

Chapter 4: The Characterizing Image

A. Spoken Images

1 AM, Oct. 1875, 400f.*

2 AM, June 1875, 649.*

3 For instance with Christina and Mary. Christina is rough and provocative when she says to Roderick: "You have gone up like a rocket, in your profession, they tell me;

are you going to come down like the stick?" (AM, July 1875, 60.) Mary is more sensitive, reserved and modest, when, after her first impression of Rome, she says to Rowland: "Here in a single hour, everything is changed. It is as if a wall in my mind had been knocked down at a stroke. Before me lies an immense new world, and it makes the old one, the poor little narrow, familiar one I have always known, seem pitiful." (AM, Sept. 1875, 273.)

4 AM, May 1881, 624.

5 AM, Feb. 1881, 183.

6 As for instance when she says to Isabel: "Now, of course, you are completely your own mistress. I don't mean you were not so before. But you are at present on a different footing; property erects a kind of barrier." (AM, March 1881, 355.)

7 AM, Jan. 1881, 16f.

8 AM, Feb. 1881, 203.

9 AM, Feb. 1881, 204.

10 AM, Aug. 1896, 205.

11 AM, Aug. 1896, 213. Other examples are: "Do you know what she had the cheek to tell me?" (AM, Aug. 1896, 214) and: "What good does it do me to be here, when I find you only a stone?" (AM, Aug. 1896, 214.)

12 Owen employs one such image which, although on the edge of the conventional, does not sound quite in accordance with his intellectual level: "I rushed down to Ricks, as you saw, with fire and sword, and the day after that I went to see her at Waterbath." (AM, Aug. 1896, 205.)

13 AM, June 1896, 732.

14 AM, Aug. 1896, 214.

15 AM, Sept. 1896, 381.

16 AM, May 1896, 637.

17 AM, July 1896, 64.

18 AM, Sept. 1896, 381.

19 AM, Feb. 1875, 146f.*

20 "I think that when you expect a man to produce beautiful and wonderful works of art, you ought to allow him a certain freedom of action, you ought to give him a long rope, you ought to let him follow his fancy and look for his material wherever he thinks he may find it! A mother can't nurse her child unless she follows a certain diet; an artist can't bring his visions to maturity unless he has a certain experience. You demand of us to be imaginative, and you deny us that which feeds the imagination. In labor we must be as passionate as the inspired sibyl; in life we must be mere machines. It won't do. When you have got an artist to deal with, you must take him as he is, good and bad together. I don't say they are pleasant fellows to know or easy fellows to live with; I don't say they satisfy themselves any better than other people. I only say that if you want them to produce, you must let them conceive. If you want a bird to sing you must not cover up its cage. Shoot them, the poor devils, drown them, exterminate them, if you will, in the interest of public morality; it may be morality would gain—I dare say it would! But if you suffer them to live, let them live on their own terms and according to their own inexorable needs!" (AM, June 1875, 646f.)

21 AM, Oct. 1881, 491.

22 AM, Oct. 1881, 487f.

23 AM, Sept. 1896, 385.

24 AM, Sept. 1896, 387.

25 Examples: *Maria Gostrey:* "I knew you had something up your sleeve." (NAR, Feb. 1903, 307); or: "I should positively like to take her in hand" (NAR, April 1903,

654); or: "It suits my book ... that he should be impossible; and it suits it still better ... that Mrs. Newsome doesn't know he is" (NAR, Sept. 1903, 473). *Madame de Vionnet:* "she's an angel of light" (NAR, June 1903, 962); or: "I don't ask you to raise your little finger for me again." (NAR, Dec. 1903, 953.) *Chad:* "All the more that I've really dished you." (NAR, July 1903, 156.) *Miss Barrace:* "you're not worth sixpence." (NAR, May 1903, 798.) *Strether:* "I feel it in my bones" (NAR, Feb. 1903, 308); "Consideration and comfort and security—the general safety of being anchored by a strong chain" (NAR, Feb. 1903, 309); "It's a question of an immediate rupture and an immediate return. I've been conceited enough to dream I can sugar that pill." (NAR, April 1903, 635); "Well, to my having a certitude that has been tested—that has passed through the fire." (NAR, July 1903, 155); "But, on the other hand, I've gone much further to meet her. She, on her side, hasn't budged an inch." (NAR, Nov. 1903, 785.)

26 NAR, July 1903, 157.

27 NYE, XXII, 237 (not in the serial version). A similar example occurs in a discussion between Miss Barrace and little Bilham. She says: "You come over to convert the savages—for I know you verily did, I remember you—and the savages simply convert *you.*" And he replies: "Not even! ... they haven't gone through that form. They've simply—the cannibals!—eaten me; converted me if you like, but converted me into food. I'm but the bleached bones of a Christian." (NAR, May 1903, 798.)

28 C, 13.*

29 C, 17.

30 C, 293.

31 See * to n. 19 of chapter 6 and the interpretation of these metaphors on p. 122.

32 M, II, 136.

B. External Characterization

33 See p. 31.

34 AM, April 1881, 466 (see also n. 95 in chapter 3).

35 NAR, May 1903, 794.

36 NAR, June 1903, 960.

37 C, 192.

38 M, I, 173 f.*

39 M, I, 43 f.*

40 M, I, 69.

C. General Characterization

1. General

41 AM, March 1875, 303.

42 AM, Sept. 1875, 276f.*

43 AM, Dec. 1880, 743.

44 AM, Feb. 1881, 184.

45 AM, March 1881, 343.

46 If Isabel is characterized as careful and reluctant, conceited and proud, Caspar Goodwood is seen as the aggressive type who has nothing to lose but everything to gain. "Now that he was alone with her, all the passion he had never stifled surged into his senses; it hummed in his eyes and made things swim round him." (AM, Oct. 1881, 490.)

47 AM, Sept. 1881, 346.

48 AM, Oct. 1881, 488.

49 A similar example concerns Pansy's pure and innocent character: "This young lady

was so neat, so complete in her manner; and yet in character, as one could see, so innocent and infantine ... She was like a sheet of blank paper,—the ideal *jeune fille* of foreign fiction. Isabel hoped that so fair and smooth a page would be covered with an edifying text." (AM, May 1881, 626.) At the beginning of the chapter that appeared the following month we read: "Pansy was really a blank page, a pure white surface, she was not clever enough for precocious coquetries." (AM, June 1881, 802.)

50 AM, April 1896, 441.
51 AM, June 1896, 723.
52 NAR, Dec. 1903, 950.
53 NAR, Jan. 1903, 149.
54 NAR, Jan. 1903, 152.
55 NAR, April 1903, 637.
56 Ibid.
57 NAR, Jan. 1903, 150.
58 NAR, March 1903, 467.
59 NAR, July 1903, 150.
60 Such individual touches are conveyed by the following images: of Strether: "he was like a man who, finding in his pocket, with joy, more money than usual, handles it a while and idly, pleasantly chinks it before addressing himself to the business of spending." (NAR, Jan. 1903, 139.) Of Maria Gostrey: "wherever she happened to be she found a dropped thread to pick up, a ragged edge to repair, some familiar appetite to ambush, jumping out as she approached, yet appeasable with a temporary biscuit." (NAR, Jan. 1903, 156.) Of Jeanne de Vionnet: "She was fairly beautiful to him—a faint pastel in an oval frame: he thought of her already as of some lurking image in a long gallery, the portrait of a small old-time princess of whom nothing was known but that she had died young." (NAR, June 1903, 954.) Of Mrs. Newsome: "'I see it all,' he [Strether] absently echoed, while his eyes might have been fixing some particularly large iceberg in a cool blue northern sea." (NAR, Nov. 1903, 786.) Of Chad: "Chad was always letting people have their way when he felt that it would somehow turn his wheel for him; it somehow always did turn his wheel." (NAR, Dec. 1903, 952.)
61 C, 70.
62 C, 76.
63 C, 178.
64 Other examples: of Merton: "He suggested above all, however, that wondrous state of youth in which the elements, the metals more or less precious, are so in fusion and fermentation that the question of the final stamp, the pressure that fixes the value, must wait for comparative coolness." (C, 42.) Of Lord Mark, as he strikes Milly: "It had helped him to place her, and she was more and more sharply conscious of having— as with the door sharply slammed upon her and the guard's hand raised in signal to the train—been popped into the compartment in which she was to travel for him." (C, 131.)
65 C, 300.
66 C, 431.
67 M, I, 128.
68 M, I, 138.
69 M, I, 329f.
70 M, II, 106.
71 M, I, 254.

2. War Images

72 "Mr. Leavenworth, with calm unconsciousness, proceeded to fire the mine" (AM, Aug. 1875, 133); it "was monstrous to suppose that she [Christina] could have sacrificed

so brilliant a fortune to a mere movement of jealousy, to a refined impulse of feminine deviltry, to a desire to frighten poor Mary from her security by again appearing in the field". (AM, Oct. 1875, 397.) Rowland gets the impression from Christina's manner, after she has surrendered and agreed to marry Casamassima, "that her battle had been fierce". (AM, Oct. 1875, 404.)

73 AM, Nov. 1880, 597.
74 AM, Aug. 1881, 213.
75 AM, April 1896, 438.
76 AM, May 1896, 632. "The action is the mother's refusal to give up the house, or the things", James wrote in his second notebook-entry concerning *The Old Things*. (N, 198.)
77 AM, June 1896, 722.
78 AM, June 1896, 723f.
79 AM, July 1896, 69.
80 Ibid.
81 "We're beaten brothers in arms." (NAR, Jan. 1903, 159.) "he had ... a conception of carrying the war into the enemy's country by showing surprise at the enemy's ignorance." (NAR, April 1903, 642.) "He's very decent, and won't be a traitor in the camp." (NAR, Sept. 1903, 461.)
82 C, 24ff.*
83 C, 67f.
84 C, 68.
85 C, 140.
86 C, 206f.
87 C, 365.
88 C, 364.
89 We have only to remember the scene in which Mrs. Stringham finds Milly sitting on a rock at the edge of a dangerous slope, "looking down on the kingdoms of the earth" (C, 104); her innocent and carefree attitude towards Europe and its society is well enough described by the word "plunge", which is used of her first acquaintance with the "obscure depths of a society constituted from far back". (C, 128.)
90 M, II, 9f.
91 M, II, 15.
92 M, II, 110.
93 M, II, 219.
94 Fanny's great gift of adaptation and her calculated vagueness are the basis of another war image: "She had taken the five minutes, obviously, amid the rest of the talk and the movement, to retire into her tent for meditation—which showed, among several things, the impression Charlotte had made on her. It was from the tent she emerged, as with arms refurbished; though who indeed could say if the manner in which she now met him [Amerigo] spoke most, really, of the glitter of battle or of the white waver of the flag of truce?" (M, I, 355f.)

3. Animal Images

95 AM, Jan. 1875, 12.
96 Comparing Roderick to Sam Singleton Rowland "remembered afresh that the sea is inhabited by big fishes and little, and that the latter often find their way down the throats of the former". (AM, Nov. 1875, 554.)
97 Such as: "we are two lame ducks" (AM, Nov. 1880, 588); or: "he's an odd fish." (AM, Sept. 1881, 354.)
98 AM, June 1881, 817.

99 AM, Oct. 1896, 522.

100 Ibid.

101 Of the animal images in *The Ambassadors* only two deserve mention. One is a characterization of Gloriani, as he affects Strether: "there was something in the great world covertly tigerish, which came to him, across the lawn, in the charming air, as a waft from the jungle. Yet it made him admire most of the two, made him envy, the glossy male tiger, magnificently marked." (NAR, May 1903, 806.) The other is a self-characterization of Strether (which is not yet to be found in the serial version): "I've come very much, it seems to me, to double up my fore legs in the manner of the camel when he gets down on his knees to make his back convenient." (NYE, XXII, 234.)

102 C, 25.*

103 C, 66.

104 C, 71.

105 C, 63.

106 C, 150.

107 C, 232.

108 The central symbol for Milly's purity and innocence, the dove, will be analysed in the chapter in which the development of James's use of iterative imagery is dealt with. One other animal image used for Milly stands in sharp contrast to those used for Mrs. Lowder, Kate and Merton by way of its conception. "It was of course as one of the weak that she had gone to him [Sir Luke Strett]—but, oh, with how sneaking a hope that he might pronounce her, as to all indispensables, a veritable young lioness!" (C, 208.) The implication, in this case, is not one of evil or wickedness, but Milly's hopes that the great doctor might pronounce her completely healthy, in full possession of her power and strength.

109 M, I, 164f.

110 M, I, 8.

111 M, II, 235 f.*

112 M, II, 245 ff.*

113 An image attributed to Maggie is of no particular significance: "And yet, by her little crouching posture there, that of a timid tigress, she had meant nothing recklessly ultimate, nothing clumsily fundamental." (M, II, 10.) A striking pictorial creation describes Maggie's oscillation between her belief that she has been wronged by her husband and Charlotte and the suppression of this suspicion as unjustified and only a silly idea of hers: "she tried to deal with herself, for a space, only as a silken-coated spaniel who has scrambled out of a pond and who rattles the water from his ears. Her shake of her head, again and again, as she went, was much of that order, and she had the resource, to which, save for the rude equivalent of his generalising bark, the spaniel would have been a stranger, of humming to herself hard as a sign that nothing had happened to her. She had not, so to speak, fallen in; she had had no accident and had not got wet; this at any rate was her pretension until after she began a little to wonder if she mightn't, with or without exposure, have taken cold." (M, II, 7.)

Chapter 5: Images Expressing the Abstract in Terms of the Concrete

A. The Poetic Metaphor

1 One of Joyce's favourite novels was James's *The Portrait of a Lady*.

2 AM, April 1875, 423. Other examples of this kind are: "he leaned back in his chair with his hands in his pockets, and flung open the gates of his eloquence" (AM,

March 1875, 308); or: "If Roderick took the words out of your mouth when you were just prepared to deliver them with the most effective accent, he did it with a perfect good conscience and with no pretension of a better right to being heard, but simply because he was full to overflowing of his own momentary thought and it sprang from his lips without asking leave" (AM, March 1875, 303); or: "the path of glory" (AM, Feb. 1875, 148); or: "you marched into the jaws of danger" (AM, June 1875, 655); or: "there were no visible clouds in his heaven, but there were cloud-shadows on his mood" (AM, May 1875, 516); or: "the shipwreck of her hopes." (AM, Oct. 1875, 400.)

3 AM, Dec. 1875, 660.

4 AM, Aug. 1875, 137.

5 Examples of this kind are, for instance: "When you have lived as long as I, you will see that every human being has his shell, and that you must take the shell into account. By the shell I mean the whole envelope of circumstances. There is no such thing as an isolated man or woman; we are each of us made up of a cluster of appurtenances. What do you call one's self? Where does it begin? Where does it end? It overflows into everything that belongs to us, and then it flows back again." (AM, March 1881, 344.) "The consciousness of success, which must now have flamed high within him, emitted very little smoke for so brilliant a blaze." (AM, June 1881, 822.) "Isabel presently found herself in the singular situation of defending the British constitution against her aunt; Mrs. Touchett having formed the habit of sticking pins into this venerable instrument. Isabel always felt an impulse to remove the pins; not that she imagined they inflicted any damage on the tough old parchment, but because it seemed to her that her aunt might make better use of her sharpness." (AM, Dec. 1880, 746.) "Madame Merle had predicted to Mrs. Touchett that after Isabel had put her hand into her pocket half a dozen times she would be reconciled to the idea that it had been filled by a munificent uncle." (AM, March 1881, 358.) "The mistress of Ricks ... presented to her companion the handsome face she had composed to hear everything. Strangely enough, it was just this fine vessel of her attention that made the girl most nervous about what she must drop into it" (AM, July 1896, 58); "the pressure she proposed to exercise would be, should success attend it, to keep him tied to an affection that had died a sudden and violent death." (AM, June 1896, 736.) "She lived now in a kind of bath of boldness, felt as if fierce light poured in upon her from windows opened wide." (AM, July 1896, 69.) "His blankness showed for a little that he felt the chill of her cold logic." (AM, Aug. 1896, 215.)

6 AM, April 1881, 449.

7 AM, Nov. 1880, 585 f.

8 As an example of a nature description by Hardy here is a passage from *Far from the Madding Crowd:* "The hill was covered on its northern side by an ancient and decaying plantation of beeches, whose upper verge formed a line over the crest, fringing its arched curve against the sky, like a mane. Tonight these trees sheltered the southern slope from the keenest blasts, which smote the wood and floundered through it with a sound as of grumbling, or gushed over its crowning boughs in a weakened moan. The dry leaves in the ditch simmered and boiled in the same breezes, a tongue of air occasionally ferreting out a few, and sending them spinning across the grass. A group or two of the latest in date among the dead multitude had remained till this very mid-winter time on the twigs which bore them, and in falling rattled against the trunks with smart taps.

Between this half-wooded half-naked hill, and the vague still horizon that its summit indistinctly commanded, was a mysterious sheet of fathomless shade — the sounds from which suggested that what it concealed bore some reduced resemblance to features here. The thin grasses, more or less coating the hill, were touched by the wind in breezes of differing powers, and almost of differing natures—one rubbing the blades heavily, another raking them piercingly, another brushing them like a soft broom. The instinctive act of humankind was to stand and listen, and learn how the trees on the right and the trees on the left wailed or chaunted to each other in the regular antiphonies of a cathedral choir; how hedges and other shapes to leeward then caught the note, lowering it to the tenderest sob; and how the hurrying gust then plunged into the south, to be heard no more" (beginning of chapter 2).

9 NAR, Feb. 1903, 299.
10 NAR, March 1903, 479.
11 NAR, April 1903, 652.
12 NAR, Sept. 1903, 478.
13 NAR, Feb. 1903, 318.
14 NAR, May 1903, 805.
15 NAR, March 1903, 468.
16 NAR, Sept. 1903, 474.
17 NAR, Oct. 1903, 616. As a further example this impressive personification of abstract matters may serve: "It faced him, the reckoning, over the shoulder of much interposing experience—which also faced him; and one would float to it, doubtless, duly, through these caverns of Kublai [sic] Khan." (NAR, Dec. 1903, 959.)
18 NAR, Dec. 1903, 954f.
19 C, 360f.
20 "in the course of the few late strolls he was finding time to take through dusky labyrinthine alleys and empty *campi,* overhung with mouldering palaces, ... where the sound of a rare footstep on the enclosed pavement was like that of a retarded dancer in a banquet-hall deserted— ... he entertained cold views ... on the principle that the shortest follies are the best" (C, 401); "This colloquy had taken place in the middle of Piazza San Marco, always, as a great social saloon, a smooth-floored, blue-roofed chamber of amenity, favourable to talk ... the great mosque-like church ... rose now, domed and pinnacled, but a little way behind them, and they had in front the vast empty space, enclosed by its arcades, to which at that hour movement and traffic were mostly confined. Venice was at breakfast ... and, except for the parties of importunate pigeons picking up the crumbs of perpetual feasts, their prospect was clear" (C, 406); "he took his course, through crooked ways, to the Piazza, where he should have the shelter of the galleries. Here, in the high arcade, half Venice was crowded close, while, on the Molo, at the limit of the expanse, the old columns of St. Mark and of the Lion were like the lintels of a door wide open to the storm ... There were stretches of the gallery paved with squares of red marble, greasy now with the salt spray; and the whole place, in its huge elegance, the grace of its conception and the beauty of its detail, was more than ever like a great drawing-room, the drawing-room of Europe, profaned and bewildered by some reverse of fortune. He brushed shoulders with brown men whose hats askew, and the loose sleeves of whose pendent jackets, made them resemble melancholy maskers. The tables and chairs that overflowed from the cafés were gathered, still with a pretence of service, into the arcade, and here and there a spectacled German, with his coat-collar up, partook publicly of food and philosophy" (C, 461f.); "The weather changed, the stubborn storm yielded, and the autumn sunshine, baffled for many days, but now hot and almost vindictive, came into its own again and, with an almost audible paean, a suffusion of bright sound that was one with the bright colour, took large possession. Venice glowed and plashed and called and chimed again; the air was like a clap of hands, and the scattered pinks, yellows, blues, sea-greens, were like a hanging-out of vivid stuffs, a laying down of fine carpets." (C, 488.)
21 C, 72f.

22 C, 313. Other examples are: "It didn't sit, the ugly motive, in Lord Mark's cool
English eyes" (C, 373); or: "The truth about Milly perched on his [Sir Luke Strett's]
shoulders and sounded in his tread, became by the fact of his presence the name and
the form, for the time, of everything in the place; but it didn't, for the difference, sit in
his face." (C, 493.)

23 M, I, 195.

24 M, I, 338.

25 M, II, 48.

26 M, I, 316f.

27 M, II, 193.

28 M, II, 322. Other examples are: "Their rightness, the justification of everything —
something they so felt the pulse of—sat there with them" (M, I, 170); or: "Her
thought, however, just at present, had more than one face—had a series that it successively presented." (M, II, 336.)

B. *Thoughts and Ideas*

29 AM, March 1875, 299.

30 AM, March 1875, 303.

31 AM, Nov. 1875, 563.

32 AM, Nov. 1875, 566.

33 AM, Dec. 1875, 656.

34 AM, Dec. 1880, 742. The ambiguous formulation of this image renders its interpretation difficult. What does James mean by "a certain impulse"? Probably the most satisfactory explanation is that it stands for passion, or, maybe, even more narrowly, for
Isabel's sexual love and desire. If this interpretation is correct and she is already
frightened by the thought of that impulse, then she must naturally show a strong
tendency to frigidity. This would be strengthened by the facts that she a) marries a man
who already has a child, b) has no children herself, c) is so terribly frightened of Goodwood's fierce and overwhelming passion which, with him, without doubt, is firmly
rooted in the sexual.

35 AM, May 1881, 647.

36 AM, Aug. 1881, 227ff.* Such a passage seems to refute Mr. Anderson's view as
expressed in *The American Henry James*, p. 188, that Isabel's return to Rome is one to
"the house of life in which she has encountered her other self". Osmond's house is
rather one of death. Mr. Anderson's thesis on the whole, as established in his book,
could be disproved in many points with James's imagery, but the recent publication
of the book has not allowed a detailed criticism to be incorporated in this study, and,
as Mr. Leon Edel has put it, to "attempt to argue with it on the level of its own circular
and often evasive Procrustean arguments, involves the reader not in James's world
but in a world of Anderson's creation". (*AL*, Jan. 1958, p. 495.)

37 See p. 35.

38 We think it very likely that *Middlemarch* had a decisive influence on the conception
of *The Portrait*. James had reviewed Eliot's novel in 1873, and his major criticism was
that it had too insignificant a setting. "With its abundant and massive ingredients
Middlemarch ought somehow to have depicted a weightier drama. Dorothea was altogether too superb a heroine to be wasted; yet she plays a narrower part than the
imagination of the reader demands. She is of more consequence than the action of
which she is the nominal centre. She marries enthusiastically a man whom she fancies
a great thinker, and who turns out to be an arid pedant. Here, indeed, is a disappointment with much of the dignity of tragedy; but the situation seems to us never to
expand to its full capacity. It is analysed with extraordinary penetration, but one may

178

say of it, as of most of the situations in the book, that it is treated with too much refinement and too little breath. It revolves too constantly on the same pivot." (*The House of Fiction*. Essays on the Novel by Henry James, ed. by Leon Edel, London 1957, p. 261).

39 AM, June 1896, 736.
40 AM, Aug. 1896, 206.
41 As this metaphor is part of a series of iterative imagery it will be analysed in the next chapter.
42 See chapter 4, C, 2.
43 AM, Aug. 1896, 215.
44 AM, Oct. 1896, 518.*
45 NAR, Feb. 1903, 314.*
46 N, 229.
47 NAR, Feb. 1903, 316.
48 NAR, March 1903, 464.
49 NAR, Aug. 1903, 301.
50 NYE, XXII, 59 (this and the two following quotations do not yet stand in the serial version).
51 NYE, XXII, 228.
52 NYE, XXII, 229f.*
53 H. G. Wells, in his *Experiment in Autobiography* (London 1934, vol. II, p. 538), writes: "I once saw James quarrelling with his brother William James, the psychologist. He had lost his calm; he was terribly unnerved. He appealed to me, to me of all people, to adjudicate on what was and what was not permissible behaviour in England. William was arguing about it in an indisputably American accent, with an indecently naked reasonableness. I had come to Rye to fetch William James and his daughter to my home at Sandgate. William had none of Henry's passionate regard for the polish upon the surfaces of life and he was immensely excited by the fact that in the little Rye inn, which had its garden just over the high brick wall of the garden of Lamb House, G. K. Chesterton was staying. William James had corresponded with our vast contemporary and he sorely wanted to see him. So with a scandalous directness he had put the gardener's ladder against that ripe red wall and clambered up and peeped over!
Henry had caught him at it.
It was the sort of thing that isn't done. It was most emphatically the sort of thing that isn't done ... Henry had instructed the gardener to put away that ladder and William was looking thoroughly naughty about it."
54 C, 46.
55 C, 54.
56 C, 319ff.*
57 C, 394f.
58 C, 569f.*
59 M, I, 10f.*
60 M, I, 339.
61 M, I, 132. With "half-a-dozen" James wants to stress the extent of Adam's wealth. There are only very few indeed who possess as much as he does. It is not convincing when Quentin Anderson interprets "half-a-dozen" as referring to the other major characters of the novel (see *The American Henry James*, p. 309, n. 23). Had James wanted to convey this meaning he most certainly would have chosen "six" instead of "half-a-dozen". Furthermore the analysis of the spiral metaphor does not permit Anderson's interpretation.

62 M, I, 151.
63 M, II, 14f.
64 M, II, 24f.*
65 M, II, 145f.
66 M, II, 146.
67 M, II, 308.

C. *Feelings*

68 AM, Feb. 1875, 160.
69 AM, Sept. 1875, 270.
70 AM, Sept. 1875, 281.
71 AM, Jan. 1881, 4.
72 AM, Aug. 1881, 226.
73 AM, Nov. 1881, 622.
74 AM, Dec. 1881, 769.
75 AM, March 1881, 358.
76 Three functionally not very significant images concern Fleda's feelings: "Fleda, at this, felt her heroism meet its real test,—felt that in telling him the truth she should effectively raise a hand to push his impediment out of the way." (AM, Aug. 1896, 203.) After her breakdown in front of Owen: "Fleda winced at what he knew; she made a wild gesture which seemed to whirl it out of the room. The mere allusion was like another embrace." (AM, Aug. 1896, 217.) Her reaction to Mrs. Gereth's announcement that she has sent all her works of art back to Poynton: "She had been sore with the wrong to Owen, she had bled with the wounds of Poynton. Now, however, as she heard of the replenishment of the void that had so haunted her, she came as near sounding an alarm, as if from the deck of a ship she had seen a person she loved jump into the sea." (AM, Sept. 1896, 382.)
77 NAR, June 1903, 946f.
78 NAR, June 1903, 955f.
79 NAR, May 1903, 793. For the close link with James's own experience see N, 373.
80 NAR, July 1903, 143f.*
81 NAR, Oct. 1903, 637.
82 NAR, Oct. 1903, 640.
83 C, 424f.
84 C, 442.*
85 C, 226.
86 C, 345.
87 M, I, 279.
88 F. O. Matthiessen, *Henry James: The Major Phase*, p. 159.

D. *States of Dependence*

89 In *Roderick Hudson* James works almost exclusively on the outwardly apparent plane of relationships. With the exception of Rowland's affection for Mary there are no hidden relations. Nor is this particular relationship one of dependence.
90 AM, June 1881, 823.
91 AM, Nov. 1881, 624.
92 AM, March 1881, 335.
93 AM, Aug. 1881, 231.
94 AM, March 1881, 339.
95 AM, Oct. 1881, 499.*
96 AM, June 1896, 721.

97 AM, June 1896, 725.
98 AM, July 1896, 72.
99 AM, June 1896, 736.
100 AM, June 1896, 731.
101 AM, Oct. 1896, 527.
102 AM, Oct. 1896, 522.
103 NAR, April 1903, 653.
104 NAR, Aug. 1903, 299.
105 In order to elucidate this change James has introduced a series of iterative and closely
   related boat metaphors. They will therefore be analysed in chapter 6, A, 1.
106 NAR, Aug. 1903, 298.
107 Ibid.*
108 C, 53.
109 C, 277.
110 C, 176.
111 C, 371.
112 C, 379f.
113 M, I, 12f.*
114 M, I, 23f.
115 M, I, 141.
116 M, I, 296.
117 M, I, 297.
118 M, I, 330.
119 M, I, 199f.*
120 M, II, 295f.*
121 M, I, 190f.
122 M, I, 48.
123 M, I, 302f.
124 M, I, 366.
125 M, II, 294.

Chapter 6: The Constructive Image

A. *Iterative Imagery*

1 The group of iterative war images in *The Old Things* has already been dealt with as a
   whole in an earlier chapter, from a different point of view. They strengthen the structure of the first part of the novel. They dramatize and emphasize the important points
   in the struggle for the possession of the spoils. This series of iterative imagery in *The
   Old Things* is a direct result of James's occupation with drama during the previous
   years.

1. Water Images

2 AM, May 1875, 522.
3 AM, July 1875, 67.
4 AM, July 1875, 69.
5 AM, Aug. 1875, 130.
6 NAR, Jan. 1903, 150.
7 NAR, Jan. 1903, 157.
8 NAR, April 1903, 647.
9 NAR, May 1903, 812.
10 NYE, XXII, 64f. (not yet in the serial version).

11 NAR, Aug. 1903, 312f.*
12 NAR, Sept. 1903, 457.
13 NAR, Sept. 1903, 467.
14 NAR, Dec. 1903, 959.
15 As for example: Merton "perceived from it, even at the moment and as he had never done before, that, since he had known these two women, no confessed nor commented tension, no crisis of the cruder sort, would really have taken form between them: which was precisely a high proof of how Kate had steered her boat". (C, 540.)
16 C, 88.
17 C, 95.
18 C, 165.
19 M, I, 27ff.*
20 M, I, 269ff.*
21 M, I, 375.
22 M, I, 379.
23 M, II, 136.
24 M, II, 262.
25 M, II, 361.

2. *Architectural Images*

26 The architectural images occurring in *The Ambassadors* are on the border-line between metaphor and symbol. They will, therefore, be analysed in the next chapter.
27 AM, Dec. 1880, 748.
28 AM, March 1881, 335.
29 AM, May 1881, 624.
30 AM, Sept. 1881, 364.
31 AM, Dec. 1881, 751.
32 M, I, 135 ff.*
33 F. O. Matthiessen writes in his chapter on *The Golden Bowl:* "In two of James' most breath-takingly elaborate efforts the Prince is at one time a Palladian church, at another a dazzling pagoda." (*Henry James: The Major Phase,* p. 82.) This statement is correct in the first instance, but only partly true in the second. The "pagoda" cannot merely be identified with the prince.
34 M, II, 5.
35 Ibid.
36 M, II, 6.
37 M, II, 3 ff.*
38 M, II, 9.
39 M, II, 26.
40 M, II, 28.

3. *Flying Images*

41 If we exclude here *The Wings* where the symbol of the dove is used somewhat differently.
42 AM, Nov. 1880, 589.
43 AM, Feb. 1881, 190.
44 AM, March 1881, 357.
45 AM, June 1881, 819. In the final edition James replaced "stone" by "faded rosebud", thus rendering the meaning of the image clearer and underlining Osmond's worthlessness.
46 AM, June 1881, 821.
47 AM, July 1881, 75.

48 AM, June 1896, 735.
49 AM, Aug. 1896, 205 f.
50 AM, Sept. 1896, 376.
51 AM, Sept. 1896, 380.

4. Princess and Dove Images in "The Wings of the Dove"

52 F. O. Matthiessen, *Henry James: The Major Phase*, p. 59.
53 C, 92.
54 C, 100f.
55 C, 104.
56 C, 142.
57 Ibid.
58 C, 211f.
59 C, 364.
60 C, 364f.
61 C, 367.
62 C, 393.
63 C, 422.*
64 C, 437.
65 C, 233f.*
66 C, 427f.*
67 C, 538.
68 C, 575.

5. Minor Forms of Iterative Imagery

69 NAR, June 1903, 963.*
70 NAR, July 1903, 149.
71 M, I, 22f.
72 M, I, 24.
73 M, I, 27.
74 Also used iteratively are the labyrinth images and those of Merton's "turning round a corner" in *The Wings*, which have already been analysed in other connections (see pp. 45 and 96).

B. Preparatory Images

75 AM, Feb. 1875, 148. In the final edition James replaced "a denser leafage" by "some wonderful flowers", thus giving the passage more colour as well as making the reference to Roderick's several works as a sculptor more obvious.
76 AM, March 1875, 310.
77 AM, Jan. 1881, 17.
78 AM, May 1881, 624.
79 AM, Sept. 1881, 361.
80 AM, June 1881, 808f.
81 AM, May 1881, 630.
82 AM, Sept. 1881, 339.
83 AM, May 1896, 631.
84 AM, May 1896, 635.
85 AM, July 1896, 71.
86 AM, Sept. 1896, 381.
87 NAR, April 1903, 645.
88 NAR, April 1903, 647.

89 Ibid.
90 NAR, June 1903, 952.
91 NAR, Dec. 1903, 967.
92 NAR, Oct. 1903, 635.
93 C, 107.
94 C, 271f.
95 C, 449.
96 Ibid.
97 C, 36.
98 C, 146.
99 C, 165.
100 The most elaborate preparation of Milly's death is to be found in the symbolic treat-
    ment of the Bronzino painting which she resembles. But here we are not in the
    presence of images in the strict sense. Therefore a closer analysis of these passages
    will follow in the next chapter.
101 C, 469.
102 C, 472.
103 M, I, 15.
104 M, I, 210.
105 M, II, 200.
106 M, I, 301.

Chapter 7: The Transition from Metaphor to Symbol

1 The same distinction can be made between James's early and late short stories. Titles
  in which the real central figure is named are predominant among the early stories (as
  for instance "Eugene Pickering", "Madame de Mauve", "Daisy Miller"). After
  James's occupation with the drama symbolical titles begin to prevail (as for instance:
  "The Death of the Lion", "The Figure in the Carpet", "The Beast in the Jungle",
  "The Bench of Desolation").
2 AM, April 1875, 434.
3 AM, March 1875, 312.
4 AM, Dec. 1875, 664.
5 Henry James, "Iwan Turgéniew", NAR, April 1874, 335. In this article James uses
  these expressions to describe Dmitri Rudin. Roderick is undoubtedly modelled to a
  great extent on this particular character of Turgenieff's (see also Kelley, C. P., *The
  Early Development of Henry James,* p. 187f.).
6 The artist's death at the end of the novel, and Rowland's return to America remind us
  strongly of a passage in one of James's notebook-entries for the year 1881. He writes
  about his return from Europe to America in September 1874: "I had come back then
  to 'try New York,' thinking it my duty to attempt to live at home before I should grow
  older, and not take for granted too much that Europe alone was possible; especially
  as Europe for me then meant simply Italy, where I had had some very discouraged
  hours, and which, lovely and desirable though it was, didn't seem as a permanent
  residence, to lead to anything." (N, 24.) Roderick's artistic life in Italy had not led to
  anything but death. We can see it as the outcome of James's own perception of the
  dangers for an American artist of a country like Italy, as he himself had experienced
  them, and as he was to express them again in his preface to *The Portrait.*
7 Where he says at one point: "My subject, all blissfully, in face of difficulties, had defined
  itself—and this in spite of the title of the book—as not directly, in the least, my young
  sculptor's adventure. This it had been but indirectly, being all the while in essence

and in final effect another man's, his friend's and patron's, view and experience of him."
(NYE, I, xvi f.) A little later James remarks that "the drama is the very drama of that
[Rowland's] consciousness". (NYE, I, xvii.)

8 AM, Jan. 1875, 4.
9 NYE, XXI, xiv.
10 N, 379. As early as the preface to *Roderick Hudson* he had written about his choice of
Northampton: "What I wanted, in essence, was the image of some perfectly humane
community which was yet all incapable of providing for it ... It was a peaceful, rural
New England community *quelconque* — it was not, it was under no necessity of being,
Northampton Mass." (NYE, I, x f.)
11 NAR, Feb. 1903, 318 ff.*
12 NAR, March 1903, 464.*
13 NYE, XXII, 228 ff.* This passage occurs in one of the parts which James restored
in the final version. It becomes apparent, therefore, that he felt an urgent need to stress
the symbolism of the two earlier passages (both parts of the serial version) by restoring
the third and conclusive one. The course of Strether's transformation thus becomes
clearer, and its meaning is made more evident.
14 NYE, XXII, 235.
15 C, 428 f.
16 C, 180.
17 C, 183. The painting to which James refers has been identified with Bronzino's portrait
of Lucrezia Panciatichi, painted between 1532 and 1540 (now in the Uffizi Galleries in
Florence). Carved into the longer green "beads" of the second and larger necklace
worn by Bronzino's Lucrezia is the legend "Amour dure sans fin" (see Allott, Miriam,
"The Bronzino Portrait in Henry James's *The Wings of the Dove*", in *MLN*, vol. 68,
No. 1, January 1953, pp. 23–25).
18 C, 375.
19 M, II, 205.
20 M, II, 222.
21 *Henry James: The Major Phase*, p. 83.
22 M, II, 241. Maggie also has a vision of "Io goaded by the gadfly" (M, II, 317), of
the "torment of the lost pilgrim who listens in desert sands for the possible, the
impossible, plash of water" (M, II, 289); or she feels a "strangeness that had already,
fifty times, brushed her, in the depth of her trouble, as with the wild wing of some
bird of the air who might blindly have swooped for an instant into the shaft of a well,
darkening there by his momentary flutter the far-off round sky" (M, II, 192), and
Charlotte's voice affects her "like the shriek of a soul in pain". (M, II, 300.)
23 M, II, 376.

APPENDIX

Here follow some passages as a whole containing images which have been analysed. This is mainly to show how organically they are intervowen into the texts of the novels.

Chapter 3

to n. 2: first version

he immediately perceived that she was greatly changed since their parting, and that the change was by no means for the worse. She was older, easier, more free, more like a young woman who went sometimes into company. She had more beauty as well, inasmuch as her beauty, before, had been the depth of her expression, and the sources from which this beauty was fed had in these two years evidently not wasted themselves. (AM, Sept. 1875, 270).

final version

he immediately perceived that she was now a person changed, and changed not to her disfigurement. She was older, easier, lighter; she had, as would have been said in Rome, more form. She had thus, he made out, more expression, facial and other, and it was beautifully as if this expression had been accumulating all the while, lacking on the scene of her life any channel to waste itself. It was like something she had been working at in the long days of home, an exquisite embroidery or a careful compilation, and she now presented the whole wealth of it as a kind of pious offering.

to n. 32: I didn't go off to the Old World to learn my business; no one took me by the hand; I had to grease my wheels myself, and, such as I am, I'm a self-made man, every inch of me! Well, if our young friend is booked for fame and fortune, I don't suppose his going to Rome will stop him. But, mind you, it won't help him such a long way, either. If you have undertaken to put him through, there's a thing or two you'd better remember. The crop we gather depends upon the seed we sow. He may be the biggest genius of his age: his potatoes won't come up without his hoeing them. If he takes things so almighty easy as—well, as one or two young fellows of genius I've had under my eye—his produce will never gain the prize. Take the word for it of a man who has made his way inch by inch, and doesn't believe that we'll wake up to find our work done because we've lain all night a-dreaming of it: anything worth doing is devilish hard to do! If your young protajay finds things easy and has a good time and says he likes the life, it's a sign that—as I may say—you had better step round to the office and look at the books.

to n. 33: "English society," as he would have said, cut him, accordingly, in two, and he reminded himself often, in his relations with it, of a man possessed of a shining star, a decoration, an order of some sort, something so ornamental as to make his identity not complete, ideally, without it, yet who, finding no other such object generally worn, should be perpetually, and the least bit ruefully, unpinning it from his breast to transfer it to his pocket. The Prince's shining star may, no doubt, having [sic] been nothing more precious than his private subtlety; but whatever the object was he just now fingered it a good deal, out of sight—amounting as it mainly did for him to a restless play of memory and a fine embroidery of thought.

to n. 36: he had taken at the station itself a line that led him without a break, and that enabled him to lead the Pococks—though dazed a little, no doubt, breathless, no doubt, and bewildered—to the uttermost end of the passage accepted by them perforce as pleasant. He had made it, for them, violently pleasant and mercilessly full; the upshot of which was, to Strether's vision, that they had come all the way without discovering that it was really no passage at all. It was a brave blind alley, where to pass was impossible, and where, unless they stuck fast, they would have—which was always awkward—publicly to back out. They were touching bottom, assuredly, tonight; the whole scene represented the terminus of the *cul-de-sac*.

to n. 64: On those lines he could still be liberal, yet it was at best a sort of whistling in the dark. It was unmistakable, moreover, that the sense of being in the dark now pressed on him more sharply—creating thereby the need for a louder and livelier whistle. He whistled long and hard after sending his message; he whistled again and again in celebration of Chad's news; there was an interval of a fortnight in which this exercise helped him. He had no great notion of what, on the spot, Sarah Pocock would have to say—though he had indeed confused premonitions; but it shouldn't be in her power to say—it shouldn't be in any one's anywhere to say—that he was neglecting her mother. He might have written before more freely, but he had never written more copiously; and he frankly gave for a reason, at Woollett, that he wished to fill the void created by Sarah's departure.

The increase of his darkness, however, and the quickening, as I have called it, of his tune, resided in the fact that he was hearing almost nothing.

to n. 75: For this had been all day, at bottom, the spell of the picture—that it was essentially, more than anything else, a scene and a stage, that the very air of the play was in the rustle of the willows and the tone of the sky. The play and the characters had, without his knowing it till now, peopled all his space for him, and it seemed somehow quite happy that they should offer themselves, in the conditions so supplied, with a kind of inevitability. It was as if the conditions made them not only inevitable, but so much more nearly natural and right as that they were at least easier, pleasanter, to put up with. The conditions had nowhere so asserted their difference from those of Woollett as they appeared to him to assert it in the little court of the Cheval Blanc while he arranged with his hostess for a comfortable climax. They were few and simple, scant and humble, but they were *the thing,* as he would have called it, even to a greater degree than Madame de Vionnet's old, high salon, where the ghost of the Empire [sic] walked. "The" thing was the thing that implied the greatest number of other things of the sort he had had to tackle; and it was queer of course, but so it was—the implication here was complete. Not a single one of his observations but somehow fell into a place in it; not a breath of the cooler evening that wasn't somehow a syllable of the text. The text was simply, when condensed, that in *these* places such things were, and that if it was in them one elected to move about, one had to make one's account with what one lighted on. Meanwhile, at all events, it was enough that they did affect one—so far as the village aspect was concerned—as whiteness, crookedness and blueness set in coppery green; there being positively, for that matter, an outer wall of the White Horse that was painted the most improbable shade. That was part of the amusement—as if to show that the fun was harmless; just as it was enough, further, that the picture and the play seemed supremely to melt together in the good woman's broad sketch of what she could do for her visitor's appetite.

to n. 76: That was the story—that she was always, for her beneficent dragon, under arms; living up, every hour, but especially at festal hours, to the "value" Mrs. Lowder had attached to her. High and fixed, this estimate ruled, on each occasion, at Lancaster Gate, the social scene; so that our young man now recognised in it something like the artistic idea, the plastic substance, imposed by tradition, by genius, by criticism, in respect to a given character, on a distinguished actress. As such a person was to dress the part, to walk, to look, to speak, in every way to express, the part, so all this was what Kate was to do for the character she had undertaken, under her aunt's roof, to represent. It was made up, the character, of definite elements and touches—things all perfectly ponderable to criticism; and the way for her to meet criticism was evidently at the start to be sure her make-up was exact and that she looked at least no worse than usual. Aunt Maud's appreciation of that to-night was indeed managerial, and Kate's own contribution fairly that of the faultless soldier on parade. Densher saw himself for the moment as in his purchased stall at the play; the watchful manager was in the depth of a box and the poor actress in the glare of the footlights. But she *passed,* the poor actress—he could see how she always passed; her wig, her paint, her jewels, every mark of her expression impeccable, and her entrance accordingly greeted with the proper round of applause. Such impressions as we thus note for Densher come and go, it must be granted, in very much less time than notation demands; but we may none the less make the point that there was, still further, time among them for him to feel almost too scared to take part in the ovation. He struck himself as having lost, for the minute, his presence of mind—so that, at any rate, he only stared in silence at the older woman's technical challenge and at the younger one's disciplined face. It was as if the drama—it thus came to him, for the fact of a drama there was no blinking—was between *them,* them quite preponderantly; with Merton Densher relegated to mere spectatorship, a paying place in front, and one of the most expensive. This was why his appreciation had turned for the instant to fear—had just turned, as we have said, to sickness; and in spite of the fact that the disciplined face did offer him over the footlights, as he believed, the small gleam, fine, faint, but exquisite, of a special intelligence. So might a practised performer, even when raked by double-barrelled glasses, seem to be all in her part and yet convey a sign to the person in the house she loved best.

The drama, at all events, as Densher saw it, meanwhile went on—amplified soon enough by the advent of two other guests, stray gentlemen both, stragglers in the rout of the season, who visibly presented themselves to Kate, during the next moments, as subjects for a like impersonal treatment and sharers in a like usual mercy.

to n. 78: it was only that with this young woman Milly had constantly proceeded, and more than ever of late, on the theory of intimate confessions, private, frank ironies that made up for their public grimaces and amid which, face to face, they wearily put off the mask.

These puttings-off of the mask had finally quite become the form taken by their moments together, moments indeed not increasingly frequent and not prolonged, thanks to the consciousness of fatigue on Milly's side whenever, as she herself expressed it, she got out of harness. They flourished their masks, the independent pair, as they might have flourished Spanish fans; they smiled and sighed on removing them; but the gesture, the smiles, the sighs, strangely enough, might have been suspected the greatest reality in the business. Strangely enough, we say, for the volume of effusion in general would have been found by either, on measurement, to be scarce proportional to the paraphernalia of relief. It was when they called each other's attention to their ceasing to pretend, it was then that what they were keeping back was most in the air. There was a difference, no doubt, and mainly to Kate's advantage: Milly didn't quite see what her friend could keep back, was possessed of, in fine, that would be so subject to retention; whereas it was comparatively plain sailing for Kate that poor Milly had a treasure to hide.

to n. 81: They might have been—really charming as they showed in the beautiful room, and Charlotte certainly, as always, magnificently handsome and supremely distinguished— they might have been figures rehearsing some play of which she herself was the author;

they might even, for the happy appearance they continued to present, have been such figures as would, by the strong note of character in each, fill any author with the certitude of success, especially of their own histrionic. They might in short have represented any mystery they would; the point being predominantly that the key to the mystery, the key that could wind and unwind it without a snap of the spring, was there in her pocket—or rather, no doubt, clasped at this crisis in her hand and pressed, as she walked back and forth, to her breast. She walked to the end and far out of the light; she returned and saw the others still where she had left them; she passed round the house and looked into the drawing-room, lighted also, but empty now, and seeming to speak the more, in its own voice, of all the possibilities she controlled. Spacious and splendid, like a stage again awaiting a drama, it was a scene she might people, by the press of her spring, either with serenities and dignities and decencies, or with terrors and shames and ruins, things as ugly as those formless fragments of her golden bowl she was trying so hard to pick up.

to n. 97: "It's not too late for *you,* on any side, and you don't strike me as in danger of missing the train; besides which people can be in general pretty well trusted, of course— with the clock of their freedom ticking as loud as it seems to do here—to keep an eye on the fleeting hour. All the same, don't forget that you're young—blessedly young; be glad of it, on the contrary, and live up to it. Live all you can; it's a mistake not to. It doesn't so much matter what you do in particular, so long as you have your life. If you haven't had that what *have* you had? This place and these impressions—mild as you may find them to wind a man up so; all my impressions of Chad and of people I've seen at *his* place—well, have had their abundant message for me, have just dropped *that* into my mind. I see it now. I haven't done so enough before—and now I'm old; too old at any rate for what I see. Oh, I *do* see, at least; and more than you'd believe or I can express. It's too late. And it's as if the train had fairly waited at the station for me without my having had the gump- tion to know it was there. Now I hear its faint, receding whistle miles and miles down the line."

to n. 122: "You keep the key of the cupboard, and I foresee that when we're married you'll dole me out my sugar by lumps." She had replied that she rejoiced in his assumption that sugar would be his diet, and the domestic arrangement so prefigured might have seemed already to prevail. The supply from the cupboard at this hour was doubtless, of a truth, not altogether cloyingly sweet; but it met, in a manner, his immediate requirements.

to n. 140: there was a card she could play, but there was only one, and to play it would be to end the game. She felt herself—as at the small square green table, between the tall old silver candlesticks and the neatly arranged counters—her father's playmate and partner; and what it constantly came back to, in her mind, was that for her to ask a question, to raise a doubt, to reflect in any degree on the play of the others, would be to break the charm. The charm she had to call it, since it kept her companion so constantly engaged, so perpetually seated and so contentedly occupied. To say anything at all would be, in fine, to have to say *why* she was jealous; and she could, in her private hours, but stare long, with suffused eyes, at that impossibility.

to n. 141: her sole strength lay in her being able to see that if Charlotte wouldn't "want" the Assinghams it would be because that sentiment too would have motives and grounds. She had all the while command of one way of meeting any objection, any complaint, on his wife's part, reported to her by her father; it would be open to her to retort to his possible "What are your reasons, my dear?" by a lucidly-produced "What are hers, love, please?—isn't that what we had better know? Mayn't her reasons be a dislike, beautifully founded, of the presence, and thereby of the observation, of persons who perhaps know about her things it's inconvenient to her they should know?" That hideous card she might in mere logic play—being by this time, at her still swifter private pace, intimately familiar with all the fingered pasteboard in her pack. But she could play it only on the forbidden issue of sacrificing him; the issue so forbidden that it involved even a horror of finding out if he would really have consented to be sacrificed. What she must do she must do by keeping her hands off him.

Chapter 4

to n. 1: "Look at me in my misery and refuse to help me! Oh, you needn't be afraid, I know I'm a fright, I haven't an idea what I have on. If this goes on we may both as well turn scarecrows. If ever a woman was desperate, frantic, heart-broken, I'm that woman. I can't begin to tell you. To have nourished a serpent, sir, all these years! to have lavished one's self upon a viper that turns and stings her own poor mother! To have toiled and prayed, to have pushed and struggled, to have eaten the bread of bitterness, and all the rest of it, sir—and at the end of all things to find myself at this pass. It can't be, it's too cruel, such things don't happen, the Lord don't allow it. I'm a religious woman, sir, and the Lord knows all about me. With his own hand he had given me his reward! I would have lain down in the dust and let her walk over me; I would have given her the eyes out of my head, if she had taken a fancy to them. No, she's a cruel, wicked, heartless, unnatural girl! I speak to you, Mr. Mallet, in my dire distress, as to my *only* friend. There isn't a creature here that I can look to—not one of them all that I have faith in. But I always admired you. I said to Christina the first time I saw you that there at last was a real gentleman. Come, don't disappoint me now! I feel so terribly alone, you see; I feel what a nasty, hard, heartless world it is that has come and devoured my dinners and danced to my fiddles, and yet that hasn't a word to throw to me in my agony! Oh, the money, alone, that I have put into this thing, would melt the heart of a Turk!"

to n. 2: "What if the watch should run down," he asked, "and you should lose the key? What if you should wake up some morning and find it stopped—inexorably, appallingly stopped? Such things have been, and the poor devils to whom they happened have had to grin and bear it. The whole matter of genius is a mystery. It bloweth where it listeth and we know nothing of its mechanism. If it gets out of order we can't mend it; if it breaks down altogether we can't set it going again. We must let it choose its own pace, and hold our breath lest it should lose its balance. It's dealt out in different doses, in big cups and little, and when you have consumed your portion it's as naif to ask for more as it was for Oliver Twist to ask for more porridge. Lucky for you if you've got one of the big cups; we drink them down in the dark, and we can't tell their size until we tip them up and hear the last gurgle. Those of some men last for life; those of others for a couple of years. Nay, what are you smiling at so damnably?" he went on. "Nothing is more common than for an artist who has set out on his journey on a high-stepping horse to find himself all of a sudden dismounted and invited to go his way on foot. You can number them by the thousand—the people of two or three successes; the poor fellows whose candle burnt out in a night. Some of them groped their way along without it, some of them gave themselves up for blind and sat down by the wayside to beg. Who shall say that I'm not one of these? Who shall assure me that my credit is for an unlimited sum? Nothing proves it, and I never claimed it; or if I did, I did so in the mere boyish joy of shaking off the dust of Northampton. If you believed so, my dear fellow, you did so at your own risk! What am I, what are the best of us, but an experiment? Do I succeed—do I fail? It doesn't depend on me. I'm prepared for failure. It won't be a disappointment, simply because I shan't survive it. The end of my work shall be the end of my life. When

I have played my last card, I shall cease to care for the game. I'm not making vulgar threats of suicide; for destiny, I trust, won't add insult to injury by putting me to that abominable trouble. But I have a conviction that if the hour strikes *here*," and he tapped his forehead, "I shall disappear, dissolve, be carried off in a cloud! For the past ten days I have had the vision of some such fate perpetually swimming before my eyes. My mind is like a dead calm in the tropics, and my imagination as motionless as the phantom ship in the Ancient Mariner!"

to n. 19: "Mr. Striker, you must know, is not simply a good-natured attorney, who lets me dog's-ear his law books. He's a particular friend and general adviser. He looks after my mother's property and kindly consents to regard me as part of it. Our opinions have always been painfully divergent, but I freely forgive him his zealous attempts to unscrew my head-piece and set it on hind part before. He never understood me, and it was useless to try to make him. We speak a different language—we're made of a different clay. I had a fit of rage yesterday when I smashed his bust, at the thought of all the bad blood he had stirred up in me; it did me good, and it's all over now. I don't hate him any more; I'm rather sorry for him. See how you've improved me! I must have seemed to him willfully, wickedly stupid, and I'm sure he only tolerated me on account of his great regard for my mother. This morning I grasped the bull by the horns. I took an armful of law-books that have been gathering the dust in my room for the last year and a half, and presented myself at the office. 'Allow me to put these back in their places,' I said. 'I shall never have need for them more—never more, never more, never more!' 'So you've learned everything they contain?' asked Striker, leering over his spectacles. 'Better late than never!' 'I've learned nothing that you can teach me,' I cried. 'But I shall tax your patience no longer. I'm going to be a sculptor. I'm going to Rome. I won't bid you good-by just yet; I shall see you again. But I bid good-by here, with rapture, to these four detested walls—to this living tomb! I didn't know till now how I hated it! My compliments to Mr. Spooner, and my thanks for all you haven't made of me!'"

to n. 28: "You can describe yourself—*to* yourself—as, in a fine flight, giving up your aunt for me; but what good, I should like to know, would your fine flight do me?" As she still said nothing he developed a little. "We're not possessed of so much, at this charming pass, please to remember, as that we can afford not to take hold of any perch held out to us. I like the way you talk, my dear, about 'giving up!' One doesn't give up the use of a spoon because one's reduced to living on broth. And your spoon, that is your aunt, please consider, is partly mine as well." She rose now, as if in sight of the term of her effort, in sight of the futility and the weariness of many things, and moved back to the poor little glass with which she had communed before. She retouched here again the poise of her hat, and this brought to her father's lips another remark—in which impatience, however, had already been replaced by a free flare of appreciation. "Oh, you're all right! Don't muddle yourself up with *me!*"

His daughter turned round to him. "The condition aunt Maud makes is that I shall have absolutely nothing to do with you; never see you, nor speak, nor write to you, never go near you nor make you a sign, nor hold any sort of communication with you. What she requires is that you shall simply cease to exist for me."

He had always seemed—it was one of the marks of what they called the 'unspeakable' in him—to walk a little more on his toes, as if for jauntiness, in the presence of offence. Nothing, however, was more wonderful than what he sometimes would take for offence, unless it might be what he sometimes wouldn't. He walked at any rate on his toes now. "A very proper requirement of your aunt Maud, my dear—I don't hesitate to say it!" Yet as this, much as she had seen, left her silent at first from what might have been a sense of sickness, he had time to go on: "That's her condition then. But what are her promises? Just what does she engage to do? You must work it, you know."

"You mean make her feel," Kate asked after a moment, "how much I'm attached to you?"

"Well, what a cruel, invidious treaty it is for you to sign. I'm a poor old dad to make a stand about giving up—I quite agree. But I'm not, after all, quite the old dad not to get something *for* giving up."

to n. 38: He had lost early in life much of his crisp, closely-curling hair, the fineness of which was repeated in a small neat beard, too compact to be called "full", though worn equally, as for a mark where other marks were wanting, on lip and cheek and chin. His neat, colourless face, provided with the merely indispensable features, suggested immediately, for a description, that it was *clear,* and in this manner somewhat resembled a small decent room, clean-swept and unencumbered with furniture, but drawing a particular advantage, as might presently be noted, from the outlook of a pair of ample and uncurtained windows. There was something in Adam Verver's eyes that both admitted the morning and the evening in unusual quantities and gave the modest area the outward extension of a view that was "big" even when restricted to the stars. Deeply and changeably blue, though not romantically large, they were yet youthfully, almost strangely beautiful, with their ambiguity of your scarce knowing if they most carried their possessor's vision out or most opened themselves to your own. Whatever you might feel, they stamped the place with their importance, as the house-agents say; so that, on one side or the other, you were never out of their range, were moving about, for possible community, opportunity, the sight of you scarce knew what, either before them or behind them.

to n. 39: The Prince's dark blue eyes were of the finest, and, on occasion, precisely, resembled nothing so much as the high windows of a Roman palace, of an historic front by one of the great old designers, thrown open on a feast-day to the golden air. His look itself, at such times, suggested an image—that of some very noble personage who, expected, acclaimed by the crowd in the street and with old precious stuffs falling over the sill for his support, had gaily and gallantly come to show himself: always moreover less in his own interest than in that of spectators and subjects whose need to admire, even to gape, was periodically to be considered. The young man's expression became, after this fashion, something vivid and concrete—a beautiful personal presence, that of a prince in very truth, a ruler, warrior, patron, lighting up brave architecture and diffusing the sense of a function. It had been happily said of his face that the figure thus appearing in the great frame was the ghost of some proudest ancestor. Whoever the ancestor, now, at all events, the Prince was, for Mrs. Assingham's benefit, in view of the people. He seemed, leaning on crimson damask, to take in the bright day. He looked younger than his years; he was beautiful, innocent, vague.

to n. 42: it was not amusement and sensation that she coveted, but knowledge—facts that she might noiselessly lay away, piece by piece, in the perfumed darkness of her serious mind, so that, under this head at least, she should not be a perfectly portionless bride. She never merely pretended to understand; she let things go, in her modest fashion, at the moment, but she watched them on their way, over the crest of the hill, and when her fancy seemed not likely to be missed it went hurrying after them, and ran breathless at their side, as it were, and begged them for the secret. Rowland took an immense satisfaction in observing that she never mistook the second-best for the best and that when she was in the presence of a masterpiece, she recognized the occasion as a mighty one. She said many things which he thought very profound—that is, if they really had the fine intention he

192

suspected. This point he usually tried to ascertain; but he was obliged to proceed cautiously, for in her mistrustful shyness it seemed to her that cross-examination must necessarily be ironical. She wished to know just where she was going—what she should gain or lose. This was partly on account of a native intellectual purity, a temper of mind that had not lived with its door ajar, as one might say, upon the high-road of thought, for passing ideas to drop in and out at their pleasure; but had made much of a few long visits from guests cherished and honored—guests whose presence was a solemnity.

to n. 82: To go down, to forsake her refuge, was to meet some of her discoveries half-way, to have to face them or fly before them; whereas they were at such a height only like the rumble of a far-off siege heard in the provisioned citadel. She had almost liked, in these weeks, what had created her suspense and her stress: the loss of her mother, the submersion of her father, the discomfort of her sister, the confirmation of their shrunken prospects, the certainty, in especial, of her having to recognise that, should she behave, as she called it, decently—that is still do something for others—she would be herself wholly without supplies. She held that she had a right to sadness and stillness; she nursed them for their postponing power. What they mainly postponed was the question of a surrender—though she could not yet have said exactly of what: a general surrender of everything—that was at moments the way it presented itself—to aunt Maud's looming "personality". It was by her personality that aunt Maud was prodigious, and the great mass of it loomed because, in the thick, the foglike air of her arranged existence, there were parts doubtless magnified and parts certainly vague. They represented at all events alike, the dim and the distinct, a strong will and a high hand. It was perfectly present to Kate that she might be devoured, and she likened herself to a trembling kid, kept apart a day or two till her turn should come, but sure sooner or later to be introduced into the cage of the lioness.

The cage was aunt Maud's own room, her office, her counting-house, her battlefield, her especial scene, in fine, of action, situated on the ground-floor, opening from the main hall and figuring rather to our young woman on exit and entrance as a guard-house or toll-gate. The lioness waited—the kid had at least that consciousness; was aware of the neighbourhood of a morsel she had reason to suppose tender. She would have been meanwhile a wonderful lioness for a show, an extraordinary figure in a cage or anywhere; majestic, magnificent, high-coloured, all brilliant gloss, perpetual satin, twinkling bugles and flashing gems, with a lustre of agate eyes, a sheen of raven hair, a polish of complexion that was like that of well-kept china and that—as if the skin were too tight—told especially at curves and corners. Her niece had a quiet name for her—she kept it quiet; thinking of her, with a free fancy, as somehow typically insular, she talked to herself of Britannia of the Market Place—Britannia unmistakeably, but with a pen in her ear, and felt she should not be happy till she might on some occasion add to the rest of the panoply a helmet, a shield, a trident and a ledger. It was not in truth, however, that the forces with which, as Kate felt, she would have to deal were those most suggested by an image simple and broad; she was learning, after all, each day, to know her companion, and what she had already most perceived was the mistake of trusting to easy analogies. There was a whole side of Britannia, the side of her florid philistinism, her plumes and her train, her fantastic furniture and heaving bosom, the false gods of her taste and false notes of her talk, the sole contemplation of which would be dangerously misleading. She was a complex and subtle Britannia, as passionate as she was practical, with a reticule for her prejudices as deep as that other pocket, the pocket full of coins stamped in her image, that the world best knew her by. She carried on, in short, behind her aggressive and defensive front, operations determined by her wisdom. It was in fact, we have hinted, as a besieger that our young lady, in the provisioned citadel, had for the present most to think of her, and what made her formidable in this character was that she was unscrupulous and immoral. So, at all events, in silent sessions and a youthful off-hand way, Kate conveniently pictured her: what this sufficiently represented being that her weight was in the scale of certain dangers—those dangers that, by our showing, made the younger woman linger and lurk above, while the elder, below, both militant and diplomatic, covered as much of the ground as possible. Yet what were the dangers, after all, but just the dangers of life and of London? Mrs. Lowder *was* London, *was* life—the roar of the siege and the thick of the fray. There were some things, after all, of which Britannia was afraid; but aunt Maud was afraid of nothing—not even, it would appear, of arduous thought.

to n. 102: see previous passage to n. 82.

to n. 111: Even the conviction that Charlotte was but awaiting some chance really to test her trouble upon her lover's wife left Maggie's sense meanwhile open as to the sight of gilt wires and bruised wings, the spacious but suspended cage, the home of eternal unrest, of pacings, beatings, shakings, all so vain, into which the baffled consciousness helplessly resolved itself. The cage was the deluded condition, and Maggie, as having known delusion—rather!—understood the nature of cages. She walked round Charlotte's—cautiously and in a very wide circle; and when, inevitably, they had to communicate she felt herself, comparatively, outside, on the breast of nature, and saw her companion's face as that of a prisoner looking through bars. So it was that through bars, bars richly gilt, but firmly, though discreetly, planted, Charlotte finally struck her as making a grim attempt; from which, at first, the Princess drew back as instinctively as if the door of the cage had suddenly been opened from within.

to n. 112: He had taken her chair and let her go, and the arrangement was for Maggie a signal proof of her earnestness; of the energy, in fact, that, though superficially commonplace in a situation in which people weren't supposed to be watching each other, was what affected our young woman, on the spot, as a breaking of bars. The splendid shining supple creature was out of the cage, was at large; and the question now almost grotesquely rose of whether she mightn't by some art, just where she was and before she could go further, be hemmed in and secured. It would have been for a moment, in this case, a matter of quickly closing the windows and giving the alarm—with poor Maggie's sense that, though she couldn't know what she wanted of her, it was enough for trepidation that, at these firm hands, anything should be: to say nothing of the sequel of a flight taken again along the terrace, even under the shame of the confessed feebleness of such evasions on the part of an outraged wife. It was to this feebleness, none the less, that the outraged wife had presently resorted; the most that could be said for her being, as she felt while she finally stopped short, at a distance, that she could at any rate resist her abjection sufficiently not to sneak into the house by another way and safely reach her room. She had literally caught herself in the act of dodging and ducking, and it told her there, vividly, in a single word, what she had all along been most afraid of.

She had been afraid of the particular passage with Charlotte that would determine her father's wife to take him into her confidence as she couldn't possibly as yet have done, to prepare for him a statement of her wrong, to lay before him the infamy of what she was apparently suspected of. This, should she have made up her mind to do it, would rest on a calculation the thought of which evoked, strangely, other possibilities and visions. It would show her as sufficiently believing in her grasp of her husband to be able to assure herself that, with his daughter thrown on the defensive, with Maggie's cause and Maggie's word, in fine, against her own, it wasn't Maggie's that would most certainly carry the day. Such a glimpse of her conceivable idea, which would be founded on reasons all her own, reasons of experience and assurance impenetrable to others, but intimately familiar to herself—such a glimpse opened out wide as soon as it had come into view; for if so much as this was still firm ground between the elder pair, if the beauty of appearances had been so consistently preserved, it was only the golden bowl as Maggie herself knew it that had been broken. The breakage stood not for any wrought discomposure among the triumphant three—it stood merely for the dire deformity of her attitude toward them. She was unable at the minute, of course, fully to measure the difference thus involved for her, and it remained inevitably an agitating image, the way it might be held over her that if she didn't, of her own prudence, satisfy Charlotte as to the reference, in her mocking spirit, of so much of the unuttered and unutterable, of the constantly and unmistakably implied, her father would be invited without further ceremony to recommend her to do so. But *any* confidence, *any* latent operating insolence, that Mrs. Verver should, thanks to her large native resources, continue to be possessed of and to hold in reserve, glimmered suddenly as a possible working light and seemed to offer, for meeting her, a new basis and something like a new system. Maggie felt, truly, a rare contraction of the heart on making out, the next instant, what the new system would probably have to be—and she had practically done that before perceiving that the thing she feared had already taken place. Charlotte, extending her search, appeared now to define herself vaguely in the distance; of this, after an instant, the Princess was sure, though the darkness was thick, for the projected clearness of the smoking-room windows had presently contributed its help. Her friend came slowly into that circle—having also, for herself, by this time, not indistinguishably discovered that Maggie was on the terrace. Maggie, from the end, saw her stop before one of the windows to look at the group within, and then saw her come nearer and pause again, still with a considerable length of the place between them.

Yes, Charlotte had seen she was watching her from afar, and had stopped now to put her further attention to the test. Her face was fixed on her, through the night; she was the creature who had escaped by force from her cage, yet there was in her whole motion assuredly, even as so dimly discerned, a kind of portentous intelligent stillness. She had escaped with an intention, but with an intention the more definite that it could so accord with quiet measures.

Chapter 5

to n. 36: It was as if he had had the evil eye; as if his presence were a blight and his favor a misfortune. Was the fault in himself, or only in the deep mistrust she had conceived for him? This mistrust was the clearest result of their short married life; a gulf had opened between them, over which they looked at each other with eyes that were on either side a declaration of the deception suffered. It was a strange opposition, of the like of which she had never dreamed, an opposition in which the vital principle of the one was a thing of contempt to the other. It was not her fault,—she had practiced no deception; she had only admired and believed. She had taken all the first steps in the purest confidence, and then she had suddenly found the infinite vista of a multiplied life to be a dark, narrow alley, with a dead wall at the end. Instead of leading to the high places of happiness, from which the world would seem to lie below one, so that one could look down with a sense of exaltation and advantage, and judge and choose and pity, it led rather downward and earthward, into realms of restriction and depression, where the sound of other lives, easier and freer, was heard as from above, and served to deepen the feeling of failure. It was her deep distrust of her husband,—this was what darkened the world. That is a sentiment easily indicated, but not so easily explained, and so composite in its character that much time and still more suffering had been needed to bring it to its actual perfection. Suffering, with Isabel, was an active condition; it was not a chill, a stupor, a despair; it was a passion of thought, of speculation, of response to every pressure. She flattered herself, however, that she had kept her mistrust to herself—that no one suspected it but Osmond. Oh, he knew it, and there were times when she thought that he enjoyed it. It had come gradually; it was not till the first year of her marriage had closed that she had taken the alarm. Then the shadows began to gather; it was as if Osmond deliberately, almost malignantly had put the lights out one by one. The dusk at first was vague and thin, and she could still see her way in it. But it steadily increased, and if here and there it had occasionally lifted there were certain corners of her life that were impenetrably black ... She could live it over again, the incredulous terror with which she had taken the measure of her dwelling. Between those four walls she had lived ever since; they were to surround her for the rest of her life. It was the house of darkness, the house of dumbness, the house of suffocation. Osmond's beautiful mind gave it neither light nor air; Osmond's beautiful mind, indeed, seemed to peep down from a small high window, and mock at her. Of course, it was not physical suffering; but for physical suffering there might have been a remedy. She could come and go; she had her liberty, her husband was perfectly polite. He took himself so seriously; it was something appalling. Under all his culture, his cleverness, his amenity, under his good-nature, his facility, his knowledge of life, his egotism lay hidden, like a serpent in a bank of flowers ... she nevertheless assented to this intimation that she too must march to the stately music that floated down from unknown periods in her husband's past—she, who of old had been so free of step, so desultory, so devious, so much the reverse of processional. There were certain things they must do, a certain posture they must take, certain people they must know and not know. When Isabel saw this rigid system closing about her, draped though it was in pictured tapestries, that sense of darkness and suffocation of which I have spoken took possession of her; she seemed to be shut up with an odor of mould and decay. She had resisted, of course: at first very humorously, ironically, tenderly; then, as the situation grew more serious, eagerly, passionately, pleadingly. She had pleaded the cause of freedom, of doing as they chose, of not caring for the aspect and denomination of their life—the cause of other instincts and longings, of quite another ideal.

Then it was that her husband's personality, touched as it never had been, stepped forth and stood erect. The things she had said were answered only by his scorn, and she could see that he was ineffably ashamed of her. What did he think of her? That she was base, vulgar, ignoble? He at least knew now that she had no traditions! It had not been in his prevision of things that she should reveal such flatness; her sentiments were worthy of a radical newspaper, or of a Unitarian preacher. The real offence, as she ultimately perceived, was her having a mind of her own at all. Her mind was to be his—attached to his own like a small gardenplot to a deer-park. He would rake the soil gently, and water the flowers; he would weed the beds and gather an occasional nosegay. It would be a pretty piece of property for a proprietor already far-reaching. He didn't wish her to be stupid. On the contrary, it was because she was clever that she had pleased him. But he expected her intelligence to operate altogether in his favor, and so far from desiring her mind to be a blank he had flattered himself that it would be richly receptive. He had expected his wife to feel with him and for him, to enter into his opinions, his ambitions, his preferences; and Isabel was obliged to confess that this was no very unwarrantable demand on the part of a husband. But there were certain things she could never take in. To begin with, they were hideously unclean. She was not a daughter of the Puritans, but for all that she believed in such a thing as purity. It would appear that Osmond didn't. Some of his traditions made her push back her skirts.

to n. 44: Her excitement was composed of pulses as swift and fine as the revolutions of a spinning top: she supposed she was going round, but she went round so fast that she couldn't even feel herself move. Her emotion occupied some quarter of her soul that had closed its door for the day and shut out even her own sense of it; she might perhaps have heard something if she had pressed her ear to a partition. Instead of that she sat with her patience in a cold, still chamber from which she could look out in quite another direction. This was to have achieved an equilibrium to which she couldn't have given a name: indifference, resignation, despair were the terms of a forgotten tongue. The time even seemed not long, for the stages of the journey were the items of Mrs. Gereth's surrender. The detail of that performance, which filled the scene, was what Fleda had now before her eyes. The part of her loss that she could think of was the reconstituted splendor of Poynton. It was the beauty she was most touched by that, in tons, she had lost,—the beauty that, charged upon big wagons, had safely crept back to its home. But the loss was a gain to memory and love; it was to her too, at last, that, in condonation of her treachery, the old things had crept back. She greeted them with open arms; she thought of them hour after hour; they made a company with which solitude was warm, and a picture that, at this crisis, overlaid poor Maggie's mahogany.

to n. 45: Strether, however, could not at this point indeed have completed his thought by the image of what she might have to thank herself *for:* the image, at best, of his own likeness—poor Lambert Strether washed up on the sunny strand, thankful for breathing-time, stiffening himself while he gasped, by the waves of a single day. There he was, and there was nothing in his aspect or his posture to scandalize: it was only true that if he had seen Mrs. Newsome coming he would instinctively have jumped up to walk away a little. He would have come round and back to her bravely, but he would have had to pull himself together. She abounded in news of the situation at home, proved to him how perfectly she was arranging for his absence, told him who would take up this and who take up that exactly where he had left it, gave him in fact chapter and verse for the moral that nothing would suffer. It filled for him, this tone of hers, all the air; yet it struck him at the same time as the hum of vain things. This latter effect was what he tried to justify—and with the success that, grave though the appearance, he at last lighted on a form that was happy. He arrived at this form by the inevitable recognition of his having been a fortnight before one of the weariest of men. If ever a man had come off tired Lambert Strether was that man; and hadn't it been distinctly on the ground that he *was* tired that his wonderful friend at home had so felt for him and so contrived? It seemed to him somehow at these instants that, could he only maintain with sufficient firmness his grasp of this truth, it might become in a manner his compass and his helm.

to n. 52: see passage to n. 13 in chapter 7.

to n. 56: "I'd do anything"—she kept it up—"for Kate."

Looking at him as with conscious clearness while she spoke, she might for the moment have effectively laid a trap for whatever remains of the ideal straightness in him were still able to pull themselves together and operate. He was afterwards to say to himself that something had at that moment hung for him by a hair. "Oh, I know what one would do for Kate!"—it had hung for him by a hair to break out with that, which he felt he had really been kept from by an element in his consciousness stronger still. The proof of the truth in question was precisely in his silence; resisting the impulse to break out was what he *was* doing for Kate. This at the time moreover came and went quickly enough; he was trying the next minute but to make Milly's allusion easy for herself. "Of course I know what friends you are—and of course I understand," he permitted himself to add, "any amount of devotion to a person so charming. That's the good turn then she'll do us all—I mean her working for your return."

"Oh, you don't know," said Milly, "how much I'm really on her hands."

He could but accept the appearance of wondering how much he might show he knew. "Ah she's very masterful."

"She's great. Yet I don't say she bullies me."

"No—that's not the way. At any rate it isn't hers," he smiled. He remembered, however, then that an undue acquaintance with Kate's ways was just what he mustn't show; and he pursued the subject no further than to remark with a good intention that had the further merit of representing a truth: "I don't feel as if I knew her—really to call know."

"Well, if you come to that, I don't either!" she laughed. The words gave him, as soon as they were uttered, a sense of responsibility for his own; though during a silence that ensued for a minute he had time to recognise that his own contained, after all, no element of falsity. Strange enough therefore was it that he could go too far—if it *was* too far— without being false. His observation was one he would perfectly have made to Kate herself. And before he again spoke, and before Milly did, he took time for more still—for feeling that just here it was that he must break short off if his mind was really made up not to go further. It was as if he had been at a corner—and fairly put there by his last speech; so that it depended on him whether or no to turn it. The silence if prolonged but an instant might even have given him a sense of her waiting to see what he would do. It was filled for them, the next thing, by the sound, rather voluminous for the August afternoon, of the approach, in the street below them, of heavy carriage-wheels and of horses trained to 'step'. A rumble, a great shake, a considerable effective clatter, had been apparently succeeded by a pause at the door of the hotel, which was in turn accompanied by a due proportion of diminished prancing and stamping. "You've a visitor," Densher laughed, "and it must be at least an ambassador."

"It's only my own carriage; it does that—isn't it wonderful?—every day. But we find it, Mrs. Stringham and I, in the innocence of our hearts, very amusing." She had got up, as she spoke, to assure herself of what she said; and at the end of a few steps they were together on the balcony and looking down at her waiting chariot, which made indeed a brave show. "Is it very awful?"

It was to Densher's eyes—save for its absurd heaviness—only pleasantly pompous. "It seems to me delightfully rococo. But how do I know? You're mistress of these things, in contact with the highest wisdom. You occupy a position, moreover, thanks to which your carriage—well, by this time, in the eye of London, also occupies one." But she was going out, and he mustn't stand in her way. What had happened the next minute was, first, that she had denied she was going out, so that he might prolong his stay; and second, that she had said she would go out with pleasure if he would like to drive—that in fact there were always things to do, that there had been a question for her to-day of several in particular, and that this, in short, was why the carriage had been ordered so early. They perceived, as she said these things, that an inquirer had presented himself, and, coming back, they found Milly's servant announcing the carriage and prepared to accompany her. They appeared to have for her the effect of settling the matter—on the basis, that is, of Densher's happy response. Densher's happy response, however, had as yet hung fire, the process we have described in him operating by this time with extreme intensity. The system of not pulling up, not breaking off, had already brought him headlong, he seemed to feel, to where they actually stood; and just now it was, with a vengeance, that he must do either one thing or the other. He had been waiting for some moments, which probably seemed to him longer than they were; this was because he was anxiously watching himself wait. He couldn't keep that up for ever; and since one thing or the other was what he must do, it was for the other that he presently became conscious of having decided. If he had been drifting it settled itself in the manner of a bump, of considerable violence, against a firm object in the stream. "Oh yes; I'll go with you with pleasure. It's a charming idea."

She gave no look to thank him—she rather looked away; she only said at once to her servant, "In ten minutes"; and then to her visitor, as the man went out, "We'll go somewhere—I shall like that. But I must ask of you time—as little as possible—to get ready." She looked over the room to provide for him, keep him there. "There are books and things—plenty; and I dress very quickly." He caught her eyes only as she went, on which he thought them pretty and touching.

Why especially touching at that instant he could certainly scarce have said; it was involved, it was lost in the sense of her wishing to oblige him. Clearly what had occurred was her having wished it so that she had made him simply wish, in civil acknowledgement, to oblige *her;* which he had now fully done by turning his corner. He was quite round it, his corner, by the time the door had closed upon her and he stood there alone ... Densher continued slowly to wander; yet without keeping at bay for long the sense again that his corner was turned. It was so turned that he felt himself to have lost even the option of taking advantage of Milly's absence to retrace his steps. If he might have turned tail, vulgarly speaking, five minutes before, he couldn't turn tail now; he must simply wait there with his consciousness charged to the brim ...

He spoke to her at once of their friend's visit and flight. "She hadn't known she would find me," he said—and said at present without difficulty. His corner was so turned that it wasn't a question of a word more or less.

to n. 58: The thought was all his own, and his intimate companion was the last person he might have shared it with. He kept it back like a favourite pang; left it behind him, so to say, when he went out, but came home again the sooner for the certainty of finding it there. Then he took it out of its sacred corner and its soft wrappings; he undid them one by one, handling them, handling *it,* as a father, baffled and tender, might handle a maimed child. But so it was before him—in his dread of who else might see it. Then he took to himself at such hours, in other words, that he should never, never know what had been in Milly's letter. The intention announced in it he should but too probably know; but that would have been, for the depths of his spirit, the least part of it. The part of it missed for ever was the turn she would have given her act. That turn had possibilities that, somehow, by wondering about them, his imagination had extraordinarily filled out and refined. It had made of them a revelation the loss of which was like the sight of a priceless pearl cast before his eyes—his pledge given not to save it—into the fathomless sea, or rather even it was like the sacrifice of something sentient and throbbing, something that, for the spiritual ear, might have been audible as a faint, far wail. This was the sound that he cherished, when alone, in the stillness of his rooms.

to n. 59: he had kept no impression of the girl's rejoinder. It had but sweetened the waters in which he now floated, tinted them as by the action of some essence, poured from a gold-topped phial, for making one's bath aromatic. No one before him, never—not even the infamous Pope—had so sat up to his neck in such a bath. It showed, for that matter, how little one of his race could escape, after all, from history. What was it but history, and of *their* kind very much, to have the assurance of the enjoyment of more money than the palace-builder himself could have dreamed of? This was the element that bore him up and into which Maggie scattered, on occasion, her exquisite colouring drops. They were of the colour—of what on earth? of what but the extraordinary American good faith? They were of the colour of her innocence, and yet at the same time of her imagination, with which their relation, his and these people's, was all suffused.

to n. 64: if their family coach lumbered and stuck the fault was in its lacking its complement of wheels. Having but three, as they might say, it had wanted another, and what had

Charlotte done from the first but begin to act, on the spot, and ever so smoothly and beautifully, as a fourth? Nothing had been, immediately, more manifest than the greater grace of the movement of the vehicle—as to which, for the completeness of her image, Maggie was now supremely to feel how every strain had been lightened for herself. So far as *she* was one of the wheels she had but to keep in her place; since the work was done for her she felt no weight, and it wasn't too much to acknowledge that she had scarce to turn round. She had a long pause before the fire during which she might have been fixing with intensity her projected vision, have been conscious even of its taking an absurd, fantastic shape. She might have been watching the family coach pass and noting that, somehow, Amerigo and Charlotte were pulling it while she and her father were not so much as pushing. They were seated inside together, dandling the Principino and holding him up to the windows, to see and be seen, like an infant positively royal; so that the exertion was *all* with the others. Maggie found in this image a repeated challenge; again and yet again she paused before the fire: after which, each time, in the manner of one for whom a strong light has suddenly broken, she gave herself to livelier movement. She had seen herself at last, in the picture she was studying, suddenly jump from the coach; whereupon, frankly, with the wonder of the sight, her eyes opened wider and her heart stood still for a moment. She looked at the person so acting as if this person were somebody else, waiting with intensity to see what would follow.

to n. 80: It was on this pleasant basis of costly disorder, consequently, that they eventually seated themselves, on either side of a small table, at a window adjusted to the busy quay and the shining, barge-burdened Seine; where, for an hour, in the matter of letting himself go, of diving deep, Strether was to feel that he had touched bottom. He was to feel many things on this occasion, and one of the first of them was that he had travelled far since that evening, in London, before the theatre, when his dinner with Maria Gostrey, between the pink-shaded candles, had struck him as requiring so many explanations. He had at that time gathered them in, the explanations—he had stored them up; but it was at present as if he had either soared above or sunk below them—he couldn't tell which; he could somehow think of none that didn't seem to leave the appearance of collapse and cynicism easier for him than lucidity. How could he wish it to be lucid for others, for any one, that he, for the hour, saw reasons enough in the mere way the bright, clean, ordered water-side life came in at the open window?—the mere way Mme. de Vionnet, opposite him over their intensely white table-linen, their *omelette aux tomates,* their bottle of straw-colored Chablis, thanked him for everything almost with the smile of a child, while her gray eyes moved in and out of their talk, back to the quarter of the warm spring air, in which early summer had already begun to throb, and then back again to his face and their human questions.

Their human questions became many before they had done—many more, as one after the other came up, than our friend's free fancy had at all foreseen. The sense he had had before, the sense he had had repeatedly, the sense that the situation was running away with him, had never been so sharp as now; and all the more that he could perfectly put his finger on the moment it had taken the bit in its teeth.

to n. 84: He had, in fine, judged his friend's pledge in advance as an inestimable value, and what he must now know his case for was that of a possession of a value to the full. Wasn't it perhaps even rather the value that possessed *him,* kept him thinking of it and waiting on it, turning round and round it and making sure of it again from this side and that?

It played for him—certainly in this prime afterglow—the part of a treasure kept, at home, in safety and sanctity, something he was sure of finding in its place when, with each return, he worked his heavy old key in the lock. The door had but to open for him to be with it again and for it to be all there; so intensely there that, as we say, no other act was possible to him than the renewed act, almost the hallucination, of intimacy. Wherever he looked or sat or stood, to whatever aspect he gave for the instant the advantage, it was in view as nothing of the moment, nothing begotten of time or of chance could be, or ever would.

to n. 95: He got up, as he spoke, and walked to the chimney, where he stood a moment bending his eyes, as if he had seen them for the first time, on the delicate specimens of rare porcelain with which it was covered. He took up a small cup and held it in his hand; then, still holding it, and leaning his arm on the mantel, he continued: "You always see too much in everything; you overdo it; you lose sight of the real. I am much simpler than you think."

"I think you are very simple." And Madame Merle kept her eye upon her cup. "I have come to that with time. I judged you, as I say, of old; but it is only since your marriage that I have understood you. I have seen better what you have been to your wife than I ever saw what you were for me. Please be very careful of that precious object."

"It already has a small crack," said Osmond, dryly, as he put it down. "If you didn't understand me before I married, it was cruelly rash of you to put me in such a box. However, I took a fancy to my box myself; I thought it would be a comfortable fit. I asked very little; I only asked that she should like me."

"That she should like you so much!"

"So much, of course; in such a case one asks the maximum. That she should adore me, if you will. Oh yes, I wanted that."

"I never adored you," said Madame Merle.

"Ah, but you pretended to!"

"It is true that you never accused me of being a comfortable fit," Madame Merle went on.

"My wife has declined—declined to do anything of the sort," said Osmond. "If you are determined to make a tragedy of that, the tragedy is hardly for her."

"The tragedy is for me!" Madame Merle exclaimed, rising, with a long, low sigh, but giving a glance at the same time at the contents of her mantel-shelf. "It appears that I am to be severely taught the disadvantages of a false position."

"You express yourself like a sentence in a copy-book. We must look for our comfort where we can find it. If my wife doesn't like me, at least my child does. I shall look for compensations in Pansy. Fortunately I haven't a fault to find with her."

"Ah," said Madame Merle, softly, "if I had a child"—

Osmond hesitated a moment; and then, with a little formal air, "The children of others may be a great interest!" he announced.

"You are more like a copy-book than I. There is something, after all, that holds us together."

"Is it the idea of the harm I may do you?" Osmond asked.

"No; it's the idea of the good I may do for you. It is that," said Madame Merle, "that made me so jealous of Isabel. I want it to be *my* work," she added, with her face, which had grown hard and bitter, relaxing into its usual social expression.

Osmond took up his hat and his umbrella, and after giving the former article two or three strokes with his coat-cuff, "On the whole, I think," he said, "you had better leave it to me."

After he had left her, Madame Merle went and lifted from the mantel-shelf the attenuated coffee-cup in which he had mentioned the existence of a crack; but she looked at it rather abstractedly. "Have I been so vile all for nothing?" she murmured to herself.

to n. 107: It struck him really that he had never so lived with her as during this period of her silence; the silence was a sacred hush, a finer, clearer medium, in which her idiosyncrasies showed. He walked about with her, sat with her, drove with her, and dined face-to-face with her—a rare treat "in his life," as he could perhaps have scarce escaped phrasing it; and if he had never seen her so soundless, so, on the other hand, he had never felt her so highly, so almost austerely, herself; pure and by the vulgar estimate "cold," but deep, devoted, delicate, sensitive, noble. Her vividness in these respects became for him, in the special conditions, almost an obsession; and though the obsession sharpened his pulses, adding really to the excitement of life, there were hours at which, to be less on the stretch, he directly sought forgetfulness. He knew it for the queerest of adventures—a circumstance that could play such a part only for Lambert Strether—that in Paris itself, of all places, he should find this ghost of the lady of Woollett more importunate than any other presence.

to n. 113: "You're at any rate a part of his collection," she had explained—"one of the things that can only be got over here. You're a rarity, an object of beauty, an object of price. You're not perhaps absolutely unique, but you're so curious and eminent that there are very few others like you—you belong to a class about which everything is known. You're what they call a *morceau de musée.*"

"I see, I have the great sign of it," he had risked—"that I cost a lot of money."

"I haven't the least idea", she had gravely answered, "what you cost"—and he had quite adored, for the moment, her way of saying it. He had felt even, for the moment, vulgar. But he had made the best of that.

"Wouldn't you find out if it were a question of parting with me? My value would in that case be estimated."

She had looked at him with her charming eyes, as if his value were well before her. "Yes, if you mean that I'd pay rather than lose you."

And then there came again what this had made him say. "Don't talk about *me*—it's you who are not of this age. You're a creature of a braver and finer one, and the *cinquecento,* at its most golden hour, wouldn't have been ashamed of you. It would of me, and if I didn't know some of the pieces your father has acquired I should rather fear, for American City, the criticism of experts. Would it at all events be your idea," he had then just ruefully asked, "to send me there for safety?"

"Well, we may have to come to it."

"I'll go anywhere you want."

"We must see first—it will be only if we have to come to it. There are things," she had gone on, "that father puts away—the bigger and more cumbrous of course, which he stores, has already stored in masses, here and in Paris, in Italy, in Spain, in warehouses, vaults, banks, safes, wonderful secret places. We've been like a pair of pirates—positively . stage pirates, the sort who wink at each other and say 'Ha-ha!' when they come to where their treasure is buried. Ours is buried pretty well everywhere—except that we like to see, what we travel with and have about us. These, the smaller pieces, are the things we take out and arrange as we can, to make the hotels we stay at and the houses we hire a little less ugly. Of course it's a danger, and we have to keep watch. But father loves a fine piece, loves, as he says, the good of it, and it's for the company of some of his things that he's willing to run his risks. And we've had extraordinary luck"—Maggie had made that point; "we've never lost anything yet. And the finest objects are often the smallest. Values, in lots of cases, you must know, have nothing to do with size. But there's nothing, however tiny," she had wound up, "that we've missed".

"I like the class," he had laughed for this, "in which you place me! I shall be one of the. little pieces that you unpack at the hotels, or at the worst in the hired houses, like this wonderful one, and put out with the family photographs and the new magazines. But it's something not to be so big that I have to be buried."

"Oh," she returned, "you shall not be buried, my dear, till you're dead. Unless indeed you call it burial to go to American City."

"Before I pronounce I should like to see my tomb."

to n. 119: It not only remained and abode with them, it positively developed and deepened, after this talk, that the luxurious side of his personal existence was now again furnished, socially speaking, with the thing classed and stamped as "real"—just as he had been able to think of it as not otherwise enriched in consequence of his daughter's marriage. The note of reality, in so much projected light, continued to have for him the charm and the importance of which the maximum had occasionally been reached in his great "finds"—continued, beyond any other, to keep him attentive and gratified. Nothing perhaps might affect us as queerer, had we time to look into it, than this application of the same measure of value to such different pieces of property as old Persian carpets, say, and new human acquisitions; all the more indeed that the amiable man was not without an inkling, on his own side, that he was, as a taster of life, economically constructed. He put into his one little glass everything he raised to his lips, and it was as if he had always carried in his pocket, like a tool of his trade, this receptacle, a little glass cut with a fineness of which the art had long since been lost, and kept in an old morocco case stamped in uneffaceable gilt with the arms of a deposed dynasty. As it had served him to satisfy himself, so to speak, both about Amerigo and about the Bernadino Luini he had happened to come to knowledge of at the time he was consenting to the announcement of his daughter's betrothal, so it served him at present to satisfy himself about Charlotte Stant and an extraordinary set of oriental tiles of which he had lately got wind.

to n. 120: Charlotte hung behind, with emphasised attention; she stopped when her husband stopped, but at the distance of a case or two, or of whatever other succession of objects; and the likeness of their connection would not have been wrongly figured if he had been thought of as holding in one of his pocketed hands the end of a long silken halter looped round her beautiful neck. He didn't twitch it, yet it was there; he didn't drag her, but she came; and those indications that I have described the Princess as finding extraordinary in him were two or three mute facial intimations which his wife's presence didn't prevent his addressing his daughter—nor prevent his daughter, as she passed, it was doubtless to be added, from flushing a little at the receipt of. They amounted perhaps only to a wordless, wordless smile, but the smile was the soft shake of the twisted silken rope, and Maggie's translation of it, held in her breast till she got well away, came out only, as if it might have been overheard, when some door was closed behind her. "Yes, you see—I lead her now by the neck, I lead her to her doom, and she doesn't so much as know what it is, though she has a fear in her heart which, if you had the chances to apply your ear there that I, as a husband, have, you would hear thump and thump and thump. She thinks it *may* be, her doom, the awful place over there—awful for *her;* but she's afraid to ask, don't you see? just as she's afraid of not asking; just as she's afraid of so many other things that she sees multiplied round her now as portents and betrayals. She'll know, however—when she does know."

Chapter 6

to n. 11: She [Madame de Vionnet] smiled in welcome at Strether; she greated him more familiarly than Mrs. Pocock; she put out her hand to him without moving from her place; and it came to him, in the course of a minute, and in the oddest way, that—yes, positively—she was giving him over to ruin. She was all kindness and ease, but she couldn't help so giving him; she was exquisite, and her being just as she was poured, for Sarah, a sudden rush of meaning into his own equivocations. How could she know how she was hurting him? She wanted to show as simple and humble—in the degree compatible with operative charm; but it was just this that seemed to put him on her side ... the consciousness of all this, in her charming eyes, was so clear and fine that as she thus publicly drew him into her boat she produced in him such a silent agitation as he was not to fail afterwards to denounce as pusillanimous. "Ah, don't be so charming to me!—for it makes us intimate, and, after all, what *is* between us, when I've been so tremendously on my guard and have seen you but half-a-dozen times?" He recognized once more the perverse law that so inveterately governed his poor personal aspects: it would be exactly *like* the way things always turned out for him that he should affect Mrs. Pocock and Waymarsh as launched in a relation in which he had really never been launched at all. They were at this very moment—they could only be—attributing to him the full license of it, and all by the operation of her own tone with him; whereas his sole license had been to cling, with intensity, to the brink, not to dip so much as a toe into the flood. But the flicker of his fear on this occasion was not, as may be added, to repeat itself; it sprang up, for its moment, only to die down and then go out forever. To meet his fellow-visitor's invocation and, with Sarah's brilliant eyes on him, answer, *was* quite sufficiently to step into her boat. During the rest of the time her visit lasted he felt himself proceed to each of the proper offices, successively, for helping to keep the adventurous skiff afloat. It rocked beneath him, but he settled himself in his place. He took up an oar, and since he was to have the credit of pulling, he pulled.

to n. 19: "I'm starting on the great voyage—across the unknown sea; my ship's all rigged and appointed; the cargo's stowed away and the company complete. But what seems the matter with me is that I can't sail alone; my ship must be one of a pair, must have, in the waste of the waters, a—what do you call it?—a consort. I don't ask you to stay on board with me, but I must keep your sail in sight for orientation. I don't in the least know myself, I assure you, the points of the compass. But with a lead I can perfectly follow. You *must* be my lead."

"How can you be sure," she asked, "where I should take you?"

"Why, from your having brought me safely thus far. I should never have got here without you. You've provided the ship itself, and, if you've not quite seen me aboard, you've attended me, ever so kindly, to the dock. Your own vessel is, all conveniently, in the next berth, and you can't desert me now."

She showed him again her amusement, which struck him even as excessive, as if, to his surprise, he made her also a little nervous; she treated him in fine as if he were not uttering truths, but making pretty figures for her diversion. "My vessel, dear Prince?" she smiled. "What vessel, in the world, have I? This little house is all our ship, Bob's and mine—and thankful we are, now, to have it. We've wandered far, living, as you may say, from hand to mouth, without rest for the soles of our feet. But the time has come for us at last to draw in."

He made at this, the young man, an indignant protest. "You talk about rest—it's too selfish!—when you're just launching me on adventures?"

She shook her head with her kind lucidity. "Not adventures—heaven forbid! You've had yours—as I've had mine; and my idea has been, all along, that we should neither of us begin again. My own last, precisely, has been doing for you all you so prettily mention. But it consists simply in having conducted you to rest. You talk about ships, but they're not the comparison. Your tossings are over—you're practically *in* port. The port," she concluded, "of the Golden Isles."

to n. 20: "We're certainly not, with the relation of our respective *sposi,* simply formal acquaintances. We're in the same boat"—and the Prince smiled with a candour that added an accent to his emphasis.

Fanny Assingham was full of the special sense of his manner: it caused her to turn for a moment's refuge to a corner of her general consciousness in which she could say to herself that she was glad that *she* wasn't in love with such a man. As with Charlotte just before, she was embarrassed by the difference between what she took in and what she could say, what she felt and what she could show. "It only appears to me of great importance that—now that you all seem more settled here—Charlotte should be known, for any presentation, any further circulation or introduction, as, in particular, her husband's wife; known in the least possible degree as anything else. I don't know what you mean by the 'same' boat. Charlotte is naturally in Mr. Verver's boat!"

"And, pray, am *I* not in Mr. Verver's boat too? Why, but for Mr. Verver's boat, I should have been by this time"—and his quick Italian gesture, an expressive direction and motion of his forefinger, pointed to deepest depths—"away down, down, down." She knew of course what he meant—how it had taken his father-in-law's great fortune, and taken no small slice, to surround him with an element in which, all too fatally weighted as he had originally been, he could pecuniarily float ...

"The 'boat,' you see"—the Prince explained it no less considerately and lucidly—"is a good deal tied up at the dock, or anchored, if you like, out in the stream. I have to jump out from time to time to stretch my legs, and you'll probably perceive, if you give it your attention, that Charlotte really can't help occasionally doing the same. It isn't even a question, sometimes, of one's getting to the dock—one has to take a header and splash about in the water. Call our having remained here together to-night, call the accident of my having put them, put our illustrious friends there, on my companion's track—for I grant you this as a practical result of our combination—call the whole thing one of the harmless little plunges, off the deck, inevitable for each of us. Why not take them, when they occur, *as* inevitable—and, above all, as not endangering life or limb? We shan't drown, we shan't sink—at least I can answer for myself. Mrs. Verver too, moreover—do her the justice—visibly knows how to swim."

to n. 32: There had not yet been quite so much [to be done], on all the showing, as since their [Adam's and Maggie's] return from their twenty months in America, as since their settlement again in England, experimental though it was, and the consequent sense, now quite established for him, of a domestic air that had cleared and lightened, producing the effect, for their common personal life, of wider perspectives and large waiting spaces. It was as if his son-in-law's presence, even from before his becoming his son-in-law, had somehow filled the scene and blocked the future—very richly and handsomely, when all was said, not at all inconveniently or in ways not to have been desired: inasmuch as though the Prince, his measure now practically taken, was still pretty much the same "big fact," the sky had lifted, the horizon receded, the very foreground itself expanded, quite to match him, quite to keep everything in comfortable scale. At first, certainly, their decent little old-time union, Maggie's and his own, had resembled a good deal some pleasant public square, in the heart of an old city, into which a great Palladian church, say—something with a grand architectural front—had suddenly been dropped; so that the rest of the place, the space in front, the way round, outside, to the east end, the margin of street and passage, the quantity of overarching heaven, had been temporarily compromised. Not even then, of a truth, in a manner disconcerting—given, that is, for the critical, or at least the intelligent, eye, the great style of the façade and its high place in its class. The phenomenon that had since occurred, whether originally to have been pronounced calculable or not, had not, naturally, been the miracle of a night, but had taken place so gradually, quietly, easily, that from this vantage of wide, wooded Fawns, with its eighty rooms, as they said, with its spreading park, with its acres and acres of garden and its majesty of artificial lake—though that, for a person so familiar with the "great" ones, might be rather ridiculous—no visibility of transition showed, no violence of adjustment, in retrospect, emerged. The Palladian church was always there, but the *piazza* took care of itself. The sun stared down in his fulness, the air circulated, and the public not less; the limit stood off, the way round was easy, the east end was as fine, in its fashion, as the west, and there were also side doors for entrance, between the two—large, monumental, ornamental, in *their* style—as for all proper great churches. By some such process, in fine, had the Prince, for his father-in-law, while remaining solidly a feature, ceased to be, at all ominously, a block.

Mr. Verver, it may further be mentioned, had taken at no moment sufficient alarm to have kept in detail the record of his reassurance; but he would none the less not have been unable, not really have been indisposed, to impart in confidence to the right person his notion of the history of the matter. The right person—it is equally distinct—had not, for this illumination, been wanting, but had been encountered in the form of Fanny Assingham, not for the first time indeed admitted to his counsels, and who would have doubtless at present, in any case, from plenitude of interest and with equal guarantees, repeated his secret. It all came then, the great clearance, from the one prime fact that the Prince, by good fortune, hadn't proved angular. He clung to that description of his daughter's husband as he often did to terms and phrases, in the human, the social connexion, that he had found for himself: it was his way to have times of using these constantly, as if they just then lighted the world, or his own path in it, for him—even when for some of his interlocutors they covered less ground. It was true that with Mrs. Assingham he never felt quite sure of the ground anything covered; she disputed with him so little, agreed with him so much, surrounded him with such systematic consideration, such predetermined tenderness, that it was almost—which he had once told her in irritation— as if she were nursing a sick baby. He had accused her of not taking him seriously, and she had replied—as from her it couldn't frighten him—that she took him religiously, adoringly. She had laughed again, as she had laughed before, on his producing for her that good right word about the happy issue of his connexion with the Prince—with an effect the more odd perhaps as she hadn't contested its value. She couldn't of course, however, be, at the best, as much in love with his discovery as he was himself. He was so much so that he fairly worked it—to his own comfort; came in fact sometimes near publicly pointing the moral of what might have occurred if friction, so to speak, had occurred. He pointed it frankly one day to the personage in question, mentioned to the Prince the particular justice he did him, was even explicit as to the danger that, in their remarkable relation, they had thus escaped. Oh, if he *had* been angular!—who could say what might *then* have happened? He spoke—and it was the way he had spoken to Mrs. Assingham too—as if he grasped the facts, without exception, for which angularity stood.

It figured for him, clearly, as a final idea, a conception of the last vividness. He might have been signifying by it the sharp corners and hard edges, all the stony pointedness, the grand right geometry of his spreading Palladian church. Just so, he was insensible to no feature of the felicity of a contact that, beguilingly, almost confoundingly, was a contact but with practically yielding lines and curved surfaces. "You're round, my boy," he had said—"you're *all*, you're variously and inexhaustibly round, when you might, by all the chances, have been abominably square. I'm not sure, for that matter," he had added, "that you're *not* square in the general mass—whether abominably or not. The abomination isn't a question, for you're inveterately round—that's what I mean—in the detail. It's the sort of thing, in you, that one feels—or at least I do—with one's hand. Say you had been formed, all over, in a lot of pyramidal lozenges like that wonderful side of the Ducal Palace in Venice—so lovely in a building, but so damnable, for rubbing against, in a man,

206

and especially in a near relation. I can see them all from here—each of them sticking out by itself—all the architectural cut diamonds that would have scratched one's softer sides. One would have been scratched by diamonds—doubtless the neatest way if one was to be scratched at all—but one would have been more or less reduced to a hash. As it is, for living with, you're a pure and perfect crystal."

to n. 37: she had made, at a particular hour, made by the mere touch of her hand, a difference in the situation so long present to her as practically unattackable. This situation had been occupying, for months and months, the very centre of the garden of her life, but it had reared itself there like some strange, tall tower of ivory, or perhaps rather some wonderful, beautiful, but outlandish pagoda, a structure plated with hard, bright porcelain, coloured and figured and adorned, at the over-hanging eaves, with silver-bells that tinkled, ever so charmingly, when stirred by chance airs. She had walked round and round it—that was what she felt; she had carried on her existence in the space left her for circulation, a space that sometimes seemed ample and sometimes narrow: looking up, all the while, at the fair structure that spread itself so amply and rose so high, but never quite making out, as yet, where she might have entered had she wished. She had not wished till now—such was the odd case; and what was doubtless equally odd, besides, was that though her raised eyes seemed to distinguish places that must serve, from within, and especially far aloft, as apertures and outlooks, no door appeared to give access from her convenient garden level. The great decorated surface had remained consistently impenetrable and inscrutable. At present, however, to her considering mind, it was as if she had ceased merely to circle and to scan the elevation, ceased so vaguely, so quite helplessly to stare and wonder: she had caught herself distinctly in the act of pausing, then in that of lingering, and finally in that of stepping unprecedentedly near. The thing might have been, by the distance at which it kept her, a Mahometan mosque, with which no base heretic could take a liberty; there so hung about it the vision of one's putting off one's shoes to enter, and even, verily, of one's paying with one's life if found there as an interloper. She had not, certainly, arrived at the conception of paying with her life for anything she might do; but it was nevertheless quite as if she had sounded with a tap or two one of the rare porcelain plates. She had knocked, in short—though she could scarce have said whether for admission or for what; she had applied her hand to a cool smooth spot and had waited to see what would happen. Something *had* happened; it was as if a sound, at her touch, after a little, had come back to her from within; a sound sufficiently suggesting that her approach had been noted.

to n. 63: "Call her my hostess as I've never had nor imagined a hostess, and I'm with you altogether. Of course," he added in the right spirit for her, "I do see that it's quite court life."

She promptly showed that this was almost all she wanted of him. "That's all I mean, if you understand it of such a court as never was: one of the courts of heaven, the court of an angel. That will do perfectly."

"Oh well then, I grant it. Only court life as a general thing, you know," he observed, "isn't supposed to pay."

"Yes, one has read; but this is beyond any book. That's just the beauty here; it's why she's the great and only princess. With her, at her court," said Mrs. Stringham, "it does pay." Then as if she had quite settled it for him: "You'll see for yourself."

to n. 65: "And yet without Susie I shouldn't have *you*."

It had been at this point, however, that Kate flickered highest. "Oh, you may very well loathe me yet!"

Really at last, thus, it had been too much; as, with her own least feeble flare, after a wondering watch, Milly had shown. She hadn't cared; she had too much wanted to know; and, though a small solemnity of reproach, a somber strain, had broken into her tone, it was to figure as her nearest approach to serving Mrs. Lowder. "Why do you say such things to me?"

This unexpectedly had acted, by a sudden turn of Kate's attitude, as a happy speech. She had risen as she spoke, and Kate had stopped before her, shining at her instantly with a softer brightness. Poor Milly hereby enjoyed one of her views of how people, wincing oddly, were often touched by her. "Because you're a dove." With which she felt herself ever so delicately, so considerately, embraced; not with familiarity or as a liberty taken, but almost ceremonially and in the manner of an *accolade;* partly as if, though a dove who could perch on a finger, one were also a princess with whom forms were to be observed. It even came to her, through the touch of her companion's lips, that this form, this cool pressure, fairly sealed the sense of what Kate had just said. It was, moreover, for the girl, like an inspiration: she found herself accepting as the right one, while she caught her breath with relief, the name so given her. She met it on the instant as she would have met the revealed truth; it lighted up the strange dusk in which she lately had walked. *That* was what was the matter with her. She was a dove. Oh, *wasn't* she?—it echoed within her as she became aware of the sound, outside, of the return of their friends. There was, the next thing, little enough doubt about it after aunt Maud had been two minutes in the room. She had come up, Mrs. Lowder, with Susan—which she needn't have done, at that hour, instead of letting Kate come down to her; so that Milly could be quite sure it was to catch hold, in some way, of the loose end they had left. Well, the way she did catch was simply to make the point that it didn't now in the least matter. She had mounted the stairs for this, and she had her moment again with her younger hostess while Kate, on the spot, as the latter at the time noted, gave Susan Shepherd unwonted opportunities. Kate was in other words, as aunt Maud engaged her friend, listening with the handsomest response to Mrs. Stringham's impression of the scene they had just quitted. It was in the tone of the fondest indulgence—almost, really, that of dove cooing to dove—that Mrs. Lowder expressed to Milly the hope that it had all gone beautifully. Her 'all' had an ample benevolence; it soothed and simplified; she spoke as if it were the two young women, not she and her comrade, who had been facing the town together. But Milly's answer had prepared itself while aunt Maud was on the stair; she had felt in a rush all the reasons that would make it the most dovelike; and she gave it, while she was about it, as earnest, as candid. "I don't *think,* dear lady, he's here."

It gave her straightway the measure of the success she could have as a dove: that was recorded in the long look of deep criticism, a look without a word, that Mrs. Lowder poured forth. And the word, presently, bettered it still. "Oh you exquisite thing!" The luscious innuendo of it, almost startling, lingered in the room, after the visitors had gone, like an oversweet fragrance. But left alone with Mrs. Stringham Milly continued to breathe it: she studied again the dovelike and so set her companion to mere rich reporting that she averted all inquiry into her own case.

That, with the new day, was once more her law—though she saw before her, of course, as something of a complication, her need, each time, to decide. She should have to be clear as to how a dove *would* act.

to n. 66: "Ah, my dear, you know how good I think her!"

"But she's *too* nice," Kate returned with appreciation. "Everything suits her so—especially her pearls. They go so with her old lace. I'll trouble you really to look at them." Densher, though aware he had seen them before, had perhaps not "really" looked at them, and had thus not done justice to the embodied poetry—his mind, for Milly's aspects, kept coming back to that—which owed them part of its style. Kate's face, as she considered them, struck him; the long, priceless chain, wound twice round the neck, hung, heavy and pure, down the front of the wearer's breast—so far down that Milly's trick, evidently unconscious, of holding and vaguely fingering and entwining a part of it, conduced presumably to convenience. "She's a dove," Kate went on, "and one somehow doesn't think of doves as bejewelled. Yet they suit her down to the ground."

"Yes—down to the ground is the word." Densher saw now how they suited her, but was perhaps still more aware of something intense in his companion's feeling about them. Milly was indeed a dove; this was the figure, though it most applied to her spirit. But he knew in a moment that Kate was just now, for reasons hidden from him, exceptionally under the impression of that element of wealth in her which was a power, which was a great power, and which was dovelike only so far as one remembered that doves have wings and wondrous flights, have them as well as tender tints and soft sounds. It even came to Densher dimly that such wings could in a given case—had, in fact, in the case in which he was concerned—spread themselves for protection. Hadn't they, for that matter, lately taken an inordinate reach, and weren't Kate and Mrs. Lowder, weren't Susan Shepherd and he, wasn't *he* in particular, nestling under them to a great increase of immediate ease?

to n. 69: "Anything, everything you ask," she smiled. "I sha'n't know then—never. Thank you," she added with peculiar gentleness as she turned away.

The sound of it lingered with him, making him fairly feel as if he had been tripped up and had a fall. In the very act of arranging with her for his independence he had, under pressure from a particular perception, inconsistently, quite stupidly, committed himself, and, with the subtlety sensitive, on the spot, to an advantage, she had driven in, by a single word, a little golden nail, the sharp intention of which he signally felt. He had not detached, he had more closely connected himself.

Chapter 7

to n. 11: But his own actual business, half an hour later, was with a third floor on the Boulevard Malesherbes—so much as that was definite; and the fact of the enjoyment by the third-floor windows of a continuous balcony, to which he was helped by this know-ledge, had perhaps something to do with his lingering for five minutes on the opposite side of the street. There were points as to which he had quite made up his mind, and one of these bore precisely on the wisdom of the abruptness to which events had finally committed him, a policy that he was pleased to find not at all shaken as he now looked at his watch and wondered. He *had* announced himself—six months before; he had written out, at least, that Chad was not to be surprised should he see him some day turn up. Chad had thereupon, in a few words of rather carefully colorless answer, offered him a general welcome; and Strether, ruefully reflecting that he might have understood the warning as a hint to hospitality, a bid for an invitation, had fallen back upon silence as the corrective most to his own taste. He had asked Mrs. Newsome moreover not to announce him again; he had so distinct an opinion on attacking his job, should he attack it at all, in his own way. Not the least of this lady's high merits for him was that he could absolutely rest on her word. She was the only woman he had known, even at Woollett, as to whom his con-viction was positive that to lie was beyond her art. Sarah Pocock, for instance, her own daughter, though with social ideals, as they said, in some respects different—Sarah who *was,* in her way, aesthetic, had never refused to human commerce that mitigation of rigor; there were occasions when he had distinctly seen her apply it. Since, accordingly, at all events, he had had it from Mrs. Newsome that she had, at whatever cost to her more strenuous view, conformed, in the matter of preparing Chad, wholly to his restrictions, he now looked up at the fine continuous balcony with a safe sense that if the case had been bungled the mistake was at least his property. Was there perhaps just a suspicion of that in his present pause on the edge of the Boulevard and well in the pleasant light?

Many things came over him here, and one of them was that he should doubtless presently know whether he had been shallow or sharp. Another was that the balcony in question didn't somehow show as a convenience easy to surrender. Poor Strether had at this very moment to recognize the truth that, wherever one paused in Paris, the imagination, before one could stop it, reacted. This perpetual reaction put a price, if one would, on pauses; but it piled up consequences till there was scarce room to pick one's steps among them. What call had he, at such a juncture, for instance, to like Chad's very house? High, broad, clear—he was expert enough to make out in a moment that it was admirably built— it fairly embarrassed our friend by the quality that, as he would have said, it "sprang" on him. He had struck off the fancy that it might, as a preliminary, be of service to him to be seen, by a happy accident, from the third-story windows, which took all the March sun; but of what service was it to find himself making out after a moment that the quality "sprung," the quality produced by measure and balance, the fine relation of part to part and space to space, was probably—aided by the presence of ornament as positive as it was discreet, and by the complexion of the stone, a cold, fair gray, warmed and polished a little by life—neither more nor less than a case of distinction, such a case as he could only feel, unexpectedly, as a sort of delivered challenge? Meanwhile, however, the chance he had allowed for—the chance of being seen, in time, from the balcony—had become a fact. Two or three of the windows stood open to the violet air; and, before Strether had cut the knot by crossing, a young man had come out and looked about him, had lighted a cigarette and tossed the match over, and then, resting on the rail, had given himself up, while he smoked, to watching the life below. His arrival contributed, in its order, to keeping Strether in position; the result of which, in turn, was that Strether soon felt himself noticed. The young man began to look at him as in acknowledgment of his being himself in observation.

This was interesting so far as it went, but the interest was affected by the young man's not being Chad. Strether wondered at first if he were perhaps Chad altered; then he saw that this was asking too much of alteration. The young man was light, bright and alert— with an air too pleasant to have been arrived at by patching. Strether had conceived Chad as patched, but not beyond recognition. He was in presence, he felt, of amendments enough as they stood; it was a sufficient amendment that the gentleman up there should be Chad's friend. He was young too then, the gentleman up there—he was very young. Young enough, apparently, to be amused at an elderly watcher, to be curious even to see what the elderly watcher would do on finding himself watched. There was youth in that, there was youth in the surrender to the balcony, there was youth, for Strether, at this moment, in everything but his own business; and Chad's thus pronounced association with youth had given, the next instant, an extraordinary quick lift to the issue. The balcony, the distinguished front testified suddenly, for Strether's fancy, to something that was up and up; they placed the whole case materially, and as by an admirable image, on a level that he found himself at the end of another moment rejoicing to think he might reach.

to n. 12: There was no great pulse of haste yet in this process of saving Chad; nor was that effect a bit more marked as he sat, half an hour later, with his legs under Chad's mahogany, with Mr. Bilham on one side, with a friend of Mr. Bilham's on the other, with Waymarsh stupendously opposite, and with the great hum of Paris coming up in softness, vagueness—for Strether himself indeed already positive sweetness—through the sunny windows towards which, the day before, from below, his curiosity had raised its wings. The feeling that had been with him at that moment had borne fruit almost faster than he could taste it, and Strether literally felt, at the present moment, that there was a precipitation in his fate. He had known nothing and nobody as he stood in the street; but had not his view now taken a bound in the direction of every one and of everything?

to n. 13: Strether spent an hour in waiting for him—an hour full of strange suggestions, persuasions, recognitions; one of those that he was to recall, at the end of his adventure, as the particular handful that most had counted. The mellowest lamplight and the easiest chair had been placed at his disposal by Baptiste, subtlest of servants; the novel half-uncut, the novel lemon-coloured and tender, with the ivory knife athwart it like the dagger in a contadina's hair, had been pushed within the soft circle—a circle which, for some reason, affected Strether as softer still after the same Baptiste had remarked that in the absence of a further need of anything by Monsieur he would betake himself to bed. The night was hot and heavy and the single lamp sufficient; the great flare of the lighted city, rising high, spending itself afar, played up from the Boulevard and, through the vague vista of the successive rooms, brought objects into view and added to their dignity. Strether found himself in possession as he never yet had been; he had been there alone, had turned over books and prints, had invoked, in Chad's absence, the spirit of the place, but never at the witching hour and never with a relish quite so like a pang.

He spent a long time on the balcony; he hung over it as he had seen little Bilham hang the day of his first approach, as he had seen Mamie hang over her own the day little Bilham himself might have seen her from below; he passed back into the rooms, the three that occupied the front and that communicated by wide doors; and, while he circulated and rested, tried to recover the impression that they had made on him three months before, to catch again the voice in which they had seemed then to speak to him. That voice, he had to note, failed audibly to sound; which he took as the proof of all the change in him-self. He had heard, of old, only what he *could* then hear; what he could do now was to think of three months ago as a point in the far past. All voices had grown thicker and meant more things; they crowded on him as he moved about—it was the way they sounded together that wouldn't let him be still. He felt, strangely, as sad as if he had come for some wrong, and yet as excited as if he had come for some freedom. But the freedom was what was most in the place and the hour; it was the freedom that most brought him round again to the youth of his own that he had long ago missed. He could have explained little enough to-day either why he had missed it or why, after years and years, he should care that he had; the main truth of the actual appeal of everything was none the less that everything represented the substance of his loss, put it within reach, within touch, made it, to a degree it had never been, an affair of the senses. That was what it became for him at this singular time, the youth he had long ago missed—a queer concrete presence, full of mystery, yet full of reality, which he could handle, taste, smell, the deep breathing of which he could positively hear. It was in the outside air as well as within; it was in the long watch, from the balcony, in the summer night, of the wide late life of Paris, the unceasing soft quick rumble, below, of the little lighted carriages that, in the press, always suggested the gamblers he had seen of old at Monte Carlo pushing up the tables. This image was before him when he at last became aware that Chad was behind.

BIBLIOGRAPHY

A. Works by Henry James

The Novels and Tales of Henry James, New York Edition, 24 volumes, London 1908/09.
The Ambassadors, The North American Review, Jan.-Dec. 1903.
The Ambassadors, London (Methuen) 1903.
English Hours, London 1905.
French Poets and Novelists, London 1908.
The House of Fiction, Essays on the Novel, ed. Leon Edel, London 1957.
The Golden Bowl, London (Methuen) 1904, 2 vols. (first English edition).
The Ivory Tower, London 1917.
Henry James and Robert Louis Stevenson, ed. Janet Adam Smith, London 1948.
The Letters of Henry James, sel. and ed. Percy Lubbock, 2 vols., London 1920.
Selected Letters of Henry James, ed. Leon Edel, London 1956.
The Middle Years, London 1917.
The Notebooks of Henry James, ed. F. O. Matthiessen and K. B. Murdock, New York 1947.
Notes on Novelists, London 1914.
Notes of a Son and Brother, London 1914.
The Old Things, The Atlantic Monthly, April-Oct. 1896.
The Painter's Eye, Notes and Essays on the Pictorial Arts, sel. and ed. John L. Sweeney London 1956.
Partial Portraits, London 1911.
The Complete Plays of Henry James, ed. Leon Edel, London 1949.
The Portrait of a Lady, The Atlantic Monthly, Nov. 1880–Dec. 1881.
Roderick Hudson, The Atlantic Monthly, Jan.-Dec. 1875.
The Scenic Art, Notes on Acting and the Drama 1872-1901, ed. Allan Wade, London 1949.
The Sense of the Past, London 1917.
A Small Boy and Others, London 1913.
The Wings of the Dove, London (Constable) 1902 (first English edition).

B. Articles on James's Imagery

Allott, Miriam. "Symbol and Image in the Later Work of Henry James." *Essays in Criticism*, July 1953, 321–36.
Anderson, Quentin. "Henry James, His Symbolism and His Critics." *Scrutiny*, vol. 15, Dec. 1947, 12–19.
Farris, Miriam. "The Element of Symbolism in the Later Novels and Stories of Henry James." Liverpool 1949 (diss.).
Gale, Robert L. "Freudian Imagery in James's Fiction." *The American Imago*, vol. 11, No. 2, 1954, 181–90.
– "Art Imagery in Henry James's Fiction." *AL*, March 1957, 47–63.
Gibson, Priscilla. "The Uses of James's Imagery: Drama Through Metaphor." *PMLA*, Dec. 1954, 1076–84.
Gibson, William M. "Metaphor in the Plot of *The Ambassadors*." *The New England Quarterly*, Sept. 1951, 291–305.
Kimball, Jean. "The Abyss and the Wings of the Dove: The Image as a Revelation." *Nineteenth Century Fiction*, vol. 10, March 1956, No. 4, 281–300.
Short, R. W. "Henry James's World of Images." *PMLA*, Dec. 1953, 943–60.

C. General Works on Imagery

Brinkmann, Friedrich. *Die Metaphern. Studien über den Geist der modernen Sprachen*. Bonn 1878.

Brown, Stephen James. *The World of Imagery*. London 1927.

Clemen, Wolfgang H. *The Development of Shakespeare's Imagery*. London 1953.

Deutschbein, Max. *Neuenglische Stilistik* (4. Teil: Vergleich, Metapher und Zitate). Leipzig 1932.

Downey, June E. *Creative Imagination, Studies in the Psychology of Literature*. London 1929.

Elster, Ernst. *Prinzipien der Literaturwissenschaft* (2. Band, 2. Teil: Die besonderen Eigenschaften des Stils). Halle 1911.

Littmann, Hildegard. *Die Metaphern in Merediths und Hardys Lyrik*. Bern (without year).

Müller, Max. *Vorlesungen über die Wissenschaft der Sprache* (2. Serie, 8. Vorlesung: Die Metaphern). Leipzig 1866.

Middleton Murry, John. *The Problem of Style*. London 1949.

Paul, Hermann. *Prinzipien der Sprachgeschichte*. Halle 1920.

Pongs, Hermann. *Das Bild in der Dichtung*. Marburg 1927.

Spurgeon, Caroline F. E. *Leading Motives in the Imagery of Shakespeare's Tragedies*. The Shakespeare Association, 1930.

- *Shakespeare's Iterative Imagery*. Annual Shakespeare Lecture of the British Academy, London 1931.

- *Shakespeare's Imagery and what it tells us*. Cambridge 1935.

The Times Literary Supplement. "Metaphors" (leading article), 14th October 1926.

D. General Works

1. Books

Anderson, Quentin. *The American Henry James*. Rutgers University, New Jersey, 1957.

Beach, Joseph Warren. *The Method of Henry James*. Philadelphia 1954.

Bewley, Marius. *The Complex Fate*. London 1952.

Bosanquet, Theodora. *Henry James at Work*. London 1924.

Brooks, Van Wyck. *The Pilgrimage of Henry James*. New York 1925.

Cary, Elisabeth Luther. *The Novels of Henry James*. New York, London 1905.

Dupee, Frederick Wilcox. *Henry James*. London 1951.

Edel, Leon. *Henry James: The Untried Years 1843–1870*. London 1953.

- *The Psychological Novel 1900–1950*. London 1955.

Edgar, Pelham. *Henry James: Man and Author*. London 1927.

Hueffer, Ford Maddox. *Henry James. A Critical Study*. London 1918.

Kelley, Cornelia Pulsifer. *The Early Development of Henry James*. University of Illinois Studies in Language and Literature, vol. 15, Urbana, Illinois, 1930.

Leavis, F. R. *The Great Tradition*. London 1948.

Lubbock, Percy. *The Craft of Fiction*. London 1921.

Matthiessen, F. O. *Henry James: The Major Phase*. London, New York, Toronto 1946.

- *The James Family*. New York 1947.

Nowell-Smith, Simon. *The Legend of the Master*. London 1947.

Phillips, LeRoy. *A Bibliography of the Writings of Henry James*. New York 1930.

Spender, Stephen. *The Destructive Element. A Study of Modern Writers and Beliefs*. London 1935.

Swan, Michael, *Henry James*. London 1952.

Trilling, Lionel. *The Liberal Imagination. Essays on Literature and Society*. London 1955.

- *The Opposing Self*. London 1955.

West, Rebecca. *Henry James*. London 1916.

Winters, Yvor. *In Defence of Reason*. New York 1947.

2. *Articles and Dissertations*

Allott, Miriam. "The Bronzino Portrait in Henry James's *The Wings of the Dove*." *MLN*, Jan. 1953, 23–25.

— "Henry James and the Fantasticated Conceit: *The Sacred Fount*." *The Northern Miscellany of Literary Criticism*, No. 1, Autumn 1953, 76–86.

Anderson, Quentin. "Henry James and the New Jerusalem." *Kenyon Review*, Autumn 1946, 515–66.

— "The Henry Jameses." *Scrutiny*, vol. XIV, No. 4, Sept. 1947, 242–51.

Benson, Arthur Christopher. "Lamb House, Rye", in *Rambles and Reflections*. London 1926, 29–37.

Brownell, William Crary. "Henry James", in *American Prose Masters*. London 1910.

Cox, C. B. "Henry James and Stoicism." *Essays and Studies*, 1955, 76–88.

Dupee, Frederick Wilcox. ed. *The Question of Henry James. A Collection of Critical Essays*. London 1947.

Durr, Robert A. "The Night Journey in *The Ambassadors*." *Philological Quarterly*, vol. XXXV, I, Jan. 1956, 24–38.

Edel, Leon. "Henry James: Les années dramatiques." Paris 1931 (diss.).

— "Henry James's Revisions for *The Ambassadors*." *N & Q*, vol. CC, Jan. 1955, 37–38.

Edgar, Pelham. "The Art of Henry James." *National Review*, July 1924, 730–39.

Fergusson, Francis. "Drama in *The Golden Bowl*." *Hound and Horn*, April/June 1934, 407–13.

— "*The Golden Bowl* Revisited." *The Sewanee Review*, vol. 63, 1955, 13–28.

Firebaugh, Joseph, J. "The Ververs." *Essays in Criticism*, vol. IV, No. 4, Oct. 1954, 400–10.

Freeman, John. "Henry James", in *The Moderns: Essays in Literary Criticism*. London 1916, 219–42.

Fullerton, Morton. "The Art of Henry James." *Quarterly Review*, vol. 212, April 1910, 393–408.

Garland, Hamlin. "Henry James at Rye", in *Roadside Meetings*, London 1931, 454–65.

Gordon, Caroline. "Mr. Verver, our National Hero." *The Sewanee Review*, vol. 63, 1955, 29–47.

Harlow, Virginia. "Thomas Sergeant Perry and Henry James." *Boston Public Library Quarterly*, July 1949, 43–60.

Harvitt, Hélène. "How Henry James Revised *Roderick Hudson*: A Study in Style." *PMLA*, March 1924, 203–27.

Hoare, Dorothy M. "Henry James", in *Some Studies in the Modern Novel*. London 1938, 3–36.

Hughes, Herbert Leland. "Theory and Practice in Henry James." Michigan 1927 (diss.).

Humphreys, Susan M. "Henry James's Revisions for *The Ambassadors*." *N & Q*, New Series, Sept. 1954, 397–99.

Kimball, Jean. "Henry James's Last Portrait of a Lady: Charlotte Stant in *The Golden Bowl*." *AL*, Jan. 1957, 449–68.

Krook, Dorothea. "The Method of the Later Works of Henry James." *The London Magazine*, July 1954, vol. I, No. 6, 55–70.

— "*The Wings of the Dove*." *Cambridge Journal*, vol. VII, No. 11, Aug. 1954, 671–89.

— "*The Golden Bowl*." *Cambridge Journal*, vol. VII, No. 12, Sept. 1954, 716–37.

Leavis, F. R. "Henry James and the Function of Criticism." *Scrutiny*, vol. XV, No. 2, Spring 1948, 98–104.

Leavis, Q. D. "A Note on Literary Indebtedness: Dickens, George Eliot, Henry James." *The Hudson Review*, vol. VIII, No. 3, Autumn 1955, 423–28.

Lee, Vernon. "The Handling of Words: Meredith and Henry James." *English Review*, June 1910.

Lerner, Daniel and Cargill, Oscar. "Henry James at the Grecian Urn." *PMLA*, vol. 66, 1951, 316–31.

Lind, Ilse Dusoir. "The Inadequate Vulgarity of Henry James." *PMLA*, vol. 66, 1951, 886–910.

Matthiessen, F. O. "James and the Plastic Arts." *Kenyon Review*, Autumn 1943, 533–50.

McIntyre, Clara F. "The Later Manner of Mr. Henry James." *PMLA*, vol. 27, 1912, 354–71.

Pierhal, Armand. "Henry James le Civilisé." *Hommes et Mondes*, 1951, 413–20.

Quinn, Patrick F. "Morals and Motives in *The Spoils of Poynton*." *The Sewanee Review*, vol. 62, No. 4, Autumn 1954, 563–77.

Randell, Wilfrid L. "The Art of Mr. Henry James." *Fortnightly Review*, April 1916, 620–32.

Sandeen, Ernest. "*The Wings of the Dove* and *The Portrait of a Lady*: A Study of Henry James's Later Phase." *PMLA*, Dec. 1954, 1060–75.

Short, R. W. "The Sentence Structure of Henry James." *AL*, vol. 18, May 1946, 71–88.

– "Some Critical Terms of Henry James." *PMLA*, Sept. 1950, 667–80.

The Times Literary Supplement. "The Significance of Henry James" (leading article), 6th Jan. 1927.

Tintner, Adeline R. "The Spoils of Henry James." *PMLA*, March 1946, 239–51.

Walbrook, H. M. "The Novels of Henry James." *Fortnightly Review*, May 1930, 680–91.

Waldock, Arthur J. A. "Henry James", in *James, Joyce and Others*, London 1937, 1–29.

Warren, Austin. "Myth and Dialectic in the Later Novels." *Kenyon Review*, Autumn 1943, 551–68.

– "Henry James", in *Rage for Order. Essays in Criticism*. Chicago 1948, 142–61.

Williams, Orlo. "*The Ambassadors*." *The Criterion*, Sept. 1928, 47–64.

CURRICULUM VITAE

I, Alexander Eugen Holder, of Basel, was born in the same town on the 24th April 1931, as the son of Eugen Holder-Siefert—revenue-officer of the Canton of Basel-Town—and his wife Clara. I attended the primary schools and the Mathematisch-Naturwissenschaftliche Gymnasium at Basel. In the spring of 1950 I passed the University Entrance Examination. I then studied English Literature, German Literature and General History at the University of Basel. In 1954 a grant by the Cooper Fond enabled me to do research work at the Bodleian Library, Oxford, for one year. From 1955–1957 I held the post of Lektor for German in the University of Oxford. In the autumn of 1957 I took up my studies again at the universities of Basel and Zürich and concluded them in June 1958 with the oral examination for the doctorate in English and German Literature and in General History at the University of Basel. In March 1958 I passed the examination in Latin of the Faculty of Philosophy and History at Basel.

In the course of my studies I attended lectures and seminars by the following professors and lecturers: *Basel:* H. Lüdeke, K. Jost, H. G. Wright, M. Schubiger, J. H. Gimson, G. T. Hughes, S. Hubbard (English); W. Muschg, F. Ranke, H. Wagner, W. Altwegg, W. Stammler, F. Strich, L. Wiesmann (German); E. Bonjour, W. Kaegi (History); J. Gantner, K. Jaspers, G. P. Landmann, H. Meng, H. van Oyen, L. Weber. *Oxford:* Lord David Cecil, N. Coghill, H. Gardner, M. Griffiths, R. Horwood, J. P. Leishman, J. Smithers, J. I. M. Stewart, Ch. Tolkien, F. P. Wilson, D. Whitelock (English). *Zürich:* E. Leisi (English).

The subject of the dissertation has been suggested to me by Professor Henry Lüdeke, and it has been written under his supervision.